Surgery, Ethics and the Law

© 2000 by Blackwell Science Asia
Pty Ltd

Published by Blackwell Science Asia
Pty Ltd

First printed 2000

Editorial Offices:
54 University Street
Carlton South
Victoria 3053, Australia

Osney Mead, Oxford
OX2 OEL, UK

25 John Street,
London WC 1N 2BL, UK

23 Ainslie Place
Edinburgh EH3 6AJ, UK

350 Main Street, Malden,
MA 02148-5018, USA

Other Editorial Offices:
Blackwell Wissenschafts-Verlag
GmbH, Kurfilrstendamm 57
10707 Berlin, Germany

Zehemergasse 6,
1140 Wein, Austria

All rights reserved. No part of this publication may be produced, stored in a retrieval system, or transmitted, in any form or by any means, electronic, mechanical, photocopying, recording or otherwise, except as permitted by the Copyright Act 1968, without the prior permission of the copyright owner.

Designed by Stephanie Thompson
Typeset by Pleasant House

Printed in Australia

DISTRIBUTORS
Blackwell Science Asia Pty Ltd
54 University Street
Carlton South
Victoria 3053, Australia
Orders
Tel: +61 3 9347 0300
Fax: +61 3 9347 5001
info@blacksci-asia.com.au
www.blacksci-asia.com.au

North America
Blackwell Science, Inc.
Commerce Place
350 Main Street, Malden
MA 02148-5018, USA
Orders
Tel: +1 617388 8250
            800759 6102
Fax: +1 617388 8255

Canada
Copp Clark Professional
200 Adelaide Street West
3rd Floor,
Toronto, Ontario M5H 1W7
Orders
Tel: +1 416597 1616
            800815 9417
Fax: +1 416597 1616

United Kingdom
Marston Book Services Ltd
PO Box 87
Oxford, OX2 ODT, UK
Orders
Tel: +44 1865 791155
Fax: +44 01865 791927
Telex: 837515

Cataloguing-in-Publication Data
Surgery, ethics and the law.
ISBN 0 86793 021 7
1. Medical laws and legislation.
2. Medical ethics.
I. Fearnside, Michael Robert.
II. Dooley, Brendan J., 1929–.
III. Gorton, Michael W.
174.2

Table of Contents

Foreword v

Contributors viii

Acknowledgements x

Preface xi

The College

Surgery, leadership and the College Fellowship 1
P.H. Carter, B.J. Dooley, M.R. Fearnside

Ethical Issues

Withholding and withdrawing treatment 7
B.M. Tobin

Organ donation and transplantation 19
D.F. Scott, D.M.A. Francis

The impaired fetus and newborn 41
N. Campbell

Ethics of resource allocation 53
J.M. Little

Outcome studies: An ethical perspective 63
C. Jordens

Legal Issues

Informed consent: Patient communication 75
B.J. Dooley, M.R. Fearnside

Informed consent: Legal issues 81
M.W. Gorton

Professional obligations 89
L. Atkinson

Why medical boards? 105
P.C. Arnold

Disciplinary and appeal processes 115
   L. Waller

Impaired surgeons 123
   J. Phillips

Legal liability of doctors 131
   B.J. Dooley, M.W. Gorton

Risk management 141
   R. Dickens

Court proceedings and subpoenas 151
   M.W. Gorton

Medical records and confidentiality 157
   M.W. Gorton

Medical reports 171
   K.W. Mills

Expert evidence by surgeons 177
   H. Selby

Doctors to the rescue 189
   M.W. Gorton

Coronial inquests and the medical profession 195
   V. Harcourt

Medical manslaughter and other crimes 207
   A. Merry, M.W. Gorton

Research

Ethical issues in clinical research 221
   M.R. Fearnside

Animal welfare and the ethics of
animal experimentation 235
   J. Ludbrook

Foreword

As medical and surgical treatments become more complex, and as an increasingly educated public moves away from the 'doctor knows best' paradigm, there is an increasing need for trainee physicians and surgeons to become concerned with the ethical and legal framework of the health care system. The Royal Australasian College of Surgeons is to be congratulated on sponsoring the substantial and authoritative book Surgery, Ethics and the Law. *The chapters, all written by acknowledged authorities in their particular fields, cover a wide panorama, examining a range of weighty and controversial subjects which illustrate many of the facets of the subject. The treatment is scholarly and well referenced, but at the same time the work is eminently readable and written from a generalist point of view. It certainly makes a valuable addition to the literature of a vital and expanding field.*

Sir Gustav Nossal
Department of Pathology
The University of Melbourne

Every surgeon must know and understand that he or she has obligations and responsibilities to their patients, to the community in which they live and work, and to their profession.

This book, sponsored by the Royal Australasian College of Surgeons, is primarily addressed to surgeons. Those readers will be provided with an informed understanding of both the ethical and the legal rule-frameworks within which a responsible surgeon practises her or his specialised discipline. This will lead, I believe, to the attainment of even higher standards in the practice of surgery in Australia and New Zealand. It is a book that may also be read by all members of the profession of medicine, by those practising in allied professions, and by their patients. For them, it will help enhance their appreciation of the whole context in which surgeons operate.

Professor Louis Waller, AO
Sir Leo Cussen Chair of Law
Monash University

I am pleased to present Surgery, Ethics and the Law, *which brings together a variety of information for surgeons, surgical trainees and other interested readers about the ethical and legal issues arising in the health care system. The Royal Australasian College of Surgeons is to be congratulated for producing such a comprehensive text.*

The chapters are broad in scope. 'Organ donation and transplantation' is very timely, with a number of States presently reconsidering their legislation on this matter. A balanced and thought-provoking discussion of the ethical issues is provided which includes the need for support and counselling of the families of organ donors and the methods by which donor organs are allocated.

There are many problems associated with allocating scarce medical resources, and the medical profession's role in their distribution is of paramount importance. 'Ethics of resource allocation' suggests a new ethical framework for considering this issue.

This book, issued at a time when many changes in the health care system are occurring, will contribute to the maintenance of the high standards of the medical profession.

Dr Michael Wooldridge
Minister for Health and Aged Care

Contributors

Peter C. Arnold, BSc MBBCh BA, Deputy President of the New South Wales Medical Board

Leigh Atkinson, MBBS(Qld), FRACS, FRCS(Edin), FRACS, FAFPHM(RACP), Neurosurgeon, Clinical Associate Professor, University of Queensland

Neil Campbell, MBBS, FRACP, Department of Neonatology, Royal Children's Hospital, Melbourne

Peter H. Carter, BA, MedAdmin, DipEd, MATEM, Management Consultant and Class Facilitator for Graduate Programs in Business and Technology, University of New South Wales, Chief Executive Officer, Royal Australasian College of Surgeons 1989–1999

Robert Dickens, FRACS, Orthopaedic Surgeon, President, Medical Defence Association of Victoria Ltd, Director, Professional Insurance Australia Pty Ltd

Brendan J. Dooley, MBBS, FRCS(Eng), FRACS, Orthopaedic Surgeon, Former Censor-in-Chief of the Royal Australasian College of Surgeons

Michael R. Fearnside, MBBS, MS, FRACS, Clinical Associate Professor, Department of Surgery, Sydney University and Department of Neurosurgery, Westmead Hospital

David M.A. Francis, MD, MS, FRCS (Eng & Edin), FRACS, Transplant and General Surgeon, Royal Melbourne Hospital, St Vincent's Hospital and Royal Children's Hospital, Melbourne

Michael W. Gorton, LLB, BComm.(Melb), FRACS(Hon), FANZCA (Hon), Partner, Russell Kennedy, Solicitors, Honorary Solicitor to the Royal Australasian College of Surgeons

Victor Harcourt, BComm, LLB, Grad.Dip.Health and Medical Law, Partner, Russell Kennedy, Solicitors

Chris Jordens, BA(Hons), MPH, Researcher, Centre for Values, Ethics and the Law in Medicine, University of Sydney

J. Miles Little, MD, FRACS, Emeritus Professor Surgery, Director, Centre for Values, Ethics and the Law in Medicine, University of Sydney

John Ludbrook, MD, DSc, ChM, BMedSc, FRCS, FRACS, AStat, former Senior Principal Research Fellow, NHRMC

Alan Merry, FANZCA, FPMANZCA, Anaesthetist, Clinical Associate Professor, Clinical Director of Anaesthesia, Green Lane Hospital, former Chair of the New Zealand National Committee of ANZCA, former Co-Chair of the New Zealand Medical Law Reform Group

Kingsley W. Mills, FRACS, Orthopaedic Surgeon, Former Member and Secretary, Victorian State Committee, Royal Australasian College of Surgeons

Jonathan Phillips, FRANZCP, President, Royal Australian and New Zealand College of Psychiatrists

Hugh Selby, BA, LLB, MSW(Michigan), Barrister, specialising in training advocates and witnesses

David F. Scott, MD, MS, FRACS, Adjunct Professor of Surgery

Bernadette M. Tobin, MA, MEd, PhD, Director of the Plunkett Centre for Ethics in Health Care, a joint University Centre of Australian Catholic University and the St Vincent's Health Care Campus

Louis Waller, AO, FASSA, Sir Leo Cussen Chair of Law, Monash University, Chairman of Appeals Committee of the Royal Australasian College of Surgeons

Acknowledgements

The editors acknowledge the authors of the various chapters for their commitment to *Surgery, Ethics and the Law*, and thank them for their valuable, and valued, contributions.

We thank Mrs Sheryn Blundstone and Ms Nerea Huidobro for their able organisation and coordination of original submissions.

We acknowledge Mrs Judith Bielicki for her advice, assistance and expertise, in her roles of sub-editor and coordinator of typesetting.

Part of the proceeds from the sale of *Surgery, Ethics and the Law* will benefit the Royal Australasian College of Surgeons Foundation.

Preface

B.J. DOOLEY, M.R. FEARNSIDE, M.W. GORTON

The world is experiencing rapid change in every area, but arguably nowhere more so than in medicine — some change for the better, and some for the worse! There is constant political, economic and bureaucratic pressure on the surgical profession to perform, as well as demands to improve and maintain quality of care with continuing education and accreditation.

There are three elements that go to make a good surgeon — knowledge, expertise and character. The Royal Australasian College of Surgeons is confident that surgeons and surgical trainees continue to be highly trained and competent, and maintain excellent standards in the fields of knowledge and expertise in surgery and medical practice. The purpose of this book is to highlight the importance of surgeons to be aware of and abreast of requirements in communication, ethics and the law that affect our relationships with patients and relatives of patients, as well as with paramedical staff and Government bodies.

Obviously, not every ethical and legal issue can be discussed in a book of this size, but the information given will stimulate discussion and, in many cases, references for further reading are given. The views given in each chapter are those of the author(s). Through reading these, surgeons will become even more aware of their responsibilities to patients and to the care of them.

Surgeons have a proud record as professionals and in accepting full responsibility and accountability in the overall management of their patients. Medicine is not an exact science. It is also an art. No doctor can be perfect, but practitioners do their best in every way. In the community at large, there is an increasing tendency for some people to take little or no responsibility for their actions and, at the same time, to place the blame on others should the outcome of their problems, particularly medical problems, be unsatisfactory. In cases of perceived or actual unsatisfactory results following treatment, it must be emphasised that surgeons should not be held responsible for adverse outcomes unless there is proven medical negligence.

This book covers a wide range of ethical and legal issues, mainly as they affect surgeons. Although directed principally at surgical trainees and surgeons, it will also inform the public at large, including health administrators, medical and paramedical practitioners, ethicists, the legal profession and governments, both State and Federal.

Surgery, leadership and the College Fellowship

P.H. CARTER, B.J. DOOLEY, M.R. FEARNSIDE

'It is my great pleasure to inform you that the assessment of your Advanced Surgical Training has been found satisfactory by this Court. Your names will be submitted to the Council with the recommendation that those who have completed Advanced Training be admitted to Fellowship of the College. Those who have yet to complete Training will be designated Provisional Fellows.

I would remind you that, in accepting this distinction, you accept also the commitment to cultivate and maintain the highest principles of surgical practice and ethical behaviour as espoused by the Royal Australasian College of Surgeons.'

This announcement by the Chairman of the Court of Examiners, with some 60 members of the Court present, marks the culmination of some 13 or more years of medical studies, including at least 6 in surgery, followed by final Fellowship examinations. For each new Fellow, it sets the scene and the standard for his or her future practice.

The responsibilities of Fellows of this College as professionals involve not only the quality of their own work but also:

(i) their participation as partners in the medical team, with the increasing importance of teamwork involving a wide range of both medical and paramedical specialists and others;

(ii) a commitment to conducting research, or at least applying the results where appropriate; and

(iii) teaching to ensure that they are succeeded by a new generation of surgeons who have at least attained, and hopefully exceeded, the standard of those currently practising.

Today, professional responsibility also extends to participation in management and administration to ensure the profession that surgeons represent does not lose out in the competition for the health dollar, which is shrinking in supply relative to demand. Important, too, is a commitment to the College as it strives to achieve its objectives.

Today's surgeon has an obligation to participate in continuing education and to audit his/her surgical work, leading to regular re-accreditation. It is also important that the surgeon maintains physical and mental health, and is in no way impaired in the care of patients as a result of poor health or the taking of drugs including alcohol. The surgeon must be a doctor and a teacher.

The objectives of the College are the sum of the objectives of its Fellows. The scene was set in the famous letter, known as the Foundation Letter, written by HB Devine, R Hamilton Russell and Sir George Syme (in 1925) to some 90 surgeons in Australia and New Zealand, complaining about a spirit of commercialism in some practitioners, particularly those inexperienced, who neglected ethical standards and undertook procedures for which they were not properly trained. They complained also of inadequately equipped hospitals. They were concerned that the public could not judge the competence of the practitioners or the adequacy of the hospitals. They invited the addressees to join them in forming a body to correct these problems. The first meeting of the Council of the infant College followed after 2 years' gestation, and resolutions were passed which effectively became the first Constitution of the College. These were:

1. To cultivate and maintain the highest principles of surgical practice and ethics.

2. To safeguard the welfare of the community by indicating that its Fellows have attained a high standard of surgical competency and are of high character.
3. To educate the public to recognise that the practice of surgery demands adequate and special training.
4. To promote the practice of surgery under proper conditions by securing the improvement of hospitals and hospital methods.
5. To arrange adequate post-graduate surgical training at universities and hospitals.
6. To promote research in surgery.
7. To bring together periodically the surgeons of Australia and New Zealand for scientific discussion and practical demonstration of surgical subjects.
8. To do all other things that might lead to the better achievement of these objects.

In addition to deriving some of its structures, symbols and processes from the UK colleges, particularly the Royal College of Surgeons of England, there was a significant influence on the new College of Surgeons of Australasia from the American College of Surgeons. It was held that 'the public should be educated to recognise that the practice of surgery demands adequate and special training', 'the standard of surgical practice in hospitals should be elevated', 'the welfare of the community should be safeguarded' and 'the highest principles should be cultivated'. It can be seen that these sentiments are mirrored to a great extent in the Chairman of the Court's exhortation to the new Fellow.

What, then, must a Fellow do who believes in all of this, as all Fellows must, to ensure that surgery maintains its place in society — a place of great respect and admiration, hard-earned by surgeons down the generations?

First and foremost, a surgeon has a duty, a commitment and a responsibility to his or her patients. This is something that is ingrained in medical teaching from the very beginning and is reinforced as that teaching moves through its undergraduate, hospital and specialist training years.

While surgery remains a 'cottage industry', surgeons are increasingly working in teams with their fellow surgeons in other specialties and sub-specialties, and more often with medical practitioners and others from non-surgical and indeed non-medical specialties. No longer can a surgeon be all things to all patients and he or she must recognise that teamwork is essential to optimal patient care.

The Royal Australasian College of Surgeons for many years has been strongly committed to fostering research, knowing that both basic and applied research in surgery and its related fields are essential to progression and advancement in treatment. The College commits to surgical research every spare dollar it can find and in 1999 will have spent around $1.5 million on research and a further $820 000 on other educational pursuits. This is second only to the NHMRC in Australia.

Commitment to teaching is something that is regarded as an integral part of the life and work of a surgeon. The College is now helping in this regard by providing programs that enable surgeons to become professional educators and teachers, maximising the effect of their teaching.

It seems that surgeons, who naturally prefer to spend as much time as possible in the operating theatre rather than worrying about such other necessary evils as management and administration, as a result of that commitment, have left much of the allocation of the resources in the hospital system, particularly the public system, to others, and as a result, others have derived benefit from this. In the last few years the College has identified a need to enhance surgeons' awareness of the importance of management and administration, and the College now teaches these subjects. For younger Fellows, courses in management, leadership and the law, and for Fellows, courses in management have been held and are being further developed.

It is the professional responsibility of the surgeon to ensure management and administrative decisions are taken on the basis of the best possible advice. The best possible advice in relation to surgical management and administration, and the allocation of the resources that go with it, is advice from surgeons. Surgeons who are trained in these fields are better able to provide that advice.

The College collectively upholds all of these principles and supports all of these initiatives. It is through participation in the College and its activities that Fellows can truly represent surgery and their patients, and make the College strong, to continue to do these things into the future.

Withholding and withdrawing treatment

B.M. TOBIN

In order to give a clear answer to questions about when it is proper to withhold or to withdraw medical treatment, we need a clear sense of what is medicine's *own business*. For without that, it is not possible to say, even in principle, let alone in any particular circumstance, when medicine has reached the limits of its endeavours and thus when treatment should be withdrawn or withheld.

Various answers are given to the questions 'what is medicine's business?' and 'what is the goal of medicine?' Two are worth mentioning, for even a brief consideration of each of them will be instructive about the nature of medicine's genuine business (or true goal).[1] Some claim that medicine aims at human happiness, others claim that it aims at the prolongation of life. I shall argue that neither answer is completely satisfactory, and that the business of medicine is rather the maintenance or restoration of health (or some desirable approximation to health) — health in a quite specific sense — and the palliation of suffering. Only if we see that medicine is a discrete human activity which has that relatively modest, relatively specific, aim will we be well-placed to understand why sometimes medicine *ought not do* what it *can do*.

Strangely, the claim that medicine's goal is human happiness is put forward by the World Health Organization when it *(re)defines* health as 'a state of complete physical, mental and social wellbeing'.

In redefining the concept of health to make it coextensive with the concept of 'happiness', the World Health Organization in effect claims that happiness is the doctor's business because health and happiness are equivalent. This cannot be quite right. For one thing, there are many ways in which people who enjoy good health can be unhappy. And the converse is often true: people who suffer from chronic illness for many years may live lives of great satisfaction, sometimes even putting the rest of us to shame in how they live life to the full. For another thing, complete social wellbeing depends on things about which medicine can do nothing, indeed on things that are often a matter of luck: earning a sufficient income, having a challenging career, enjoying the companionship of good friends and having a happy family life, etc. Complete mental wellbeing similarly depends on things about which medicine can do little; for instance, on one's imagination, sensitivity, judgment, fellow feeling, intelligence, etc. A professional golfer learns that having one of her breasts removed would improve her golf swing. Having carefully considered the matter, she concludes that improving her golf swing would make up for losing a normal breast.[2] Whether or not one thinks such a procedure would be a worthy one, it lies outside medicine's business. And whatever one thinks about cosmetic surgery that does not aim to correct an inborn or acquired abnormality or deformity, whether one thinks it a worthy or unworthy practice, it lies outside medicine's business.

The first thing to note about the other claim — that medicine aims at (perhaps among other things) the prolongation of life or the prevention of death — is that it is a relatively modern claim. Historically, there is good evidence that it was not until the 18th century that it was even considered part of the doctor's duty to prolong life.[3] Speculating that it may have been Francis Bacon who first introduced the idea, Daniel Callahan makes the obvious point: it is a necessarily modern notion, for it was inconceivable until relatively recently when doctors found that they *could* actually prolong life![4] However perplexed and confused doctors at times may feel about their role (when, for example, families pressure them against their better judgment into administering life-prolonging treatments to their patients) mere prolongation of life cannot be a goal, let alone *the* goal of medicine.

Sometimes, of course, saving life or, better, avoiding premature death, is a part of medicine's genuine business: the restoration or maintenance of health, and the relief of the symptoms of illness. The immediate point of much emergency care is the avoidance of accidental or premature death and, post-operatively, just making sure that a patient does not die from the surgery may be the point of much of what is done. However, that immediate purpose needs to be seen in the light of the deeper purpose of what is being attempted.

A doctor of any experience will be familiar with cases (like that of a patient who has been comatose for a long time, or that of a patient who suffers from end-stage respiratory failure) in which life has been prolonged well beyond the time at which there was a reasonable hope of returning the person concerned to some reasonably healthy state. The conditions in which such patients are often kept alive speak of what is, and what is not, medicine's business in a much more vivid way than any words can on the subject. This is not, of course, to say that a doctor may abandon such patients; but, in offering the kind of comfort care one provides for a patient who is dying, a doctor's conduct spans the borderline between what one can reasonably expect of a doctor *qua* doctor (using medical expertise to relieve the symptoms of illness, improving the circumstances in which the patient dies) and what one can reasonably expect of him or her *qua* companion (comforting a fellow mortal as death approaches).

Medicine's ultimate business is neither the pursuit of happiness nor even the prolongation of life. It is rather the maintenance or restoration of health (or some desirable approximation to health) and the relief of suffering. So we need to reflect on what the concept of health entails. The English word 'health' comes from words that denote wholeness ('to heal' is to make whole). The Greek language has two words for health: *hygieia* which means living well and *euexia* which means 'well-habitness' or 'good bodily habits'.[a] While the

---

[a] Bodily health does not depend only on the well-working of the body: it depends also on the well-ordering of the psyche.

English word emphasises a condition of the whole body, the Greek emphasises proper functioning and activity. We can sum them up by saying that health is the well-working of the human organism as a whole. Health, in this specific sense, is the business of medicine. Of course, often you have to go beyond medicine to find the best means for attaining health (good diet, sufficient rest and exercise, clean water, etc. are all necessary for good health). So although health and only health is the true business of doctors, it is not the business only of doctors.

Several features of the concept of health (the well-working of the human organism as a whole) need to be noted if we are to be well-placed to recognise the limits of medical endeavour.

First, health is not merely the absence of disease. The advent of wellness clinics and other health promotion initiatives, as well as the older institution of baby health clinics, attest to this fact. Second, health is the object of a body of knowledge and understanding about which doctors are (or ought to be) experts. Illness (like health) is both an objectively verifiable and subjectively experienced condition. Although these two aspects of illness generally go together, illness may go unrecognised (or 'unfelt') and feelings of illness are significant whether the doctor finds something wrong or not. Third, health is relative to the individual and to his or her stage in life: the idea of normal biological functioning from youth to old age conditions our sense of what counts as the restoration or maintenance of health.

Although health and illness are both objectively verifiable conditions about which doctors are more or less expert, questions about how far health is to be pursued, and in what ways and at what cost, are matters primarily for the individual whose health is at stake. The primary responsibility for seeking and preserving one's health (living a healthy life, avoiding the things that are destructive of good health, seeking medical interventions to restore one's health, etc.) rests on the individual. To enable their patient to make his or her own health care decisions wisely, doctors (and other health professionals) must take care to explain clearly and simply the nature of a proposed procedure, any risks inherent in it to which the patient is likely to attach significance, and the patient's prognosis if the procedure is not undertaken. But the responsibility for deciding what to do about one's health is ultimately a matter for the individual. And so it follows that doctors must respect refusals of treatment no matter how unwise those refusals might seem to be. There is more to life than health, and it is up to each individual to decide how far he or she wants to go in the pursuit of health.

Given the assumption that medicine's goal is the proper functioning of the human organism as a whole, we are now in a position to clarify its proper limits. When may (or ought) treatment be withheld or withdrawn? Traditional medical ethics has a clear answer to this question: when treatment would be futile. Here, it is important to note that the concept of futility has a subtle variety of meanings which cannot be captured in any single definition. What we can say, as a matter of principle, is this: when medical treatment no longer serves the goal(s) of medicine for a particular patient, when it no longer cures illness, when it no longer maintains that person in a reasonably satisfactory condition, when the benefits it promises for that person are outweighed by the burdens it will impose, when it no longer palliates the symptoms of illness, when it no longer saves life, then it is reasonably judged to be futile. Certainly, reliable judgments of futility require experience, an empathetic capacity to see a patient as a fellow human being and not merely as a diseased organism, and the readiness to see when medicine has reached its proper limits.

The difficulty that doctors have in recognising, or accepting, that futile medical treatment ought to be withheld or withdrawn is heightened when that treatment is life-prolonging. Here, it helps to remember a point made earlier. Our concept of health is sensitive to a wide range of differences, one set of which are differences in age: what counts as the restoration or maintenance of (some approximation of) health will reflect age-related differences in biology. This claim in no way supports the immoral idea that health care resources should be allocated on the basis of age. Generally, medicine ought not try to resist the biological disintegration that comes with increasing age, except (and it is a significant exception) to relieve pain and other undesirable symptoms of that disintegrating biology.[b] There is a wide range of such symptoms: urinary tract infections which cause burning and scalding, fungal infections in the mouth which are uncomfortable and cause halitosis, nausea, sleeplessness, etc. There is much for medicine to do, even when curing illness is no longer possible. By challenging the idea that life prolongation is the real goal of medicine, one is challenging less what doctors do and more how they think and speak about what they do.[1]

However, when an elderly person's life is drawing to an end, medicine ought not set out merely to postpone death. Generally, medicine ought to try to recognise when someone is dying (and that may be long before the onset of a final 'terminal' illness) so as then to shift its emphasis from cure to comfort care, and to improving the quality of the time that remains. Doctors are often reluctant to admit that a person is dying. (So, too, are the rest of us, and sometimes we bring this reluctance into the doctor's consulting rooms and put great pressure on doctors to 'do something' in the face of the impending death of someone we cannot bear to let go.) As a result, doctors often continue to emphasise the possibility of cure, or even long-term palliation, to the detriment of the patient. For one thing, a patient (distracted by the burdens of treatment and the hope that some treatment may be effective) may be denied the opportunity to adjust to the prospect of death. For another thing, he or she may be denied the best available palliative care.

Interestingly, Daniel Callahan has argued that some of the problems that occur in the care of the dying arise from contemporary views of death. He argues that, in the last hundred years, since medicine has been able to do something about postponing death, our view of death has changed subtly. It used to be experienced as a natural event, something that happened to us, not something

---

[b] This is a different point from one which is sometimes made: that it is morally legitimate to ration health care by age. In itself, the age of the patient is as irrelevant a criterion for distributing health care as is, say, the sex of the patient.

caused by us. But now (he says) we have collapsed the distinction between causality and culpability. While we used to see death as caused by old age or illness, now we think that it is caused by our failure to avert it. And so, he concludes, with the advent of effective medicine that could save life and extend it, a fatalism about death has given way to a new, corrupted sense of moral obligation to use medical means to combat death. Properly understood, the sanctity of life principle implies that it is wrong deliberately to kill another human being: today, it is often (mis)taken to require a positive struggle against death. Death has thus become an evil to be avoided for as long as possible, and what can be done to resist it ought to be done (or so it is thought). This conception of death as indefinitely avertable exerts a terrible tyranny on both the culture in general and the health care professions in particular, the manifestations of which can be discerned right across the whole range of positions (from the most conservative to the most liberal) in contemporary bioethics.

To summarise so far: given that medicine's business is the maintenance or restoration of (some semblance of) health, and that health care decisions are primarily the responsibility of the person whose health is at stake, there are two circumstances in which medical treatment ought to be withheld or withdrawn: when it is futile, and when it is refused.

Competent adult patients are entitled to refuse medical treatment that they do not want.[c] In several Australian jurisdictions, guardianship legislation enables a guardian to make decisions for an incompetent patient. Otherwise, in the case of incompetent patients, the (senior) doctor has to decide whether treatment is likely to be sufficiently therapeutic to justify the burdens it may or will impose. It would, of course, be irresponsible of the doctor not to consult both the patient's family and/or special friends, and any other caregivers, in order to ensure that a decision to withdraw or

---

[c] This is a matter of common law and, in several Australian jurisdictions, a matter of statute law in the Australian Capital Territory (*Medical Treatment Act, 1994*), South Australia (*Consent to Medical Treatment and Palliative Care Act, 1995*) and Victoria (*Medical Treatment Act, 1988*).

to withhold treatment takes into account what they may think is in the patient's best interests, what they may know (if anything) of what the patient would have wanted, how they are placed to continue to provide care for the patient, etc.

Is withdrawing or withholding life-sustaining treatment the equivalent of intending to bring about death? Notice first that the question—is the withdrawal of life support the equivalent of the doing of an act intended to lead to death?—arises outside the context of clinical medicine as well as inside. In ordinary life, there are plenty of circumstances in which no such inference can be made. John Finnis mentions the case of the British climber in the Andes who, some years ago, finally cut the rope on which his friend was dangling, lest he himself be dragged over the precipice, and who later found (to his amazed delight) that the friend he had thought certain to be killed had fallen unscathed into deep snow: that man had no intent to bring about his friend's death.[5]

Finnis makes the relevant point this way: 'one intends to bring about X if, and only if, the bringing about of X is either an end or a means in the proposal which one shapes by deliberation and chooses to adopt'. That is to say that one intends to bring about death only if bringing about death is either the end (or purpose) of what one does or the means by which one achieves one's end (or purpose). If one withdraws life-sustaining treatment precisely on the grounds of its futility, one need not be aiming at or intending the patient's foreseeably certain death. One's purpose or intent may simply be to honour the patient's wish to be relieved of (or wish to free others from) the burdens of that treatment. One's purpose or intent may simply be to cease to administer a non-therapeutic treatment. Of course, in a particular case, a doctor may very well intend to bring about death by withholding or withdrawing life-sustaining treatment: the salient point is that the withdrawal of life support is not in itself the equivalent of intending to hasten death. What the doctor actually does intend will be a factual question.

A similar question arises about palliative measures that foreseeably shorten a patient's life: is the administration of palliative treatments that shorten life the equivalent of intending to bring about death? Once again, the answer is no. The doctor who responds to the feelings of suffocation endured by a patient with end-stage throat cancer by lightly sedating him, in the certain knowledge that depressing his respiratory system will shorten his life, may be intending, may be striving, to relieve this terrifying symptom of the patient's illness, easing his suffering as he dies. Once again, what the doctor actually does intend will be a factual question: no doubt some doctors do intend to hasten death by using (or rather by abusing) 'palliative' measures.

Discussion of when it is appropriate to withdraw or withhold life-sustaining medical treatment, and when it is appropriate to relieve the symptoms of illness in a manner which foreseeably shortens life, generally gives rise to questions about euthanasia, in particular to questions about what constitutes euthanasia and to questions about whether euthanasia of any sort ought to be legalised. This is not the place for a discussion of the latter questions (except to note that, whether or not one thinks bringing about the death of another person in order to relieve that person's suffering is a worthy human practice, it lies outside the healing business of medicine). But it is the place to discuss the former questions; that is, to distinguish from euthanasia the withdrawing or withholding of futile life-sustaining treatment, together with the relief of symptoms of illness in a manner which foreseeably shortens life. Euthanasia is the intentional bringing about of death, motivated by concern for the person's suffering.[d] It may take one of various forms: it may be at the patient's request (voluntary) or in the absence of the patient's request (involuntary); it may be active (by an act such as the administration of a lethal injection) or passive (by an omission such as a failure to administer a treatment in order to bring about death). It follows that one and the same kind of act (say, sedating a patient) may on some occasions be good medical practice (that is, relief of a terrifying symptom of illness) and on other occasions constitute the intentional bringing about of death. Similarly, it follows that one

---

[d] The motive is salient. The intentional hastening of death motivated by a desire to save costs, or to ensure that someone will inherit sooner rather than later, or to relieve the patient's family of their grief or tiredness, or … etc, is not euthanasia.

and the same kind of omission (say, the withholding or withdrawing of artificial ventilation) may on occasion be good medical practice (that is, ceasing a treatment which can neither assist recovery nor maintain a tolerable condition) and on other occasions constitute the intentional bringing about of death. What matters, both in ethics and in law, is what the doctor chooses to do (whether by act or by omission).

As for the law, it will be well to note that the withdrawing or withholding of futile treatment is not only good medical practice but it is perfectly legal. In Australia, the law 'imposes on a medical practitioner a duty to exercise reasonable care and skill in the provision of professional advice and treatment'.[e] So the legally significant question to be asked about withdrawing or withholding life-sustaining treatment will be the question of whether there is a duty to maintain treatment. There is no duty (either in ethics or in law) to maintain futile treatment, even if that treatment is life-sustaining.[f]

It is one thing to do what I have tried to do, to set out in principle the goal(s) of medical treatment and the limits of medical endeavour, it is another to say something genuinely enlightening about the daily practical challenges that face doctors: challenges to their compassion, to their technical skill and to their judgment. Such challenges come from a variety of sources: from families who are unable to accept the death of someone they love, from families for whom the imminent death of a loved relative brings to the surface deep wounds of regret and remorse, from families who wish to inherit sooner rather than later. They also come from changes in the self-image of the medical professions (e.g. from those in the medical profession who think of themselves as possessing knowledge and skill which may, without loss, be put to any purpose that consumers seek and not merely to their health needs).

---

[e] Nature of duty of care, Halsbury's *Laws of Australia*, 280-2000.

[f] 'It is lawful for a doctor to withdraw treatment that is futile'. Halsbury's *Laws of Australia*, 280-3030. '...It is lawful to withdraw or withhold treatment at the request of a competent adult patient, or treatment that is futile. In some cases this principle may extend to not offering all treatments that may be available if that is not recommended by the treating doctors for a critically ill patient.' Halsbury's *Laws of Australia*, 380-3510.

One thing at least is clear: a sure sense of what medicine is about, and thus what its limits are, is at least the right starting point for reflection on what is best to do, and to refrain from doing, for a particular patient.

ACKNOWLEDGEMENTS

I am grateful to Brian Horan, Terence O'Connor and Michael Fearnside for helpful comments on an earlier draft.

REFERENCES

1. Kass L. The end of medicine and the pursuit of health. In: *Towards a More Natural Science: Biology and Human Affairs*. New York: The Free Press, 1985; 157–186.
2. Simmons L. On not destroying the health of one's patients. In: Odeberg DS, Laing JS (eds). *Human Lives: Critical Essays on Consequential Bioethics*. Hampshire: Macmillan, 1997; 144–160.
3. Amundsen DW. The physician's duty to prolong life: A medical duty without classical roots. *Hastings Center Report*, 1978; **8**: 23–30.
4. Callahan D. *The Troubled Dream of Life: In Search of a Peaceful Death*. New York: Simon & Schuster, 1993; 59.
5. Finnis J. Bland: Crossing the Rubicon? *The Law Quarterly Review*, Volume 109, July 1993.

Organ donation and transplantation

D.F. SCOTT, D.M.A. FRANCIS

Introduction

Since becoming a clinical reality more than 40 years ago, organ transplantation has raised many ethical issues. Transplantation is practised widely in developed countries and is almost a routine therapeutic procedure, indicating that moral controversies have been largely resolved within the medical and wider communities. General acceptance of clinical transplantation stems from the clear demonstration that successful organ replacement is beneficial, in that it both prolongs life and enhances the quality of life of recipients. The results of patient and graft survival after transplantation of the heart, lung, liver, kidney and pancreas in Australia and New Zealand are shown in Table 1.[1-4] The enormous enthusiasm with which clinical and experimental transplant programs have been pursued has been justified by the realisation that transplantation offers either the only or the best form of therapy in many cases of end-stage organ failure, and potentially can be applied to large numbers of patients.

The severe worldwide shortage of donor organs is the main impediment to transplantation and has resulted in ever-increasing numbers of chronically ill patients waiting for long periods of time for transplants. Currently in Australia more than 1500 patients are waiting for kidney transplants, nearly 200 are waiting for heart or

Table 1. Clinical organ transplantation in Australia and New Zealand

Organ	Number	Patient survival (%) 1 year	Patient survival (%) 5 years	Graft survival (%) 1 year	Graft survival (%) 5 years
Heart[1]	1099[a]	87	79	87	79
Lung[1]	411[b]	80	63	80	63
Heart-lung	1117[c]	79	51	79	51
Liver[2]	1336[d]	82	74	82	74
Kidney[3,4]					
- cadaver	11 477[c]	92	83	84	73
- live donors	1595[e]	N/A	N/A	94	86
Pancreas	95	90	90	75	70

a, 1984–97; d, 1985–98;
b, 1990–97; e, 1963–97.
c, 1986–97; N/A, Not available.

lung transplants, 55 for liver transplants, 25 for pancreas transplants and 450 for corneal transplants. Of patients with heart and liver failure, approximately 30% die before a cadaveric organ becomes available.

Controversial ethical issues have revolved largely around the use of living organ donors, the definition of death in relation to cadaver organ donors, the ways of obtaining donor organs, the allocation of donated organs, and the use of animals as organ donors for human recipients.

Organ donation is an outstanding act of human kindness, and must be acknowledged as such by recipients, the medical profession, and society in general. It exemplifies the concept of caring for fellow human beings and the respect our society has for the sanctity of human life. All of the major religions support organ donation, acknowledging that organ donation without coercion is a supremely humane and beneficial act. Organ donation has stimulated considerable ethical debate because of issues relating to the definition of death, the rights of individuals to decide whether or not to be organ donors, and the inherent difficulties of dealing with sudden death, bereavement, and human suffering.

Organ donors may be living healthy individuals (live donors). Such donors account for about 30% of renal transplants performed currently in Australia and New Zealand.[3] Cadaveric donation occurs after brain death is diagnosed. Permission for donation is obtained from the family of the deceased, or the deceased may have recorded his/her wish to be an organ donor prior to death.

The right to be an organ donor

The ethical principle of autonomy dictates that individuals have the right of self-determination of their future without external restraint. While most people would defend strongly this principle of having the right to do what they like with their bodies, either for good (e.g. physical and mental exercise) or for harm (e.g. smoking), most also would accept that they have the right to be an organ donor if they so wish, unless disqualified on medical or social grounds. However, few take the opportunity to exercise their autonomy by declaring their wish to become a donor, either as a live, or more particularly, a cadaver donor even though they accept the enormous benefits of transplantation. The utilitarian principle becomes submerged by societal and personal restrictions, to the detriment of others. At a time when organ donors are very scarce, the medical community must ensure that people are aware of this right, and donation must be seen to be a means of expressing autonomy, even after death.

Responsibility to the organ donor

Those involved in transplantation have responsibilities to both the organ donor and the recipient. The decision to donate an organ ideally should be taken after careful and informed consideration of all aspects of the matter. This process may be restricted by emotions and stresses felt by a potential live donor or the family of a potential cadaveric donor. It is incumbent upon medical practitioners first to provide an environment that facilitates discussion and decision making, and second to ensure that the facts concerning the process of donation, the potential sequelae, and the likely outcomes for the donor and the recipient are presented openly and comprehensibly to potential donors and their families.

Respect for the donor is paramount, irrespective of whether the donor is a living person or a corpse. The process of organ removal must be conducted with the same attention to detail and solemnity as any surgical procedure. With the advent of cadaveric multi-organ procurement, perhaps involving retrieval of heart, lungs, liver, kidneys, pancreas, blood vessels, corneas, skin, bones, spleen and lymph nodes, some health-care professionals have felt that respect for the donor has been lost. Medical and nursing staff have been offended when busy surgical teams, trying to minimise ischaemic damage to organs, appear to have no time to acknowledge the deeply held ethic of respect for the dead. The apparent moral conflict of respecting the dead while at the same time rapidly removing vital organs suitable for transplantation has been largely resolved by open acknowledgement of the importance of the act of donation, consciously respecting the dead, and being sympathetic to the feelings of others in what may be a very emotionally charged situation. Similarly, live donors occasionally have admitted to feelings of being ignored after their operation, and have perceived that medical interest was transferred to the recipient along with the donor organ.

Our responsibility to organ donors includes not only skillful removal of organs in the operating room but continues indefinitely in the form of adequate follow-up of live donors, and support and counselling of families of cadaver donors. The latter is an area that has not been well-funded or undertaken actively until recently, but clearly is of immense importance if we are to maintain community support for organ donation.

Responsibility to the organ recipient

Transplant surgeons also have a responsibility to the recipient, in addition to the normal care given to any surgical patient. We must ensure that the donor organ is of a sufficiently high standard to allow for the expectation of a successful outcome. In practice, this means taking reasonable steps to ensure that the donor is free of transmissible diseases (e.g. infection, cancer), and that the donor organ is, as far as possible, free from problems that could adversely affect the outcome (e.g. parenchymal disease, surgical injury).

The shortage of donor organs has necessitated a relaxation of the criteria of acceptability of organ donors. With the increasing use of older organ donors for example, the quality of some retrieved organs is less than optimal. Such organs would not have been used in a time of plentiful supply, but now have become a precious resource. Occasionally, the surgeon is faced with the ethical dilemma of feeling obliged to transplant an organ of less than optimal quality which possibly could lead to reduced graft function or survival, causing recipient morbidity or mortality.[5] The transplant surgeon has to make some risk–benefit analysis before advising and obtaining consent from the patient. Most would feel that the potential recipient has a moral right to know that a less-than-optimal donor organ has been procured and that it could possibly lead to a less satisfactory outcome. Similarly, most would feel that the patient also has the right of autonomy and is free to decline the organ.[6]

Live organ donation

Non-maleficence

Medical practice follows the principles of beneficence (i.e. achieving what is good for the patient) and non-maleficence (i.e. avoiding harm to the patient). Live donor transplantation goes against these principles, and this dilemma was realised even in the very early days of clinical renal transplantation. Francis Moore in 1964 summarised the unique situation of the live donor: 'For the first time in the history of medicine a procedure is being adopted in which a perfectly healthy person is injured permanently in order to improve the well being of another. Some laboratories have viewed this matter with such misgivings that under no circumstances have they used tissues from volunteer donors'.[1] This view is no longer shared by the majority of renal transplant centres, largely because the live donor operation has been shown repeatedly to be safe, both in the short and long term, and because of the significantly better results of live donor compared with cadaver donor renal transplantation (Table 1). Also, there is now considerable pressure from individuals who wish to exercise their right of autonomy by donating a kidney to someone to whom they are genetically or emotionally related, rather than having that person wait for several years, perhaps fruitlessly, in the hope of obtaining a cadaver organ.

Nevertheless, performing an operation on a living individual which is of no physical benefit to that person and which carries a risk, albeit small, of dying or permanent disability, goes against one of the major ethical pillars of medicine – 'above all, do no harm' or non-maleficence. Transplant personnel have genuine concerns about the risks to live donors. Such anxieties are alleviated to some extent by thorough investigation of potential live donors and by excluding those with any factor that may impinge adversely on their future health, by repeatedly and comprehensively explaining the potential risks and sequelae of the procedure, by encouraging exchange between potential donors and those who have donated, and by establishing short- and long-term management protocols based on recognised best practices. Even then, many transplant surgeons feel more comfortable removing a kidney from a cadaver donor than from a living donor, and look forward to the day when there is an adequate supply of donor organs from either human cadavers or non-human sources.

Regenerative tissues and non-regenerative organs

Today, there are few qualms about donating blood or bone marrow, because these tissues are regenerative and the process of donation is associated with minimal risk to the donor. Donation of non-regenerative organs generally implies greater risk, because the process of removal is more involved and because of the long-term potential risk of disease or injury to the remaining organ or tissue. The element of risk to the donor is a recurring theme in any ethical discussion about live organ donation, and it has an important bearing on the assessment of suitability of potential live donors.

Professional paternalism

Occasionally, conflict arises between an individual insistent on donating an organ and the transplant unit which believes that it is not in the person's best interest. Such professional paternalism[5] directly conflicts with the individual's autonomy. It is based on estimates of risk to the donor and predictions of the likelihood of outcome, which of course are imprecise and cannot be guaranteed. Rejecting a potential live donor denies his/her autonomy. However, from an ethical standpoint, first it exemplifies the principle of non-maleficence as perceived by the transplant unit, and second it respects the autonomy of the medical practitioners, a right to which they are entitled. There is no ethical requirement for a practitioner to acquiesce to a patient's request if it is not accepted practice or if the practitioner believes that it is not in the patient's interest. The issue of conflict between professional paternalism and donor autonomy is perhaps most relevant to the donation of segments of liver and pancreas from live donors. A parent may be particularly strongly motivated to accept major surgical risks for the sake of their sick or dying child. Many parents would 'die' to save their child, perhaps forgetting that there are other children and family members to be cared for and that perfect health may not be restored with transplantation. For the recipient, such procedures can be life-saving in the case of the liver, and can bring about enormous improvement in the quality of life for diabetics in the case of the pancreas. Thus, it may be very difficult to view such cases with objectivity and to calculate the risk–benefit ratio. Clearly, the risk to the donor of an operative procedure associated with significant mortality and morbidity must be balanced against the potential benefit to the recipient, so that all involved are comfortable with the proposed transplant.

Altruism

The desire to save a loved one, whether genetically or emotionally related, is an extremely strong motivating force and one which must be respected. It is the reason why some donors are quite prepared to accept substantial risk to give another a good chance of being restored to health. Altruism within the closeknit family of a member in need of an organ transplant kindles an internal pressure to donate and can bring about enormous self-sacrifice. Such pressure is an inherent part of familial altruism and is distinct from coercion. It may go unnoticed by the donor, who thinks organ donation is quite a natural thing to do. Altruism in organ donation has its own reward. The great majority of live donors gain enormous self-esteem and satisfaction from seeing that they have actively demonstrated their feelings for a loved one by providing the one thing that the recipient truly needed, and most would say that they would repeat the experience if possible.[7]

Live donor renal transplantation in Australia and New Zealand was restricted to genetically related individuals until 1990. Up to 1998, 74 renal transplants had been performed between genetically unrelated but emotionally related individuals, including spouses, in-laws, adoptive parents, and friends.[4] As with other live donor transplants, activity was stimulated largely by the severe shortage of cadaver organs. With improved immunosuppressive regimens and better overall management of donors and recipients, the results of live-unrelated renal transplants are comparable with those from live-related donors.[8] Living-unrelated organ donation is a true expression of altruism. The bonds that exist between such donors and their recipients may be stronger than between family members. Most transplant centres believe that such transplants should be restricted to highly motivated emotionally related pairs, and that every effort should be taken to exclude coercion and commercialisation.

Occasionally, a transplant unit is contacted by an altruistic stranger who wishes to donate a kidney to someone unknown to them. Typically, this occurs after media releases about patients, often children, in need of transplantation. The motivation of such individuals is complex. They have an extreme sense of altruism without any sense of coercion, and can be seen to exemplify a true sense of unselfishness. However, most are ignorant of the criteria for and process of live organ donation. Although donation of regenerative tissues (blood and bone marrow) from altruistic strangers is a well-established medical practice, the profession has remained sceptical about solid organ donation from such people. Concern may be expressed about the risks of the donation procedure, but the risk to an altruistic stranger kidney donor is the same as for a live-related kidney donor. Doubts may be raised about the individual's psychiatric state, ability to comprehend the donation process, and possible subsequent exploitation of the recipient, and such volunteers are rejected out of hand. This denial of autonomy may be seen as an example of professional paternalism. With proper assessment and counselling, it may be appropriate to accept such truly altruistic donors.

Use of minors as organ donors

Inherent in the concept of autonomy is the ability and the right to decide one's fate, particularly when it comes to decisions about one's body. The age of consent is defined legally and minors cannot give consent for surgical procedures. It is presumed that a child cannot comprehend fully the nature of the situation which requires an operation for the cure of a surgical illness. By the same argument, it would be wrong to assume that a child could give informed consent for removal of a donor organ. Consent of a parent or legal guardian overrides a child's autonomy during illness — a situation which is deemed entirely ethical because the operation is clearly in the interest of the child.

Live organ donation is quite different. The procedure is not in the direct interests of the donor and, in the case of renal donation from a young child, could lead to renal impairment several decades later. However, courts in the USA have allowed parents to donate kidneys and bone marrow from their under-age children on the basis that the child will benefit from the donation because the sibling will be restored to health, and family stresses and financial burdens will be reduced. In Australia, it is forbidden by law to remove non-regenerative tissues from a living child for transplantation. Regenerative tissues may be removed from a minor for transplantation to a brother, sister or parent, with the written informed consent of the parent.[9]

Paid donors

Occasional reports have appeared in the media over the last decade concerning the sale of organs, particularly kidneys and corneas, from donors in the Middle East, the Indian subcontinent and Asia. Some of these donations are motivated simply by a desire for personal financial gain, a practice which has been condemned strongly by the transplant community. Paid donations do not result solely from greed, but from extreme poverty and in circumstances the sale of a non-vital organ seems to be the only way for the donor and his/her family to achieve economic survival. Such acts may be seen as indirect altruism, where an individual is prepared to put up with short-term pain and suffering for long-term financial and economic benefit of themselves and others. These two scenarios are different, and it has been argued that, with proper controls, paid organ donation (rewarded gifting) might be acceptable in some communities and cultures.[9]

Recipients of such kidneys generally come from countries where there is a shortage of donor organs, who pay thousands of dollars to an intermediary to have the transplant, and who then return to their home country. The scope for exploitation of both donor and recipient is enormous. Allegedly, donors frequently do not receive the money promised to them, receive minimal or no pre-operative assessment to ensure accepted criteria for donation are met, and receive no follow-up. Recipient care is poor, and a significant proportion of recipients have developed AIDS. Graft survival is reduced, and recipient mortality is increased.[10, 11]

Publicity surrounding 'organ trade' by unscrupulous entrepreneurs has the potential to impact adversely on organ donation in general, even in countries far from where the practice exists. The important issue is that the trafficking in organs and derivation of profit from the suffering and exploitation of others is unethical, while the act of donation itself is not. The Transplantation Society has made a strong stand against commercialisation of organ donation, and has recommended that all countries legislate to forbid all commercial dealings in tissues and organs, which the Society feels should be given freely without financial consideration.[12]

Laparoscopic donor nephrectomy

The recent introduction of laparoscopic nephrectomy for benign and malignant diseases has stimulated interest in applying the technique to live donors. As with all new surgical procedures, ethical standards require that the technique is evaluated properly, and this is especially important in its application to the unique procedure of live donor nephrectomy — an elective major operation of no physical benefit to the patient. Principal contentious issues relate to the safety of the procedure for the donor (e.g. intraoperative bleeding, damage to adjacent structures, prolonged operating time, post-operative complications), and the implications for the recipient (e.g. immediate graft function, non-immunological complications). The quality of the removed kidney must be such as to allow at least equivalent graft survival and complication rates as the open procedure.

The unproven efficacy of the laparoscopic technique has been recognised by the Royal Australasian College of Surgeons and currently is being assessed by the Australian Safety and Efficacy Register of New Interventional Procedures–Surgical (ASERNIP-S) under the auspices of the College.

Cadaver organ donation

While we readily accept the enormous benefits of successful cadaver donor transplantation, organ donation from cadavers is poorly accepted in our community. Consequently, Australia and New Zealand have the lowest rates of cadaver organ donation of any Westernised country[13] (Table 2). This is perhaps surprising, because we like to think we are nations in which everyone gets 'a fair go', being bound together by a strong sense of 'mateship' and social justice. As a society, belief in the utilitarian principle seems to wither when it comes to cadaver organ donation.

The paradox of ready acceptance of transplantation on the one hand, and refusal to participate in its fundamental prerequisite on the other, is due largely to the circumstances in which the opportunity of cadaver organ donation arises. Potential donors have nearly always suffered sudden unexpected deaths, some from

Table 2. Cadaver donor rates (1995)[14]

Country	Cadaveric donor rate per million population
Spain	27.0
USA	20.9
UK	15.8
Canada	14.4
Switzerland	13.0
Australia	10.3
Italy	10.1
New Zealand	10.0
Greece	5.6

traumatic or other unnatural causes. Medical and nursing staff not only have to cope with their own feelings of distress, but also have to support emotionally shocked and grieving families. Some believe that an approach to the family for organ donation is inappropriate and an additional burden with which the family has to cope. Fortunately, almost 20% of cadaver donations occur because the issue is raised by the bereaved family,[15] a truly heroic act at a time of acute distress. In this instance, the family may be carrying out the wishes of the deceased, and see the act of donation as the only positive aspect of an immense tragedy — a fact which gives immeasurable support through their grieving for many years.

Surveys have shown that up to 80% of the Australian community are prepared to have their own organs donated after their death, but less than half would donate organs from their spouse or offspring. This is borne out by the finding that, of families approached for tissue or organ donation from a suitable potential donor, only 40% gave permission.[14] However, whatever the decision of the family, whether to donate or not, it must be respected. The decision not to donate can be seen as upholding the principle of autonomy, while at the same time ignoring the principle of beneficence, by denying another individual the chance of a better life.

Reluctance to donate cadaveric organs is multifactorial. Regrettably, health care professionals may not identify suitable potential donors because of what they perceive as an intrinsically unpleasant task of seeking consent. This issue has been addressed to some extent by the introduction in some parts of the US of 'required request' laws, which require medical practitioners to ask permission for organ donation from all families of medically suitable donors. Such laws take the onus away from practitioners, who therefore need not feel that an action initiated by them has added further hurt to the bereaved family.

Cultural attitudes towards death and the dead, and the way in which some ethnic groups involve the extended family when making important decisions, also influence the decision to donate. Misinterpretations of religious edicts are impediments to organ donation, some families citing religious grounds to justify refusal, even though all major religions support organ donation.

The diagnosis of death

Perhaps more than in any other area of clinical practice, it is essential that the community has confidence in the ethical standards and abilities of medical practitioners who certify death. Death is defined in all States and Territories in Australia by essentially similar laws. Part IX, paragraph 41 of the Human Tissue Act 1982[9] of Victoria states:

> *'For the purposes of the law of Victoria, a person has died when there has occurred:*
>
> *(a) irreversible cessation of circulation of blood in the body of the person; or*
> *(b) irreversible cessation of all function of the brain of the person.'*

Part (b) of this paragraph is relevant to organ donation, because organs must have an adequate circulation and oxygen supply until the time of removal from the donor, so that ischaemic damage is minimised.

The two key elements of this definition of death are first that the condition is 'irreversible', and second that 'all function' of the brain has ceased. The irreversible nature of severe depression of brain function (apnoeic coma) requires an initial diagnosis consistent with irremediable brain damage (e.g. intracranial haemorrhage, brain injury), exclusion of any reversible factors leading to coma (e.g. depressant or neuromuscular blocking drugs, hypothermia, metabolic and endocrine conditions), and a reasonable period of observation of the patient. Cessation of brain function is recognised by non-function of the brainstem, the part of the brain that is concerned with cortical activation and generation of consciousness, maintenance of respiration, co-regulation of heart rate and blood pressure, and passage of all sensory input (except sight and smell) into the brain and all motor pathways from the brain. Brainstem function can be assessed simply and accurately at the bedside by the presence or absence of reflexes of cranial nerves, the nuclei of which are distributed throughout the brainstem. Provided that irreversibility has been established, absence of brainstem reflexes equates with death of the brainstem and, therefore, death of the brain as a whole, although it does not necessarily imply death of every cell in the brain or in the rest of the body. The clinical criteria for brainstem death are shown in Table 3.

Not surprisingly, some find it difficult to accept fully the concept of brain death — that a person can be dead and yet the heart is beating, breathing occurs with the aid of a machine, urine is produced and the peripheries are warm, and so on. At times, ill-informed media have contributed to public fear and confusion with erroneous and misleading reports about brain death and organ donation,[a] to the detriment of the community in general and those awaiting transplantation in particular.

Table 3. Clinical criteria of brainstem death

1. Apnoea. Absent respiratory movement during disconnection from the ventilator with the Pa_{CO_2} greater than 50 mmHg or 6.65 kPa.
2. No pupillary response (3rd cranial nerve nucleus). No pupillary movement in response to bright light.
3. No cornea reflex (5th and 7th cranial nerve nuclei). No blinking in response to touching the cornea with a sterile throat swab.
4. No vestibulo-ocular reflex (3rd, 6th and 8th cranial nerve nuclei). No eye movement or deviation towards the ear into which ice-cold water is instilled.
5. No motor response to painful stimuli (5th and 7th cranial nerve nuclei). No facial muscular response to painful stimuli applied either to the trigeminal nerve area or the limbs.
6. No gag reflex (9th and 10th cranial nerve nuclei). No gagging movement with stimulation of the posterior pharyngeal wall with the endotracheal tube or to bronchial stimulation with a suction catheter passed into the trachea.

[a] Panorama: Transplants—are the donors really dead? British Broadcasting Corporation Channel 1, 13 October 1980.

Opting in and opting out

Currently in Australia and New Zealand, donors have to 'opt in' if they or their families wish them to be organ donors; that is, they have to make a definite decision to donate. An opting in system assumes that the individual is not a donor, and the onus is on the donor before death or the family after death to make an affirmative decision to volunteer organs. Clearly, many people do not think about organ donation and 'opting in' makes it easy to ignore what to some is a difficult issue. To some extent, an opting in system denies the utilitarian ethic and makes donation unnecessarily hard.

In an attempt to increase the number of cadaver organ donors, some countries have passed opting out or 'presumed consent' legislation. Under such laws, a medically suitable cadaver is regarded automatically as an organ donor and organs may be removed unless the individual expressly stated or appropriately registered before death that his or her organs were not to be used for transplantation. This system has increased the rate of organ donation in some countries (e.g. Austria, Belgium, Singapore) but not all (e.g. France, some parts of the USA). The advantage of an opting out system is that everyone is presumed to be an organ donor until proven otherwise, a principle exemplifying utilitarianism and altruism. A definitive commitment against organ donation has to be made in order to not become a donor after death. Acceptance of presumed consent legislation has been greater in communities that are more ethnically homogeneous. Many transplant surgeons would not remove organs from donors if the family objected or had not given consent, even though they were entitled legally to do so.

Organs from executed criminals

Executed criminals have been used as a source of cadaver kidneys in China,[15] and other Asian countries. The practice raises many ethical issues and allows for considerable exploitation of donors and recipients. An unscrupulous judiciary could be encouraged to bring in a guilty verdict and pass a death sentence, knowing that the organs could be sold subsequently. Recipients from outside China have claimed to pay over US$25 000 for such kidneys (less for mainland Chinese). The income passes to the State, and the prisoner has no option to consent or object to organ removal. It is not possible to know whether brain death is diagnosed before the organs are removed. The mortality and morbidity from infectious complications in recipients is unacceptably high,[11] indicating that donors are not screened adequately before execution. The Transplantation Society has forbidden its members to be involved in obtaining or transplanting organs from executed criminals.[14]

Use of anencephalic donors

Anencephalic infants are born without a functioning cerebral cortex and resemble individuals in a persistent vegetative state in that they breathe spontaneously, have a gag reflex and may exhibit sleep–wake brain cycles. Although no meaningful relationship could ever be established with the world around them even if they survived, such individuals are not brain dead and therefore do not meet the criteria for cadaver organ donation. Any ethical dilemma about using anencephalics as organ donors, even after they become brain dead, has been largely defused by the realisation that such tiny organs have a very poor chance of being transplanted successfully. Anencephalic infants are not regarded as suitable potential organ donors.

Conflict of interest

When the potential live donor and organ recipient are both under the care of the same clinician, it could be construed that a conflict of interest exists. However, given that the practitioner understands the principles of non-maleficence and beneficence, such conflict is unlikely to occur. Logically, there is no sense in sacrificing one individual in order to save another, or inducing significant permanent morbidity in one so as to reduce morbidity in another. Any potential conflict of interest is resolved by the donor and recipient being assessed and cared for by different clinicians.

Similarly, there must be no question of conflict of interest in either the diagnosis of brain death or the provision of cadaver organs. Determination of death of a potential donor must be made without any interest in a potential recipient, a concept which is ensured by

State laws within Australia.[9] Members of the transplant team are not responsible for diagnosing brain death and are not involved in care of potential cadaver donors, both duties being performed by intensivists.

Organ allocation

Allocation of cadaver donor organs to recipients must be based on acceptable ethical standards if society is to maintain confidence in organ donation and transplantation. Allocation may be a complex issue and is based upon several ethical principles. Because of organ scarcity, some transplant communities follow the utilitarian principle by allocating donor organs to those recipients who have the greatest chance of a prolonged and successful outcome. For example, the renal transplant community within Australia is in general agreement that cadaver kidneys should be allocated primarily on the basis of tissue matching — a factor which has been shown over many years to strongly favour a successful outcome. However, utilitarianism is tempered by the need to 'rescue' some individuals even though such action may not lead to the best overall outcome. Occasionally, a patient is in urgent need of transplantation because of specific medical problems and is given a degree of priority. Similarly, patients who have been waiting for a kidney transplant for more than 5 years also receive some priority because the suffering and adverse long-term effects of prolonged dialysis are seen as medically and ethically legitimate reasons to hasten transplantation. Few would argue that such a scheme is unjust.

The egalitarian principle that all patients should have equal access to the opportunity for donor organs necessarily excludes such factors as perceived social worth, ability to pay, gender, age and ethnic origin from being taken into consideration when allocating donor organs. It has been argued that paediatric patients represent a special case and that priority should be given to them. Such proposals stem from the emotional response, engendered by children suffering from chronic debilitating illnesses, rather than logic. A similar case could be put forward for the elderly who may have suffered over a long period of time and may be running out of time. In fact, all age groups have their own unique features which can be used to support a case for prioritisation, and so age *per se* is not a factor in the allocation process. Ethnicity may adversely affect the chance of receiving a donor organ when allocation is based on tissue matching. Because some ethnic minorities rarely donate cadaver organs, tissue types that are found commonly in those ethnic groups are infrequently present in the donor organ pool, and so potential recipients within those groups are frequently allocated well-matched organs. Most would see that the solution to this problem is to change attitudes towards donation rather than to promote an allocation policy that would lead to inferior results.

Lack of compliance with medical therapy is a continuing cause of graft failure, accounting for approximately 3% of failed kidney transplants.[2] Recipients of organs have a duty to take great care of the precious gift that they have received solely because of the beneficence of another individual. Some would argue that patients who have been unable to comply with medical treatment should not be re-allocated another organ until they demonstrate clearly that they are prepared to accept all the responsibilities associated with transplantation. While removal from a transplant waiting list as a punitive measure would be regarded as unethical, it would also be seen as ethically unacceptable to allocate an organ to an individual when there was a significant risk of failure due to non-compliance.

Xenotransplantation

Because of the enormous unfulfilled need for organ donors, the option of raising animals to provide organs for human transplantation (xenotransplantation) is being investigated actively. Animals considered as potential donors include chimpanzees, baboons and pigs. Although genetically closest to humans and having some immunological advantages, chimpanzees are unlikely to be accepted as a donor source because the species is threatened with extinction. Baboons are greater in number and are also likely to have immunological advantages over other species but, like chimpanzees, arouse considerable public sentiment which would prohibit their use. Also, the small size of their organs would generally exclude their use in adult transplantation, except for cell transplants such as pancreatic islet or nerve cells.

The preferred source, and the one under most intense research effort, is the pig. Two million pigs are slaughtered annually for human consumption in Australia, and the community reaction to the use of pigs may well be favourable. Breeding of pigs specifically for human organ transplantation raises issues of care of animals, a particular concern to animal welfare groups. The science of breeding pigs for successful human transplantation is ongoing but much remains to be done. To date, deletion of pig genes and insertion of human genes into the pig has resulted in modification of proteins which stimulate immediate rejection of transplanted pig organs by the clotting of blood vessels. Sufficient control of the xenograft reaction has been achieved to allow organs which would have failed in the host within minutes to survive for 1–2 weeks.

Genetically altered pigs must breed and develop in a pathogen-free environment, to ensure that no porcine infectious agents are transmitted with the donor organ to human recipients. This poses formidable practical problems, such as depriving pigs of their normal activities, the need to deliver large quantities of sterilised food, and the exclusion of rodents, fungi, protozoa, bacteria and viruses from the pigs' environment. The logistics of sterile surgery with adult pigs which may weigh 100–150 kg at maturity will also be difficult. Piglets would have to be delivered by caesarean section and isolated from their mother to maintain a germ-free environment. Even then, there will be concern that infectious agents [e.g. retroviruses or prions such as those that cause bovine spongiform encephalopathy (BSE or 'mad cow disease')], may not be eliminated. Without stringent controls, xenotransplantation could provide an opportunity for animal-derived infectious agents to jump the species barrier and create a new epidemic such as occurred with the human immunodeficiency virus (HIV), which moved from a benign disease in monkeys to a fatal and rapidly spreading disease in humans.

The xenograft rejection response, both acute and delayed, may be more severe than the allograft response as there is greater genetic dissimilarity between donor and recipient, and therefore more potent immunosuppressive drugs may be required. This is likely to cause a greater incidence of human opportunistic infections and an increased cancer risk in surviving recipients. Again, there will be increased concern about pig-derived pathogens in heavily immunosuppressed recipients. These factors have to be weighed against the probable success of xenotransplantation, which is likely to be less than the current average 80–90% 1 year graft survival of human solid organ transplants.

Interest groups in the community will take opposing views on the dilemma about whether to support xenotransplantation. There is an urgency to provide treatment for critically ill patients dying of organ failure and there is a developing scientifically valid approach to using genetically modified pig organs as replacement grafts. Others will oppose the intensive animal husbandry necessary to modify the pigs genetically and raise them in an isolated sterile laboratory with considerable environmental deprivation.

The dilemma of xenografts needs considerable discussion in the medical and lay communities. At the time of publication, the science of controlling xenograft rejection by genetic engineering and the use of more potent immunosuppressive drugs is not yet at a stage which will allow success comparable with cadaveric organ transplantation. Barriers to uniformly successful xenotransplantation are likely to be reduced by further research but it is not known when.

The full risks of xenotransplanted infections will remain unknown until xenotransplants are tried. There is likely to be further microbiological refinement to identify organisms which pose a threat to patients, but it is not possible to eliminate unknown potential pathogens. Is this sufficient reason for the community to decide not to proceed and to ban clinical trials? Already a number of patients have received pig cells and tissues in Sweden and the USA, and to date, pig viruses have not been identified in surviving recipients many years later. Strong consensus needs to form about whether the need is greater to help those with life-threatening illness with a xenograft that has a reasonable chance of success, or to protect the recipient and eventually the community from the potential risks of infection with hitherto unknown pathogens. Science will refine the current knowledge but will not be able to provide complete answers. Local hospital ethics committees, national scientific advisory bodies and the public need to be involved in these decisions. The level of likely success of xenotransplants will be determined initially by testing genetically altered pig organ transplants in non-human primates — the current ethical restrictions of which are considerable. The risk of transmitted infections will not be known with any confidence until after a trial of xenotransplantation in humans. In planning such trials, the requirement to fully monitor the recipient, as well as close contacts and hospital staff, for signs of well-recognised infections or previously unknown infective illness is absolute. Finally, specimens from the donor animal and organ recipients will need to be stored in case new diseases appear at a later date. When these conditions are introduced and accepted, society may have confidence that xenotransplantation will benefit critically ill patients with an acceptable level of risk to the community.

Conclusions

Organ donation and transplantation have stimulated considerable ethical debate since becoming a clinical reality more than four decades ago. Many ethical issues have been resolved as society has evolved and has become more accepting of change, and the success and benefits of transplantation have become evident to all. The challenge of the future is for all involved in transplantation to ensure that their practices are based on sound ethical and scientific principles, and to keep their respective communities informed about transplant practices in an open and frank manner. We must be prepared to engage with purpose those who wish to examine ethical and contentious issues, so that transplantation — a means of saving human life and reducing suffering — is advanced.

REFERENCES

1. Australian and New Zealand Cardiothoracic Transplant Registry. *Seventh Annual Report, 1984-1997*.

2. Sheil AGR. *Australia and New Zealand Liver Transplant Registry*. Camperdown: Australian National Liver Transplant Unit, 1999.

3. Disney APS, Collins J, Russ GR, Herberrt K, Walker R, Kerp P. *ANZDATA Registry Report 1998*. Adelaide: Australia and New Zealand Dialysis and Transplant Registry, 1998.

4. Disney APS et al. *ANZDATA Registry Report 1997*. Adelaide: Australia and New Zealand Dialysis and Transplant Registry, 1997.

5. Lloveras J. The elderly donor. *Transplant. Proc.* 1991; **23**: 2592–2595.

6. Sells RA. Informed consent from recipients of marginal donor organs. *Transplant. Proc.* 1999; **31**: 1324–1325.

7. Gouge F, Moore J, Bremer BA *et al*. The quality of life of donors, potential donors, and recipients of living-related donor renal transplantation. *Transplant. Proc.* 1990; **22**: 2409–2413.

8. Cecka JM, Terasaki P. Living donor kidney transplants: superior success rates despite histoincompatibilities. *Transplant. Proc.* 1997; **29**: 203.

9. *Human Tissue Act (Victoria) 1982*. Melbourne: Government Printer.

10. Salahudeen AK, Woods HF, Pingle A *et al*. High mortality among recipients of bought living-unrelated donor kidneys. *Lancet* 1990; **336**: 725–728.

11. Cheng IKP, La KN, Au TC *et al*. Comparison of the mortality and morbidity rate between proper and unconventional renal transplantation using organs from executed prisoners. *Transplant. Proc.* 1991; **23**: 2533–2536.

12. The Council of the Transplantation Society. Commercialism in transplantation: The problems and some guidelines for practice. *Lancet* 1985; **ii**: 713–716.

13. Matesanz R, Miranda B. *Organ Donation for Transplantation: The Spanish Model*. Madrid: Grupo Aula Medica, 1996; 190.

14. Policy Statement: Ethics Committee of The Transplantation Society.

15. Jager L, Pollock G, Scully G. *Victorian Transplant Co-ordinators Donor/Transplant Annual Report 1996*, 1997.

FURTHER READING

Childress JF. *Who should Decide? Paternalism in Health Care*. New York: Oxford University Press, 1982; 3–27.

Dossetor JB. Rewarded gifting: Ever ethically acceptable? *Transplant. Proc.* 1992; **24**: 2092.

Moore PD. New problems for surgery. *Science*, 1964; **144**: 388–392.

The impaired fetus and newborn

N. CAMPBELL

Teamwork, new technologies, and evidence-based medicine have improved survival and quality of life across the range of diseases peculiar to the fetus and newborn. Nevertheless, there are still babies for whom modern care can do nothing more than prolong the interval before death or else ensure survival with very poor quality of life. While there is a broad consensus that life-sustaining treatment should be withheld or withdrawn from at least some impaired babies, there remains vigorous ethical debate about the detail, and some of the legal aspects are unclear.

Closely related to these issues is the new status of the fetus as a patient. Ultrasound scanning, amniotic fluid, fetal blood, and chorionic villous sampling now allow diagnosis of a range of fetal disorders. These in turn raise ethical and legal questions surrounding termination of pregnancy, fetal therapy including surgery, and timing and method of delivery.

Impairments in babies for whom withholding life-sustaining treatment may be considered include:

1. Those for whom life will be short despite treatment (e.g. anencephaly, Trisomy 18, and Potter's syndrome).
2. Those for whom survival is possible, but with serious intellectual impairment (e.g. various brain malformations, or severe asphyxia).

3. Those for whom survival is possible but with severe physical disabilities (e.g. thoracic meningomyelocoele).
4. Those for whom survival is possible but only with prolonged burdensome treatment (e.g. short bowel syndrome from atresia or volvulus requiring lifelong parenteral nutrition).

Termination of pregnancy for fetal impairment remains ethically controversial but is widely practised. When families have chosen to continue pregnancy, fetal surgery has been attempted for such conditions as diaphragmatic hernia, obstructive uropathy, and hydrocephalus, but case selection and efficacy remain problematic.

It is obvious that many impairments require the involvement of paediatric surgeons, and while newborn intensive care is a team-endeavour involving several subspecialties, surgeons need to be active team members and are often the most appropriate team 'leader'. It follows that paediatric surgeons need a good grasp of ethical and legal issues.

There are basic ethical differences between babies and adults:

1. Babies are 'incompetent'; all decisions must be made by others on their behalf.
2. Decisions to provide or withhold treatment are made at the beginning of a potential life, rather than towards the end of a life.
3. Prognosis, both for survival and degree of impairment, is usually less clear in babies than in adults of advanced age with terminal diseases.
4. Decisions to treat babies with conditions causing severe life-long disabilities have a greater impact on the lives of others — parents, siblings, and the community — than is usually the case with decisions in adults.

The surgeon or physician has an additional difficulty. Rather than dealing with just one (adult) patient, he must try to act for two parties — the parents and the baby — whose interests might be seen as conflicting.

Given these differences, the ethical and legal debate can be summarised as follows:

1. Are there babies from whom life-sustaining treatment should be withheld or withdrawn?
2. If there are, then are they babies for whom death is inevitable despite treatment, or are they also babies who can survive but with a very poor quality of life?
3. What kind of treatment may be withheld — only 'high technology' treatments such as mechanical ventilators and complex surgery, or less complex treatments like oxygen therapy and antibiotics, or basic care such as tube feeding?
4. Who should make the decisions — parents, or doctors, or hospital ethics committees, or the law courts?

In practice, life-sustaining treatments including surgery are frequently withheld or withdrawn from severely impaired babies. Published data from Australia, the UK and North America show that 30–80% of deaths in neonatal intensive care units follow the withholding of treatment, rather than being the inevitable outcomes of disease.[1-6]

Reasons given for treatment withdrawal in these and other published reports[7-16] include judgments concerning the child's likely quality of life should he/she survive, but there is a spectrum of views of what is an 'acceptable' quality and what is not. Some report withdrawing treatment only from babies who will be so impaired that they will probably be unaware of their own existence.[1,6-8] Others report withdrawal for lesser degrees of intellectual impairment, and also for severe physical disabilities with normal or near-normal intellect.[3,9-15]

With respect to forms of treatment withheld, once again there is a spectrum of views. Some reports express the view that only complex invasive life-support treatments may be withheld.[9-11] Others report withholding less complex treatments such as intravenous fluids and antibiotics. Other reports express the view that any treatment likely to prolong life, including the provision of nutrition and fluid by nasogastric tube or gastrostomy, should be withheld.[3] Surgical procedures such as oesophageal atresia repair, relief of congenital bowel obstructions, and myelomeningocoele repair are also withheld from time to time.

Most decisions are made by the health-care team and parents in concert. There is, once again, a spectrum of views as to who makes the decision in cases of conflict. Many reports state that parents' views should be accorded great weight, but if they differ from the health team's views they should not prevail.[7,8] Other reports state the view that it is the parents' values that should prevail, and so decisions belong solely to them provided that they are adequately informed, counselled, and supported.[1,3,13]

Ethics committees are widely involved in the USA, but not in Australia, the UK and Europe. Numerous cases have reached the law courts in the USA and UK, but there have been only two in Australia in recent years. Those reaching the courts are thus only the minutest proportion of all cases of treatment withdrawal.

Numerous government and semi-government agencies and professional bodies around the world have published discussion papers or policy statements concerning treatment of the impaired newborn. In general they support, as sound medical practice, withholding life-sustaining treatment in certain circumstances, including those in which decisions are based on quality-of-life judgments.

In Australia, such bodies include the Health Department of Western Australia; the South Australian Health Commission; the Australian Human Rights Commission; the National Health and Medical Research Council; and the Australian College of Paediatrics (the ACP, now the Paediatric Division of the Royal Australasian College of Physicians). The committee which produced the ACP's policy statement was chaired, appropriately, by an eminent paediatric surgeon.

Legally, areas of uncertainty exist in withholding or withdrawing treatment. These uncertainties arise because first there are no actual statutes giving parents or doctors the right to withhold treatment from babies who would otherwise survive, and second there are legal sanctions against causing harm, especially death.

Most available legal guidance to clinicians comes from cases that have appeared before the courts in the UK, Canada, and USA.

Some of these court decisions appear conservative; that is, they suggest that courts might not sanction some decisions made almost every day by parents and doctors. Further, some judgments appear to be based on misunderstandings of medical matters, the principles on which judgments are based change from time to time, and decisions of lower courts are from time to time reversed on appeal to higher courts. All of these matters lead to uncertainty.

The impaired newborn has the same legal right to medical treatment as any other person; the clinician owes the same duty of care to impaired babies as to any other patient. It is unlawful to discriminate against any patient on the basis of disability. The law starts out with a very strong presumption in favour of supporting life. However, it does not require the continuation of treatment when it is "futile", nor when death is "inevitable", nor when "the burdens of treatment outweigh any possible benefit". The guiding principle upon which the law insists is that all decisions and treatments must be those which serve the baby's "best interests".

The terms in inverted commas above recur regularly in legal writings and court judgments. However, they are too vague to be guides for action for health workers and families. Modern high-technology care has reduced the impairments in which death is inevitable. In many situations death can only truly be said to be inevitable after all available treatments have been tried and the baby eventually dies. Life-sustaining treatments have never been systematically offered in conditions such as anencephaly, so stating in these conditions that death is inevitable is a self-fulfilling prophecy.

When is treatment futile? When death is the outcome despite all treatment, or also when treatment results in survival but with extremely poor quality of life? When do burdens of treatment outweigh benefits? Only when, after all burdens, the baby dies, or when the burdensome treatment results in survival with severe disabilities? What constitutes a baby's best interests? Can it ever be in a baby's best interests to be dead rather than alive? Do the baby's interests require a certain level of quality in survival? Are a disabled child's best interests served if treatment is mandated by law when his parents believe his life will not be worth living? Or do his best interests require that he has parents who feel strongly that he must be given all treatment, and therefore are highly motivated to devote themselves to a lifetime of care?

Courts have allowed that quality-of-life judgments may be taken into account, but only in ways that are not helpful as guides to doctors and parents. For example, judgments have been served that it might be lawful to withhold treatment if a child's life would otherwise be one of continuous unbearable pain and distress (a scenario that does not exist in the real world), or if the child would have intellectual disability approaching the adult condition known as persistent vegetative state (a state much harder to be sure of in babies and infants than in adults).

Parents have the legal authority to make decisions for impaired babies. The doctor must have the parents' informed consent before he/she can treat, as for any other child. Either parent can make decisions for their child, whether or not the parents are married. However, as mentioned, parents' decisions are lawful only if they serve the baby's best interests. The doctor cannot lawfully either provide or withhold treatment at the parents' direction if it is not in the child's best interests.

In cases of unresolvable disagreement between the parents, or between the parents and the clinicians, the legal remedy is to take the case to a court for resolution. Any interested party can seek intervention by a court. In cases that have come before Australian and UK courts, the initiators have included, variously, social workers disagreeing with doctors and parents, family members other than parents questioning parents' and doctors' decisions, doctors disagreeing with parents, and health authorities, doctors, and parents in agreement, but seeking the support of a court because of uncertainty.

In Australia the relevant courts are the highest courts in each State, or the (Commonwealth) Family Court. Hospital solicitors are best placed to initiate such proceedings, and to guide clinicians through the legal labyrinth. Although this is the proper process according to the law, it is seldom used. This is because disagreements are very uncommon, and when they occur clinicians believe it is preferable to solve them by other means.

Given the foregoing — that decisions to let impaired babies die are frequent, that they are almost always based on quality-of-life judgments, that such cases are seldom brought before the courts but when they are the courts make decisions which seem conservative when compared with decisions made by parents and doctors — it might be inferred that there are serious tensions between what the law requires and what is actually done, and that doctors and parents may therefore be at considerable risk of legal sanctions, including charges of murder or manslaughter.

This is not really the case. There is a substantial body of informed opinion, based upon public debate and the judgments handed down by courts, which in my view can be fairly summarised as follows. The agencies of the law acknowledge and support, as right and proper, that the great majority of decisions to withhold treatment from babies are made by conscientious doctors and devoted parents acting in good faith for what they perceive to be the best. The law has no interest in intruding into such situations. However, when cases are brought before the courts, the law has a paramount duty to protect respect for life and the interests and wellbeing of all children. They will therefore incline towards decisions which cannot be construed as lessening respect for life, or diminishing the protection of the interests and wellbeing of children. They are thus more likely than not to decide in favour of continuing treatment, at least for the time being, except in the most extreme circumstances.

However, if cases in which parents and doctors have withheld treatment are brought to the law's attention, it is unlikely that legal sanctions will result, provided it is clear that parents and doctors have acted reasonably and in good faith.

Furthermore, judgments in the courts appear to be evolving towards more liberal decisions. Quality-of-life considerations are more accepted and concepts of what constitute a child's best interests are being widened to include the child's relationships with parents and the community — in effect, to take into account the interests of others. Recently courts have accepted that withholding nourishment and fluids artificially administered (by nasogastric tube or gastrostomy) may be in a person's interests and therefore lawful.

This body of opinion should be reassuring to parents and doctors acting in good faith, but uncertainties remain, and even a remote prospect of legal sanctions is distressing.

Based upon the public debate, court rulings, and my own experience, the following is my suggested approach to the management of seriously impaired babies. When a baby is born with impairments likely to cause death or very poor quality of life, the option of withholding treatment should form part of the discussions with parents from the outset. Several subspecialists are usually involved with severely impaired babies. They should all have input into discussions with parents, but a senior experienced clinician — surgeon or paediatrician — should be clearly identified as the team leader, co-ordinating the others and conducting most of the discussions with the family. The senior consultant should be empathetic, gaining parents' trust early, and conveying to them that the health-care team is concerned for them and their baby, that their views and values are very important, and that they have substantial 'control' in what is happening to them and their baby.

The full extent of the baby's impairments — diagnosis and prognosis — must be delineated and documented exhaustively. If withholding treatment becomes a serious possibility, the decision-making process must be as open as possible and fully documented. Discussions between consultant and parents must be ongoing, in language the parents understand, using interpreters when necessary, and avoiding as far as possible medical and scientific terminology. Parents should be encouraged to seek advice and support from other family members, friends, spiritual advisors and anyone else they would like. Second opinions from consultants from other institutions should be offered in some situations. Parents may be offered written literature and, in some circumstances, introduced to other families with disabled children.

In general, the values, attitudes, and opinions of the parents, counselled and supported as outlined, should prevail. Most parents are able to take in and comprehend information and advice over time. When involved actively in the decision-making process they perceive the decision to be theirs, and are willing to accept the responsibility.

Occasionally parents arrive at decisions that are impossible for health workers to accept. Usually this involves the parents insisting that invasive treatments, including sometimes major surgery, be continued when survival is unlikely, or when the child has little or no prospect of future awareness. Rarely it involves parents refusing consent to treatment that has a high chance of resulting in survival with good quality of life, albeit impaired. Both situations are very uncommon when the process outlined above has been followed. Parents are more likely to insist on continuing treatment if the option of non-treatment is raised late in the child's course, if a single consultant has not been involved from the outset, and if rapport and trust have not been established early.

When parents insist on continuing treatment, it should be continued in good faith, except that major surgery should be delayed if possible. At the same time, discussions should continue with the family, maintaining respect and avoiding confrontation. My experience is that consensus is almost always reached.

When parents refuse consent for appropriate treatment, again treatment should be continued, even though there is, for a time, no valid authority. Again, surgery should be delayed if possible, while discussions continue. Again, in my experience, willing consensus is eventually reached.

Seeking legal advice in these situations is unlikely to help. Given the present state of the law it is almost impossible for a lawyer to give advice other than to proceed to court. Once such advice has been given it is almost impossible for clinicians to ignore.

With the accumulated experience of participating with many hundreds of families making decisions for their impaired babies, most clinicians believe court action should be avoided. It seems inherently right that families make their own decisions for their own babies. Experience teaches us that most decisions arise out of love and involve sacrifice of parental needs and desires, rather than being motivated by parental self-interest. Families who remain in control of their own destiny and that of their impaired baby cope much better with grief if treatment is withdrawn and the baby dies, or with the life-long care of their disabled child if they opt for treatment. When decisions are imposed against family wishes it may lead to a lifetime of bitterness and unresolvable grief, or alienate them from the care of a surviving disabled child.

All aspects of the decision-making and withdrawing processes should be documented in detail over time, including the reasons for withdrawal, subspecialist opinions, parents' views and the details of palliative care.

Returning to the impaired fetus, legal and ethical matters are less unclear. Termination of pregnancy is lawful under the same conditions applying to all terminations. Although these conditions vary in detail from State to State, in essence they are that the mother requests termination, and medical opinion agrees that continuation of the pregnancy would threaten the mother's physical or mental health, broadly interpreted. The consent of the father is not required. However, it is desirable from the ethical point of view to ensure his approval unless the mother refuses him involvement.

There is no gestational age beyond which termination becomes always unlawful. Given that fetuses born from 23 weeks' gestation onwards are frequently offered care and survive, termination of fetuses after 22 weeks is very controversial. It is possible that legal problems may arise in the future when termination is performed beyond 22 weeks.

Pregnancies are often terminated when the fetus is found to have impairments which are easily treated in babies born alive. Although this is lawful (provided medical opinion agrees that continuation of the pregnancy would threaten the mother's physical or mental health), there is controversy among paediatricians and surgeons as to whether it is ethical. It is reasonable at least to ensure that families make informed decisions when they are considering termination. Institutions providing antenatal fetal diagnosis should also provide to families who are found to have an impaired fetus, access to paediatric surgical advice as to the treatability of their fetus's impairment, before termination is decided upon.

There is mounting evidence that for many women the psychological trauma resulting from termination is at least as great as that resulting from the death of a live-born baby, and for some women the trauma is worse. Such psychological distress can be severe and life-long. Everyone involved in terminations of impaired pregnancies should be aware of such possibilities. Institutions providing termination of pregnancy should provide comprehensive psychological support services from the time of detection of fetal impairment to well beyond the termination.

Fetal surgery remains experimental. It should be attempted only in tertiary academic perinatal centres conducting research programs in fetal surgery. It is a team endeavour requiring a range of subspecialists and clinical scientists. International Societies and Fetal Treatment Registries have been formed to collate the world's experience in fetal therapies. Rather than working in isolation, teams attempting fetal surgery should integrate their activities with those international bodies.

REFERENCES

1. Whitelaw A. Death as an option in neonatal intensive care. *Lancet* 1986; **2**: 328–331.

2. Yu VYH. Selective non-treatment of newborn infants. *Med. J. Aust.* 1994; **2**: 627–629.

3. Campbell N. When care cannot cure: medical problems in seriously ill babies. In: Beller FK, Weir RF (eds). *The Beginning of Human Life*. Dordrecht: Kluwer Academic 1994; 327–334.

4. Wall SN, Partridge JC. Withdrawal of life support in the ICN: decisions and practice by neonatologists. *Pediatr. Res.* 1993; **33**: 30A (Abstract).

5. Ryan CA, Byrne P, Kuhn S, Tyebkhan J. No resuscitation and withdrawal of therapy in a neonatal and a pediatric intensive care unit in Canada. *J. Pediatr.* 1993; **123**: 534–538.

6. Kelly NP, Rowley SR, Harding JE. Death in neonatal intensive care. *J. Paediatr. Child Health* 1994; **30**: 419–422.

7. Fost N. Counseling families who have a child with a severe congenital anomaly. *Pediatrics* 1981; **67**: 321–324.

8. Royal College of Paediatrics and Child Health (UK). *Withholding or Withdrawing Life Saving Treatment in Children — A Framework for Practice*. London, 1997.
9. Outterson C. Newborn infants with severe defects: a survey of paediatric attitudes and practices in the United Kingdom. *Bioethics* 1993; **7**: 420–435.
10. Singer P, Kuhse H, Singer C. The treatment of newborn infants with major handicaps: a survey of obstetricians and paediatricians in Victoria. *Med. J. Aust.* 1983; **2**: 274–278.
11. Bay B, Burgess M. A survey of Calgary paediatricians' attitudes regarding the treatment of defective newborns. *Bioethics* 1991; **5**: 139–149.
12. Sauer P. Ethical decisions in neonatal intensive care units: the Dutch experience. *Pediatrics* 1992; **90**: 729–732.
13. Duff R. Counseling families and deciding care of severely defective children: a way of coping with 'Medical Vietnam'. *Pediatrics* 1981; **67**: 315–320.
14. *Report of the Task Force on Ethical and Legal Issues Concerning Disabled and Extremely Low Birthweight Newborn Infants*. Adelaide: South Australian Health Commission. 1991; 6–7.
15. Campbell N. Withholding and withdrawing active medical treatment in critically ill infants and children. In: Taeusch HW, Christiansen H, Buescher E (eds). *Pediatric and Neonatal Tests and Procedures*. Philadelphia: WB Saunders 1996; 197–204.
16. Australian College of Paediatrics. Non-intervention in children with major handicaps: legal and ethical issues. Report of a working party. *Aust. Paediatr. J.* 1983; **19**: 217–222.

FURTHER READING

Skene L. *Law and Medical Practice: Rights, Duties, Claims and Defences*. Sydney: Butterworths, 1998.

Ethics of resource allocation

J.M. LITTLE

Introduction

Principle-based ethics have contributed enormously to our understanding of medical ethics. The four well-known principles have become so familiar as to have been christened the 'Georgetown mantra' after the university where they were first enunciated. It is difficult to find fault with those principles — beneficence, the act of doing good for each patient; non-maleficence, the avoidance of doing harm; respect for the individual autonomy of each patient as a decision maker; and justice, the principle of equal treatment for each person, regardless of their personal or cultural attributes.

Principle-based ethics were devised with the clinical dyad in mind — the distinctive relationship between a patient and his/her doctor. It has been easy to broaden the base of these kinds of ethics to include relationships with families and other support groups. A new model of medicine, however, has grown up in the last 20 years or so, and promises to remain and to grow in importance over the first century of the new millennium. It has made the application of principle-based ethics more difficult.

In the late 1970s, Dr James Maloney, a cardiac surgeon from Los Angeles, wrote an article in which he predicted the present crisis in medicine in the USA.[1] He saw clearly that, as the costs of medicine rise, external controls will increasingly be used to control those costs.

This has indeed happened. The various formulae (such as disease-related groupings (DRG)) have been tried as ways of normalising medical and surgical practice. More recently, the health maintenance organisations (HMO) and managed care have gained effective control over practice principles and delivery. There is great unrest in the USA, and some States have introduced corrective legislation to reduce the potential for inequity and poor practice which managed care and the commercial principles of the HMO have spawned.[2]

We have not reached the same point in Australia, but external forces are increasingly acting on medicine. Science and technology have made many things possible. We take for granted coordinated trauma services, oncology services, cardiac units and transplantation, all of which have appeared in my practising lifetime. These goods have come at huge cost. That cost cannot be met by simple payment from patients to the health-care system. Modern Western liberal societies retain a belief in the value of individual human life, both for its quantity and its quality. Once the State accepts some responsibility for health, outside interference in health and medicine become inevitable. A significant part of the funding for health must come from the State. The State is therefore a legitimate stakeholder in the health endeavour.

The State is, however, not the only other stakeholder in addition to patients, their families and support groups and the health-care worker. Because health has become a huge enterprise in which the State is involved, a series of bureaucracies has arisen to manage the complex affairs of health. Health departments, administrators and managers are also stakeholders, taxed with the practical implementation of the health policies generated by politicians. The difficulties involved in achieving service delivery within constrained budgets have given rise to health economics as a special field of study, and it also has a legitimate interest in health services.

At the same time, there have been profound social changes. The Consumer Movement and the Rights Movement have generated new pressures and new ways of discourse, which have enabled aggrieved patients and their families to seek legal redress for their grievances. The law has become yet another party with a vested interest in health, as have the media, the medical technology companies and the health insurance agencies.

The crowded office and the costs of health

Thus, there are at the beginning of the 21st century, many stakeholders in health, and many constraints on its practitioners. The old dyadic model of the medical encounter, which has served so well for so long, is no longer adequate. Consultations take place in a 'crowded office'. This means that principle-based ethics are, by themselves, no longer adequate. Of their four principles, only the principle of justice seems able to cope with some of the pressures that operate on medicine. Originally meant to remind us that we should treat all people as equals, they can be construed to mean that we should conduct each clinical transaction in such a way as to preserve the interests of the legitimate stakeholders. As economists remind us, each commitment we make to expensive treatment carries an opportunity cost.[3,4] That cost may be purely financial, or it may be in terms of human capital. In other words, our decisions have to take into account the service we may be able to render here and now *and* the service that we (or our colleagues) may *not* be able to render later, because of the resources committed to the patient at this time.

We can perhaps see this kind of decision most starkly in countries where true rationing has been implemented. In Italy, for example, in the early days of liver transplantation each unit performing transplants had a cap placed on the numbers that could be performed. Once the unit reached that number, the budget was closed, and the clinicians were compelled to find other ways to deal with their patients. At first, they referred their excess patients to other countries without such rationing, but this soon overtaxed the other national transplant units, which then refused to take further referrals.

Australia does not have this kind of rationing yet, but it could come. A *de facto* rationing does exist when, for example, cardiac units develop policies which exclude patients from certain categories of surgery on the grounds of co-morbidity. They reason that it is not justified to provide surgery for the very old, for example, because the inevitable co-morbidities of age preclude satisfactory results. To offer such services to the very old, the reasoning goes, uses scarce resources, and does nothing to improve the quality of what is left of life. This kind of reasoning has some justifications, but also has inherent dangers. It slips easily into discrimination on the grounds of age, or ageism, where decisions are made simply on the basis of numerical age, rather than on an individual assessment of the medical indications and contraindications.

We can see readily that principle-based ethics do little to help us in situations of this kind. The principle of beneficence suggests that we must do *something* of benefit for our elderly patients. The principle of non-maleficence requires that we avoid doing harm. But which is the greater harm — doing nothing and allowing the person to die without hope or help, or doing something which may not work and which may preclude someone else from undergoing effective treatment?

The principle of autonomy requires that we respect the patient's right to make informed choices. How do we respect the patient's autonomy if he or she expresses a strong wish to undergo the surgery, whatever the risk? And what sort of justice to the individual is done by refusing treatment? And is the injustice done to this individual by denying treatment outweighed by the *possible* benefit to someone else because there are resources preserved by the denial of treatment?

Constructing new ethics

Principle-based ethics leave us with many questions. Their grounding in the dyadic patient–doctor relationship remains useful, but restricts their applicability to these broader problems. If medical ethics are to be useful in the new century, they must be reconstructed in order to cope with the new demands, including genetic screening and engineering, cloning, cancer screening programs, reproductive technology, and the health and welfare of disadvantaged groups.

Speculation about the structure of such an ethical system is not possible within this brief chapter, but some suggestions about its elements may be helpful.

Virtue ethics

First, the new ethics need to remain grounded in traditional medical virtues. Pellegrino and Thomasma suggest that beneficence and fidelity to duty are the central virtues that should motivate the actions and decisions of health-care workers.[5] These become more acutely important in the era of resource constraint, because they need to be invoked when certain kinds of treatment are simply not available. If resource constraints dictate that the medically frail must be excluded from scarce, expensive, labour-intensive treatments (e.g. cardiac transplantation), then beneficence and fidelity to duty require us to find other ways to lessen the sufferings of those who cannot be treated.

Rights and duties

Second, a new formulation of rights and duties will be needed. Rights and duties make up a complex network of mutually sustaining relationships.[6] We have no rights unless someone observes a duty to implement them. Rights include guarantees that we can do, possess, receive and be protected from certain things. Some rights are simple liberties. Others are rights that must be claimed. Some are legally guaranteed, some guaranteed by morality. Rights are best construed as having *prima facie* status, as existing 'other things being equal'.

For practical purposes, rights can be seen as more or less binding agreements that humans in societies should be protected against events and procedures that threaten their security or limit their capacity to flourish. Duties are those obligations which balance the rights and desires of individuals against the welfare of others and of the larger community. While patients may be seen as having rights of access to health care, they may also be held to owe duties of honest disclosure, reasonable compliance with treatment if they continue under the care of the doctor who recommends the treatment, and an understanding of the limits of medical treatment.

For doctors, there are at least five categories of duty: a pastoral duty of care to provide skilled and ethically modulated services, an epistemological duty to know what should be known and to contribute to medical knowledge, a duty of collegiality, a duty to know and work within the law, and a duty to practise health care in ways which observe community welfare. These communitarian duties are becoming rapidly more important and more demanding as the health budget is progressively stretched by the technologies and expectations of modernity.

Doctors' rights are complex. They have the implicit right to obtain the confidential information that makes up the medical history, the right to conduct a physical examination and to perform various more or less invasive procedures which would in other contexts constitute an assault. They have the right to expect to be appropriately rewarded for what they do. These are the *Aesculapian rights* which pass to doctors by virtue of their knowledge, their training and their licence to practise. Then there are certain rights that protect the mutuality of trust between doctor and patient. It seems reasonable that doctors should have the right to expect free and honest disclosure of all that is relevant to the clinical problem, and compliance within the limits of patient autonomy with the recommended treatment. Doctors also should have a right to possess a limited trust in the patient to present with what is genuinely perceived by the patient to be a problem within the domain of health. Attempts to manipulate doctors to secure advantage or avoid responsibility should be causes of distrust. Doctors should also be able to expect collegial support from their colleagues, within the reasonable bounds of acceptable professional behaviour. Most importantly, the doctor should hold a right to express and follow his/her own conscience.

Systematic examination of complex issues under a model of rights and duties will, of course, not solve all ethical problems, but it does help us to remember some of the important issues that can remain untouched by principle-based ethics.

Community values and discourse ethics

Third, the new medical ethics will need to reflect community values.

The bad effects of resource constraints are borne by the community in which they occur. Finding out what things communities value, and the priorities assigned to them, is clearly a difficult process, but it is not something that can be dismissed as too difficult. The Oregon project in the USA was one attempt to capture public opinion in order to determine what medical services Oregon should provide, and which it should exclude.[7,8] The process has been criticised for its flaws,[9] but it represents at least a sincere attempt to measure priorities before making policy decisions. In Australia, the Constitutional Convention of 1997 represented another attempt to examine an issue, using representation as a means of insight into public opinion. These kinds of exercises produce a variant of what have been called 'discourse ethics'.[10,11] Ethics of this kind have the strength of expressing the values of all stakeholders rather than simply the values of those who make policy or deliver services.

However, for discussions of this kind to work, those who represent the legitimate stakeholdings will need to understand the basic rules which, explicitly or implicitly, govern effective discourse. These rules seem self-evident, but are in fact demanding. Those who are interested in reading further will find helpful material in the work of Alexy,[12] Grice,[13] Devlin,[14] and Devlin and Rosenberg.[15] All are agreed that speakers in each discourse should work within agreed definitions of the terms used, should speak clearly and to the point, and should respect the right of others to put their own consistent views. Gray[16] and Arrow *et al.*[17] have described ways to resolve differences that arise due to ideological differences and differences arising from vested interests.

Although there are useful guidelines for public discussions, there is still an inadequate understanding of the conceptual differences that people bring with them to these discussions. Consider as a simple example, the different nuances that stakeholders bring to the word 'outcomes'. Doctors tend to think of outcomes as the results of management, the rates of survival or symptom relief, of mortality and complication rates. Evidence-based medicine depends on standardised measures of outcome in order to establish norms for satisfactory treatment. Economists and policy makers think of 'outputs', measurable units of productivity which can be subjected to cost–benefit, marginal cost and opportunity cost analyses as measures of 'efficiency'. Patients and their families frequently perceive the process of care as a part of the outcome. In palliative care, indeed, the process *is* the outcome. The word, which seems so simple and satisfactory as a starting point for discussion, carries conceptual baggage which may make it ambiguous and misleading in actual use, unless the rules of effective discourse are carefully observed.

It is particularly important to distinguish the times when a word is used in a moral sense, from the times when it is used in a performative sense. This distinction can be understood by thinking about the word 'care'. Care carries a heavy moral implication. No one can argue against the desirability of 'good care' for the ill. But care also slips into a performative sense. The legal 'duty of care' implies objective standards of care, to which health care workers must conform. Hidden within the one word are two notions of care. We can 'care for' patients in the performative sense without 'caring about' them in the moral sense. Management protocols provide rules for 'caring for'. Our consciences and our compassion provide guides to 'caring about'. Patients and their families quite commonly make this distinction when they tell us that they were well enough looked after by medical staff, but that no one seemed concerned to treat them as individuals with particular problems, fears and aspirations.

Ethonomics

Finally, the new ethics will have to recognise the validity of economic and material constraints, and the inevitable interests of other stakeholders in health. This will mean that policy makers, economists, managers and health-care workers need to understand one another, the values and the language they use in their daily activities.[18] They will need to recognise the grounding functions which justify the health endeavour, and the moral imperative to deliver the best care possible within the inevitable constraints. The implications of this are immense. Determining the level of services that can be provided will be an exercise in responsibility and accountability which demands collaboration. For the same reasons, medical research will need to be planned in light of the new ethics, with careful consideration of the availability of the end products of the research, the opportunity costs of the research itself and the technology it may produce. Whatever the new ethics may look like, they will affect every branch of health, and every kind of medical research.

REFERENCES

1. Maloney JV. Presidential address: The limits of medicine. *Ann. Surg.* 1981; **194**: 247–255.
2. Hitchens C. Bitter medicine. In: *Vanity Fair*. 1998; 24–35.
3. Mooney G. *Economics, Medicine and Health Care*. 2nd edn. Hertfordshire: Harvester, Wheatsheaf, 1992.
4. Mooney G. *Key Issues in Health Economics*. Hertfordshire: Harvester, Wheatsheaf, 1994.
5. Pellegrino ED, Thomasma DC. *The Virtues in Medical Practice*. New York: Oxford University Press, 1993.
6. Freeden M. *Rights*. Milton Keynes: Open University Press, 1991.
7. Haas M, Hall J. The Oregon Plan. *Public Health Bulletin NSW*, 1992; **3**: 50–51.
8. Thorne JI. Oregon Pro: As the nation waits, Oregon moves forward. *Bull. Am. Coll. Surg.* 1993; **78**: 8,10,12 passim.
9. Liu JT-Y. Oregon con: Oregon's experiment: Just another Medicaid cutback. *Bull. Am. Coll. Surg.* 1993; **78**: 9,11,13 passim.
10. Benhabib S, Dallmayr F (eds). *The Communicative Ethics Controversy*. Cambridge, MA: MIT Press, 1990.
11. Habermas J. *Moral Consciousness and Communicative Action*. Cambridge: Polity Press, 1992.
12. Alexy R. A theory of practical discourse, In: Benhabib S, Dallmayr F (eds).*The Communicative Ethics Controversy*. Cambridge, MA: MIT Press, 1990; 151–190.
13. Grice HP. *Studies in the Way of Words*. Cambridge, MA: Harvard University Press, 1989.
14. Devlin K. *Goodbye, Descartes: The End of Logic and the Search for a New Cosmology of the Mind*. New York: John Wiley and Sons, Inc, 1997.
15. Devlin K, Rosenberg K. *Language at Work: Analyzing Communication Breakdown in the Workplace*. Stanford, CA: CSLI Publications, 1997.
16. Gray B. Conditions facilitating interorganisational collaboration. *Human Relations* 1985; **38**: 911–936.
17. Arrow K, Mnookin RH, Ross L, Tversky A, Wilson R (eds). *Barriers to Conflict Resolution*. New York: WW Norton and Co, 1995.
18. Little M. Assignments of meaning in epidemiology. *Soc. Sci. Med.* 1998; **47**: 1135–1145.

Outcome studies:
An ethical perspective

C. JORDENS

Background

Interactions between patients and clinicians take place in a social space that is increasingly crowded with different interests. The interest of the State is ever-present due to its role as a funder of health services; but as the State strives to control public expenditure on health care, its presence is also expressed through control and surveillance carried out by managers and administrators who are empowered to implement policies of 'economic rationalisation'.

The consumer movement has brought new social influences to bear on decision-making structures that were previously the exclusive domain of health experts. The influence of the legal profession is becoming more apparent as levels of medical litigation rise. Various groups, clinical researchers and health economists, health industries and the media, claim to have a legitimate stake in health services, and therefore seek to influence, more or less overtly, what goes on in the clinic.

Some applaud these developments as a sign of increasing openness in the health professions, while others lament them as unwanted intrusions. We point to the reality of the 'crowded consultation room' in order to make two general points about medical ethics. First, if ethical analysis is framed exclusively in terms of the clinician–patient relationship, it is unlikely to help clinicians negotiate the changing social environment in which they practise. To remain relevant, medical ethics must account for the broader network of relationships within which clinicians and patients encounter each other. This leads us to adopt a stakeholder model for ethical analysis.

Second, different stakeholders justify their interest and activity in health care, using words and ideas that are drawn from different fields of knowledge and practice, or different discourses. Difficulties in communication are thus a major feature of interactions between different stakeholdings. Furthermore, there is a real premium on concepts that gain general acceptance across the wider health-care endeavour, as these create the possibility of mutual understanding. The notion of 'outcome' is one example of such a concept. 'Accountability', 'evidence' and 'care' are others. A common problem that arises in relation to such key concepts is that different stakeholders attach different meanings and values to them. The confusion to which this gives rise leads us to view discourse ethics as an increasingly indispensable aspect of medical ethics.[1]

We shall now discuss the evaluation of outcomes in health care from an ethical perspective, framing the issue as a problem for discourse ethics.

Basing evaluation on outcomes: What is the common denominator?

When different stakeholders commit themselves to basing evaluation on outcomes, three simple, interdependent assumptions remain stable, irrespective of the context: (i) that the commitment presupposes an evaluative effort; (ii) that outcomes are differentiated from a process; and (iii) that outcomes are privileged in evaluation.

Each assumption points to the value-ladenness of outcomes in a different way. The first prompts us to consider why evaluation is considered obligatory in the first place. From what moral basis does this obligation arise? In relation to whom or what does one feel, or is one made to feel, accountable? The second point reminds us that outcomes exist only in relation to some goal-directed activity.[2] To name something as an outcome is to nominate a specific moment or event, within some wider process or sequence of events, as the point at which the actual effects of some endeavour will be evaluated.[3] This point is captured in the following question: For the purpose of evaluating this particular activity, which of its consequences shall be taken into account?[4]

This leads us to the third point. From an ethical perspective, to privilege outcomes in evaluation is to adopt a consequentialist approach. In other words, it implies that doing the right thing means choosing, from among the actions available, the one that will probably result in the most good for those parties affected by the action. What constitutes 'good' rests in turn on a theory of value. In other words, even though basing evaluation on outcomes always constitutes an agreement to be judged on one's results in some sense, the evaluation of those results rests on some prior notion of what is valued; it assumes an answer to the question: How shall we evaluate the consequences to which we are appealing? If some parties stand to benefit while others stand to lose, an additional question arises: How are we going to weigh the gains and losses of those affected?[4]

When these core assumptions are put to work in the context of different stakeholdings, important differences emerge. We shall now explore some of these differences on the basis of the three points outlined above, comparing 'micro' (clinical) and 'macro' (system-wide) perspectives on health.

The 'micro' perspective

At a micro level, outcome studies include any study that tracks the results of intervention by considering what happens to individuals. This applies whether the study is prospective or retrospective, and whether the study aggregates many observations to arrive at a single estimate of risk or benefit. This evaluative practice reflects the fact that, at a clinical level, outcomes are differentiated from the process of treating individual patients, and the consequences that are taken into account are therefore those that accrue to individual patients. Clinical outcome studies do not usually examine the consequences of intervention for parties other than the patient, and so they do not raise the question of how to weigh gains and losses to a range of affected parties.

The question of how consequences are evaluated (i.e. which consequences constitute benefits to patients and which constitute risks or disbenefits) refers us to the question of a theory of value. Until fairly recently, clinicians were assumed to know what was best for patients, and this was reflected in both the choice of outcomes in evaluation, and in clinical decision-making, where the patient's role was seen as one of simply consenting or not consenting to a course of treatment chosen by the clinician. While the probability of a given outcome is furnished by an evidence-base built up of outcome studies, the value of an outcome, however, is derived from the lives and experiences of patients. Consider, for example, a surgical procedure of which the likely consequence (based on quantitative estimates of risk in clinical outcome studies) includes impotence. The value of this outcome to a particular patient will depend on whether he is sexually active, and if so, how important this is in the context of his life and relationships.

Thus, from the point of view of clinical practice, individual life and experience constitute the 'value base' for clinical evaluation, and outcome studies find their ethical justification in the fact that clinicians and patients are able to make better informed decisions.[5]

Some formal methods of clinical decision-making attempt to factor patient values into decision-making by allowing patients to assign weights or 'utilities' to the probable outcomes of alternative therapeutic actions.[6,7] Whether it is achieved by explicit, formal methods or not, taking patient values into consideration in clinical decision-making clearly draws the patient into the decision-making process. This is usually seen as reflecting greater respect for patient autonomy,[8] although it can also be seen as inviting patients to share with their physicians the burdens of decision.[9] It is important to note, however, that what constitutes a relevant outcome is still largely determined from a clinical — which usually means pathophysiological — perspective.

This is not a problem provided that clinically defined outcomes coincide with the dimensions of experience that are important to patients. If, for example, we wanted to evaluate a new way of treating compound fractures in otherwise healthy patients, we might choose control of pain and distress as a short-term outcome, and restoration to normal function as a long-term outcome.

These outcomes are highly likely to coincide with what matters to patients in the short and long term, irrespective of their individual differences. Where restoration to the *status quo ante* is not possible, as is often the case in the context of serious chronic illness, serious gaps may open up between clinically defined outcomes and what matters to patients. For example, outcomes such as tumour size and survival may reflect what is measurable in some areas of cancer medicine, more than what is important about the illness and its treatment from the standpoint of the patient's experience. If issues such as 'burden of suffering' or 'reasonable hope' loom large in experience, but are absent from clinical evaluation, we have to ask: What is the 'values base' of the chosen outcomes? Quality-of-life measures are one response to this problem, but as our previous example concerning impotence suggests, different domains of life and experience vary in importance to different individuals, and to the same individual over time.[10-14] Another response to the problem is to enrich notions of outcome by listening to patients' accounts of their illness and treatment, so as to discern what is important and common in experiential terms across a defined spectrum of illness.[15] Qualitative research methods can provide systematic approaches to doing this, although translating the results of such research into measurement is another question altogether.[16] Yet another approach is to involve, in clinical research of a given illness, people who have had personal experience of it.

In general, demands for rigorous measurement in areas of practice that deal with chronic illness or complex patterns of co-morbidity should not lead to the measurement of wrong things. By cleaving only to what is measurable, evaluation may become detached from its 'values base' in the lives and experiences of patients. Neu observed: 'for many long-term patients, changes in the inputs to their care — changes in the way they are treated on a daily basis — could be a lot more important than changes in the underlying health status'.[17] Knowing how to use outcome measurement wisely includes knowing the limits of its usefulness.

The 'macro' perspective

In public health, outcomes are defined in distinction to the process of intervening in populations so as to improve health and reduce the burden of ill-health. From this perspective, the clinical treatment of individuals appears as one component of a much wider spectrum of activity that spans preventive and health promotion programs, and potentially includes any intervention which influences the health of populations even though it might lie outside the aegis of health systems. Improvements to water and food supplies and other aspects of the social and physical environment fall into the latter category.

At this macro level, the consequences of interventions that are taken into account are changes in the health of populations, measured statistically.[18] Recent thinking has attempted to reorient this activity away from measuring health in negative terms (i.e. in terms of burden of disease, morbidity and mortality, etc.) towards measures of 'health gain'. Behind this shift is a reconsideration of the broader goal or purpose of health systems. Rather than being seen primarily as a means of rescuing the casualties of disease and injury, they are increasingly viewed as a social resource for producing a specific social good, namely, health-related welfare.[19] Putting aside the question of precisely what this notion encompasses, we can say that, at the macro or population level, health-related welfare is what is valued, and the consequences of health interventions are, therefore, evaluated in terms of the degree to which they produce this good.

Unlike the micro perspective, which takes into account only those consequences that accrue to specific individuals receiving an intervention, the macro perspective attempts to encompass consequences to all parties affected by a given intervention. This is done by considering the intervention's opportunity cost, or the best alternative use of the health dollars funding the intervention.[20,21] This is part of an economic discourse of efficiency which, like the productive model outlined above, reflects the contemporary influence of economics in public health.

Examining the opportunity cost of resource allocation decisions means weighing up gains and losses to a range of parties. (As we have seen, this question is not raised by clinical outcome studies.) Extensive consideration is given to questions of this nature in the discourse of policy-making, where the response is often framed in terms of finding a way to aggregate individual preferences or utilities. Some commentators draw attention to the conceptual problems inherent in such an approach.[17] Others question the apparent underlying assumption that an objective basis can be found for making value-laden decisions, and raise ethical concerns about the link being forged between resource allocation and evidence of clinical efficacy.[22,23] In addition to these concerns, we would like to ask: What is the value base of outcome evaluation at the macro or system-wide level?

The influence of neoclassical economics has led to the introduction of metaphors into health care that are both useful and limiting. The production model discussed above is one such metaphor. The metaphor of patients as consumers or 'rational utility-maximisers' is another. Individual utility may well be the value base of the marketplace, but is it also, therefore, the value base of health-care systems? We would argue that it is not. At the macro level, the obligation to evaluate arises from an explicit or implicit agreement to make the best use of the health dollar. In turn, the health dollar represents a portion of the common weal. The relevant value base in this case would, therefore, appear to be the community rather than the individual, and resource allocation decisions would appear to require a determination of community preferences rather than a weighing up of individual preferences. Whether you accept this argument depends, of course, on whether you believe that communities are more than the sum of the individuals in them, and whether it is sensible to speak of communities expressing preferences. In other words, the issue turns on philosophical and political beliefs about the nature of society. There is simply no escaping this and, moreover, evaluative practices are not neutral with respect to such beliefs. Those who insist on making individual preferences the value base in policy decisions are in effect denying the existence of community. Those who see community as the proper value base for decisions concerning the common weal reject neo-classical economics in favour of a communitarian approach.[24] Our own view is that communities exist to the extent that the processes of decision-making allow. Thus, processes of collective decision-making, such as those embodied in Australia's 1999 Constitutional Convention, in citizen juries and in the Oregon experiment,[25-27] allow the expression of a community; and a community exists to the extent that such processes actually occur. This is to see community as a process of discussion and shared decision-making to which one is committed or not.

Intermediate, managerial perspectives

By contrasting only micro and macro perspectives on health care, we have oversimplified the picture somewhat. There are clearly intermediate, managerial perspectives on outcomes that fall between clinical- and system-level perspectives on health care. At this level, the obligation to evaluate arises from the performative accountability of managers to organisations and organisational goals; outcomes are differentiated from the process of implementing work process control, and existing performative standards or benchmarks form the background against which outcomes gain their value.[28,29]

Summary

Discussion about outcomes and outcome studies is frequently undermined by the assumption that because different stakeholders are talking about outcomes, they must be talking about the same thing. Our research and experience tells us otherwise, and we have attempted to clarify matters by describing first what remains *constant* when different stakeholders agree to base evaluation on outcomes, and second what *varies* across different stakeholdings in terms of the meanings and values at stake in notions of outcome. By way of summary, it is useful to think of the clinician, the manager and the policy-maker as stakeholders who stand in different relationships of accountability:[30] the first to individuals, the second to organisations, and the third to communities. Each relationship has a different mode of regulation: the first moral, the second performative, and the third economic. In different stakeholdings, outcomes are defined separately from processes and assigned value on different bases, and different kinds of questions and issues preoccupy those who view the system from a micro as compared to a macro perspective.[31] In any discussion between stakeholders, it is important to recognise and acknowledge that these differences in meaning and value underlie the common commitment to base evaluation on outcomes. Without such an acknowledgement, there is a high likelihood that the discussion will proceed at cross-purposes, and the central issue of values will become lost in irresolvable debates about measurement.

A final point that needs to be made is that evaluation constitutes a kind of surveillance that clinical practice and public health systems impose upon themselves, and it can cause ethical tensions where it alters relationships of accountability. For example, the requirement to rigorously evaluate treatments creates a tension between a clinician's duty to contribute to medical science by enrolling patients in clinical trials, and a pastoral duty to advance the individual interests of those patients. Turning clinicians into fund holders to make them aware of the opportunity costs of what they do creates a similar tension in their pastoral duty to individuals, and while it may make the costs clear to them, it may also place them in a morally uncomfortable position. Evaluative requirements are also imposed by one stakeholder upon another in complex networks of surveillance and control, and this can give rise to similar problems. Burdening clinicians (and nurses in particular) with endless paperwork that serves the managerial goal of work process control has serious opportunity costs in terms of patient care.

In short, those who strive to make medicine economically accountable must also be held morally accountable for the effects of their influence within the clinic. The advantage of adapting a stakeholder model to ethical analysis is that it makes visible the many social influences that are currently brought to bear in the clinic. We hope this helps clinicians make sense of the complex and changing social environment in which they practise.

REFERENCES

1. Habermas J. *Moral Consciousness and Communicative Action.* Cambridge: Polity Press, 1992.

2. Wilkin D. Selecting an instrument to measure the outcomes of health care. In: Stewart M, Tudiver F, Martin JB, Dunn EV, Norton PG (eds). *Tools for Primary Care Research.* Newbury Park: Sage 1992; 50–63.

3. Armstrong D. Health outcomes: The socio-historical context. In: Macbeth H (ed.) *Health Outcomes: Biological, Social and Economic Perspectives.* New York: Oxford University Press, 1996; 4–30.

4. Brody BA, Engelhardt HT, Section B. The major moral considerations. 1. Appealing to the consequences of our actions. In: Brody BA, Englehardt HT (eds). *Bioethics: Readings and Cases.* New Jersey: Prentice-Hall, 1987.

5. Kerridge I, Lowe M, Henry D. Ethics and evidence based medicine. *BMJ* 1998; **316**: 1151–1153.

6. Clarke JR. A scientific approach to surgical reasoning: V Patients' attitudes. *Theor. Surg.* 1991; **6**: 166–176.

7. Sox HC et al. *Medical Decision Making.* Boston: Butterworths, 1988.

8. Lynn J, DeGrazia D. An outcomes model of medical decision making. *Theor. Med.* 1991; **12**: 325–343.

9. Katz J. *The Silent World of Doctor and Patient.* New York: The Free Press, 1984.

10. Baldwin S, Godfrey C, Propper C. *Quality of Life.* London: Routledge, 1990.

11. Bullinger M. Quality of life: A definition, conceptualisation and implications—a methodologist's view. *Theor. Surg.* 1991; **6**: 143–148.

12. Cella CF, Tulsky DS. Quality of life in cancer: Definition, purpose and method of measurement. *Cancer Invest.* 1993; **11**: 327–336.

13. Muldoon MF et al. What are quality of life measurements measuring? *BMJ* 1998; **316**: 542–545.

14. Williams JI. Strategies for quality-of-life assessment: A methodologist's view. *Theor. Surg.* 1991; **6**: 152–157.

15. Little M et al. Liminality: A major category of the experience of cancer illness. *Soc. Sci. Med.* 1998; **47**: 1485–1494.

16. Kessler RC, Mroczek DK. Measuring the effects of medical interventions. *Med. Care* 1995; **33**: A5109–A5119.

17 Neu CR. Individual preferences for life and health: Misuses and possible uses. In: Kane RL, Kane RA (eds). *Values and Long-term Care.* Lexington, MA: D.C. Heath, 1982; 261–275.

18. Opit LJ. The measurement of health service outcomes. In: Holland WW, Detels R, Knox G (eds). *Oxford Textbook of Public Health.* Oxford: Oxford University Press, 1991; 159–172.

19. Hall J, Shiell A. CHERE, *Health Outcomes: A Health Economics Perspective*. CHERE Discussion paper series no. 19. Sydney: Centre for Health Economics Research and Evaluation,1993.

20. Mooney G. *Economics Medicine and Health Care.* New York: Harvester Wheatsheaf, 1986.

21. Mooney G. *Key issues in health economics.* Hertfordshire: Harvester Wheatsheaf, 1994.

22. Evans DE. Summary: Assessment of 21st Century bioethics. In: *Ethics Fatigue: The Fracturing of Medical Ethics*. Third annual seminar of the Centre for Values, Ethics and the Law in Medicine. 1998. The University of Sydney: Centre for Values, Ethics and the Law in Medicine, 1999.

23. Hope T. Evidence-based medicine and ethics. *J. Med. Ethics* 1995; **21**: 259–260.

24. Mooney G. 'Communitarian claims' as an ethical basis for allocating health care resources. *Soc. Sci. Med.* 1998; **47**: 1171–1180.

25. Liu JT-Y. Oregon con: Oregon's experiment: Just another Medicaid cutback. *Bull. Am. Coll. Surg.* 1993; **78**: 9,11,13 passim.

26. Haas M, Hall J. The Oregon plan. *NSW Public Health Bull.* 1992; **78**: 8–14.

27. Thorne JI. Oregon pro: As the nation waits, Oregon moves forward. *Bull. Am. Coll. Surg.* 1993; **78**: 8,10,12 passim.

28. Zimmerman DL, Daley J. Using outcomes to improve health care decision making: Primer. Boston, MA: Management Decision and Research Centre; Veterans Affairs Health Services Research and Development Service. 1997; 24.

29 Campion FX, Rosenblatt MS. Quality assurance and medical outcomes in the era of cost containment. *Surg. Clin. North Am.* 1996; **76**: 139–159.

30. Tannenbaum SJ. Say the right thing: Communication and physicians accountability in the era of medical outcomes. In: Boyle PJ (ed). *Getting Doctors to Listen: Ethics and Outcomes Data in Context.* Washington DC: Georgetown University Press, 1998; 204–223.

31. Baume P. Health system reform. *Health Outcomes Bull.* 1994; 1–4.

Informed consent:
Patient communication

B.J. DOOLEY, M.R. FEARNSIDE

For centuries, the medical ethic has been concerned primarily with doctors acting in the best interests of patients, and not intentionally doing harm during or as a result of advice or treatment. The latter would be malpractice.

The notion of informed consent followed increasing calls from the community in the 1960s and 1970s for individual patients to become a party to a clinical decision made about treatment and advice which directly affected them. Patients should be encouraged to make their own decisions, based on this information. Conversely, information that is vital to their decision-making should not be withheld, particularly if such information could persuade them not to have the treatment advised. In such situations, again, the law would regard this as malpractice. Doctors had always leaned towards protecting their patients from anxiety and concern, by shouldering the burden of bad news themselves and, in many ways, standing clear of patients under their care. Consent for an operation was considered to have been obtained when the patient signed a General Consent to Treatment on admission to hospital.

One of the authors of this chapter (BJD) was a member of the Working Party of the Health Care Committee of the National Health and Medical Research Council, which formulated General Guidelines for Medical Practitioners on Providing Information to Patients.

These guidelines state: 'The guidelines are based on the general principle that patients are entitled to make their own decisions about medical treatments or procedures, and should be given adequate information on which to base those decisions.

- Information should be provided in a form and manner which help patients understand the problem and treatment options available, and which are appropriate to the patient's circumstances, personality, expectations, fears, beliefs, values and cultural background.
- Doctors should give advice. There should be no coercion, and the patient is free to accept or reject the advice.
- Patients should be encouraged to make their own decisions.
- Patients should be frank and honest in giving information about their health, and doctors should encourage them to be so.'

The guidelines reflect the Common Law right of legally competent patients to make their own decisions about medical treatment, and their right to grant, withhold or withdraw consent before or during examination or treatment. The guidelines of the NHMRC do not change the law, nor do they set a mandatory standard. Rather, they reflect the doctor's existing Common Law responsibility always to take reasonable care. In appropriate circumstances, divergence from the guidelines would not inevitably be regarded as negligent or unprofessional behaviour.

It should be noted that the guidelines may be consulted in disciplinary or civil proceedings in deciding whether a doctor has behaved reasonably in giving information, although ultimately it will be the role of the Court to decide the reasonableness of a doctor's behaviour in a given case.

It should be recognised by all, in particular by doctor and patient, that in any case provision of full information is impossible. On the one hand, even doctors do not know or understand many aspects of diseases, their treatment and complications, and the patient, on the other hand, is not educated in them and in most cases understands little of the information given. However, despite these problems, the patient should be informed of the possible or likely nature of the illness or disease, the approach to investigation, diagnosis and treatment: what all this entails, the expected benefits, common side-effects and material risks of any intervention whether this be an investigation or a treatment, whether the intervention is conventional or experimental, who will undertake the intervention, and what will be their costs.

It should be discussed with the patient what the options are for all the investigations, diagnosis and treatment, rough percentages, the degree of uncertainty of any diagnosis reached, and the degree of uncertainty about the outcome. In other words, the patient should be familiar with what the expected outcome would be if untreated, what the expected outcome would be if treated, and the alternatives available. The patient should also have a rough idea of the time and rehabilitation involved to reach the optimum outcome.

On informing patients of the risks involved, it should be explained whether the intervention is complex or straightforward, and the risks, particularly if they are major such as loss of limb, loss of sight, and even death, should certainly be discussed. It is recognised that the patient's temperament, attitude and level of understanding may influence what information is given, but certainly every patient should receive a basic amount of information, sufficient for him/her to make a decision.

Information should be withheld only in extremely limited circumstances of therapeutic privilege, where a doctor judges on reasonable grounds that the patient's physical or mental health might be seriously harmed by the information, or if the patient expressly directs the doctor to make the decisions and does not want the offered information. It is quite common in practice where, on commencing to give what one might call informed consent, the patient states: 'I don't want to hear anything about the risks. Just get on with the job'. Even in these cases, the doctor should give the patient basic information about their illness, the seriousness of it, proposed intervention and the reasons for that. It is also recognised that, in an emergency, when immediate intervention is necessary to preserve life or to prevent serious harm, it may not be possible to provide information. In the case of minors, informed consent should be given by the guardian or, as in most cases, by one or both parents. The legal position may be more complex and, in some cases (e.g. affecting sterilisation), there will be need for consent by the court or an official State body.

In presenting information, it may be necessary to see the patient a second time, with relatives; when the patient is not fluent in English, a competent interpreter, preferably an adult member of the family, should be present. The patient should not be rushed, and should be given sufficient time to make a decision. The patient should be encouraged to ask questions, and consult with family, friends or advisors. The patient should be assisted in seeking other medical opinions, where this is requested or when the doctor feels it would help. At the same time, it is realised that further opinions can add to confusion!

In most cases, for many proposed investigations and treatment, it is not necessary for a doctor and patient to enter into prolonged discussion about the advantages and disadvantages of the intervention. To give an example, in the treatment of a laceration, the doctor should enquire about the patient's general health, his/her state of immunisation against tetanus, advise on the possible risks of scarring which may influence the method of wound closure and debridement, and note the possibilities of septic infection. On the other hand, if the patient needs an organ transplant, as discussed elsewhere in this book, an extended period of informed consent is mandatory. Commonsense dictates the extent of informed consent, and only very rarely should it become an issue in alleged medical negligence. In general terms, the more serious the condition, the greater the requirement for discussion and explanation. This is particularly so where there are material hazards to treatment proposed, which must be balanced against likely benefits. Also, in the case of cosmetic surgery and in situations where the patient's expectations are unduly excessive, careful informed consent is indicated.

There must always be discussion with the patient and, in particular, discussion should end with the doctor asking the patient

'Are there any further questions? Do you wish to come back for further discussion before making a final decision?'

Obtaining written informed consent to general treatment, particularly only on admission to hospital, is insufficient, and consent specific to the procedure is necessary. A written request by the patient for a particular treatment rather than a consent might be a more reasonable approach.

Informed consent is best provided against a background of the traditional relationship between doctor and patient. Neither author, both of whom have been in practice for a considerable time, has found difficulty in reviewing his own practices and behaviours, giving what he feels is adequate informed consent. Surgeons have found it particularly helpful to have written guidelines for patients on particular procedures, and both surgeon and patient can make this a basis for the discussion. In Western countries, for most of this century surgeons have acted according to the Bolam Principle, after a case in England (*Bolam v. Friern Hospital Management Committee* [1957] 2 ALR 118) where the judge stated 'A doctor is not guilty of negligence if he has acted in accordance with a practice accepted as proper by a reasonable body of medical men skilled in that particular art'. However, that is insufficient now. The contemporary model is to apply the standard to the 'particular patient for whom treatment is to be determined'. This model takes more account of the individual patient, any social, cultural or ethnic issues which may influence him/her, and any 'worst fear' concerns he/she may have. The information given must assist the patient to come to a reasonable decision. This model was adopted by the High Court of Australia in 1992, (in the case of *Rogers v. Whitaker* [1992], 119 ALR 628) where the Court declared that when deciding what information is 'material' (and therefore must be disclosed to the patient) the particular circumstances of the patient were the central issue. Therefore, the quantum of information could not be predetermined by consideration of what is accepted practice by the medical profession. This opinion rejected the Bolam Principle. In particular, the Court considered a risk to be material if a person in the patient's position, if warned of the risk, would be likely to attach significance to it.

Alternatively, a risk would be material if the doctor was aware that the particular patient would attach significance to it if warned.

In other words, the patient would not proceed with the treatment if aware of a particular risk that would be of significance to him/her.

FURTHER READING

Beauchamp JF, Childress TL. *Principles of Biomedical Ethics,* 3rd Edn. New York: Oxford University Press, 1989.

Informed Decisions about Medical Procedures. Published jointly by the Law Reform Commission of Victoria (Report 24), Australian Law Reform Commission (Report 50), and the New South Wales Law Reform Commission (Report 62), Melbourne and Sydney, 1989.

General Guidelines for Medical Practitioners on Providing Information to Patients. Canberra: National Health and Medical Research Council, 1993.

Little M. *Humane Medicine.* Melbourne: Cambridge University Press, 1995; 122–141.

Informed consent: Legal issues

M.W. GORTON

The duty

In *Rogers v. Whittaker* (1992) 119 ALR 628, the High Court confirmed the existing obligations of doctors to exercise reasonable care and skill in providing advice and treatment to patients. The standard of care and skill required is that of the ordinary skilled person exercising the particular specialist skills involved. While the law has always recognised that a doctor has a duty to warn a patient of a material risk inherent in any proposed procedure or treatment, the High Court has formulated a higher standard for doctors.

> 'A risk will be considered material if, in the circumstances of the particular case, a reasonable person in the position of the patient, if warned of the risk, would be likely to attach significance to it or if the medical doctor is, or should reasonably be, aware that the particular patient, if warned of the risk, would be likely to attach significance to it.'

Thus, when considering the need to inform a patient of a particular risk, there will be two separate matters that require consideration:

1. Would a reasonable person, in the position of the patient, be likely to attach significance to the risk?

2. Is the doctor aware, or should the doctor be reasonably aware,

that this particular patient would be likely to attach significance to that risk?

The High Court decision places a high burden on practitioners to ensure that all material risks are considered, and that the particular circumstances of the patient are considered.

Factors to consider

1. Would the risk influence the decisions of a reasonable person in the position of the patient? The risk might be so slight that no reasonable person would be influenced by it.

2. Obviously, the more drastic the intervention or procedure, the more necessary it is to inform of risks and consequences.

3. The desire for information by the patient necessitates greater disclosure, and even if the patient says that he/she has no desire for information, the doctor might have to evaluate carefully the patient's real wishes. In *Rogers v. Whittaker*, the patient was particularly inquisitive and anxious about the procedure.

4. In some cases, the temperament and health of the patient might be considered. It may be that disclosing information may be injurious to the physical or mental health of the patient in some cases. The doctor can apply reasonable judgment as to what and how to disclose.

5. The case of *Kalokerinos v. Burnett* (1996) CA 40243/95 in the New South Wales Court of Appeal has taken the concept of informed consent a step further. Where a doctor referred a patient to a specialist, noting an appointment, and giving details to the patient, the doctor nonetheless was held to be negligent when the patient ultimately did not keep the appointment. The shortcoming for which the doctor was ultimately held responsible was not explaining adequately to the patient the consequences of not attending the future appointment. The Court accepted the evidence of the patient that, had she been adequately informed, she would have kept the appointment and ultimately avoided the health consequences which subsequently occurred. However, of assistance to doctors generally, was the

recognition of the contributory negligence of the patient herself, where 20% of the claim was attributed to the patient's own negligence.

6. The existence of emergency situations, or lack of opportunity for proper counselling or discussion, can affect the obligations to disclose. Clearly, in an emergency environment, the information that may be disclosed may be minimal or not possible at all.

7. Special issues arise in relation to the obtaining of consent from (giving adequate information to) children, teenagers and the intellectually disabled.

8. Medical defence organisations and some recent studies support the view that patients are less likely to sue their doctor if an adequate and caring explanation is given when an adverse outcome (or even negligence) occurs. Information and education for patients is one way doctors can reduce their risk of litigation. Part of the problem in recent times is that patients, encouraged by some doctors, have come to expect perfection and are disappointed, even angry, when less than perfect results are obtained.

Causation: Linking loss to the negligence

Even where a doctor may not have given adequate information to a patient, the doctor is not automatically liable for the negligence if it can be shown that the patient would otherwise have had the procedure or agreed to the treatment. In the case of *Domeradski v. Royal Prince Alfred Hospital* (unreported), the New South Wales Supreme Court indicated that it would be open for a jury to find that there was a failure to warn the patient of the risk of stroke and that such a warning should have been given, and also that the jury could determine whether the patient would have changed his mind or decided otherwise if the information had been given. In such cases, the onus is on the patient to show that he/she would not have agreed to the procedure or treatment if properly informed. In the case of *Rogers v. Whittaker*, it was accepted that the patient would not have undergone the procedure if adequately informed.

The problem for the medical profession

The decision in *Rogers v. Whittaker* ignores the fact that practitioners do not operate in a perfect world and that, in many cases, all of the requirements of proper informed consent may be very difficult to achieve. These difficulties include:

1. Informed consent may require detailed and time-consuming discussions with the patient. The Medical Benefits Schedule does not necessarily recognise or reward such endeavour.

2. Communication skills of doctors, and indeed patients, vary considerably. Should training courses for doctors now include communications skills? Patients have different abilities or willingness to take in information, or make decisions about their treatment. There will be reactions from fear to aggression, or to meek compliance. This will affect the type of communication with the patient.

3. Other cultural factors may play a part. Obviously, for patients of an ethnic background, the availability of interpreters becomes an issue. Where a child of the patient acts as an interpreter, there may be differing abilities to communicate the message adequately.

4. The circumstances in which practitioners have an opportunity to convey information is never perfect. The ability to have one, two or even three meetings with a patient to discuss the issue is difficult in most cases. In an emergency, it may be impossible. For anaesthetists, radiologists and others with limited contact with a patient, it becomes very difficult. In hospital situations, where hospital administration controls most of the patient contact, the opportunity for the surgeon may be limited.

Delegation

Of course, doctors in busy hospitals do not act in a perfect world, and do not have unlimited time in which to consider properly all of the issues and risks, regardless of how remotely they may affect the patient's decision. Many doctors, unwisely, will delegate the task of explaining the risks to patients to assisting doctors, trainees or other hospital staff. Doctors are entitled to delegate this responsibility to others, but they bear the liability if the others do not properly advise patients. Doctors who leave informed consent to assisting or junior doctors run the risk that the other doctors do not do the job properly.

It is clearly the responsibility of the treating doctor to obtain informed consent from the patient, and to advise the patient of all material risks. If this is not done properly, the treating doctor bears the legal responsibility.

Doctors who rely simply on consent forms, hospital administration or other bureaucratic processes, run a substantial risk.

> 'Consent should be obtained by the person who will touch the patient. The doctor who delegates his responsibility to a hospital employee, such as a nurse, takes the risk that the consent obtained may be inadequate.'

Trainees

There is now sufficient case law to suggest that one of the material risks involved in any procedure, which ought to be advised to patients, is the fact that it may be undertaken by a trainee or inexperienced doctor, rather than the treating consultant or proceduralist. Several American and Canadian cases raise these issues:

> In *Buie v. Reynolds* Okl App 571 (Oklahoma), the Judge noted:

>> 'A resident did perform the operation thereby engaging in a type of ghost surgery which is condemned by the law as malpractice and by the American Medical Association as a fraud and a deceit and a violation of a basic ethical concept.'

A surgeon may not, says the AMA article, permit surgery residents in training to perform operations on private patients under the supervision of the patient's surgeon without the knowledge or consent of the patient.

> In *Pugsley v. Privette* 263 SE 2d 69 (Virginia), a surgeon was held liable in battery for operating on a patient, despite the fact that the patient had signed a consent form. The patient had insisted that her

own physician do the operation, rather than the actual surgeon involved.

A comment by the Court in *Consadine v. Camp Hill Hospital* (1982) 133 DLR (3D) 11 (Nova Scotia), was that it was 'quite incredible that the operating surgeon had never spoken to the patient prior to the surgery — even though there was no actual negligence shown in the surgery performed'.

The question arises whether the fact that a trainee or inexperienced doctor will be involved in the procedure, or may be carrying out some or all of the procedure, is a material matter which ought to be disclosed to the particular patient in the particular case.

The recent decision of the High Court of Australia in *Chappel v. Hart* (1998) HCA 55, provides clear support for the proposition that such disclosure is required. *Chappel v. Hart* is a case in which it is alleged that Hart was not warned of the particular risks of a procedure. Hart said that if warned of the risks she would not have undergone the procedure. The case is very similar to *Rogers v. Whittaker*. It was alleged that the doctor was of average experience in relation to the particular procedure, and that more experienced doctors may have produced a better result. It seems implicit from the case, although it was not finally decided, that Hart should have been warned that the doctor was only of average competence in relation to this procedure, and that there were more experienced surgeons available. It was stated:

> 'If the foreseeable risk to Mrs Hart was the loss of an opportunity to undergo surgery at the hands of a more experienced surgeon, the duty would have been a duty to inform her that there were more experienced surgeons practising in the field.'

Later, it was stated:

> 'Mrs Hart swore that if she had been told by [the doctor] of the risks to her voice, she would not have gone ahead with the operation by him. She would have sought further advice. She would have wanted the operation performed by the most experienced person available.

> *Professor B was posited as such a person. The evidence showed that he had performed many more operations of this kind than [the doctor] had.'*

Ultimately, the Court's decision did not determine this issue. However, it provides a telling argument for the suggestion that a doctor might have to warn of the fact that he/she is junior or inexperienced in relation to particular procedures.

If it is, therefore, material that a doctor may have to disclose his/her relative level of experience, then it can clearly be a matter for disclosure that a trainee or inexperienced doctor would undertake some or all of a medical procedure.

Most of the community will accept that public hospitals are training hospitals, and that junior doctors and trainees must gain experience and learn under supervision. However, the Courts are likely to require also that patients be adequately informed when a trainee or junior doctor will be performing a procedure, and probably the level of supervision involved.

It would not be sufficient that a general consent form indicated that the hospital was a training hospital, and that certain procedures would be undertaken by trainees from time to time. Such a general formulation or general advice would not satisfy the requirements for the informed consent to be specific to the patient in the particular circumstances.

Of course, patients can be advised in a way that it is non-threatening and does not jeopardise the training situation which applies in hospitals. Patients can be advised that a junior doctor will be undertaking the procedure, under close supervision of the consultant, and with the consultant available to monitor and step in when necessary.

Standard consent and information sheets

It has been suggested that the use of standard consent forms and information sheets will be sufficient to maintain informed consent. As has now been noted in a number of journals and guidelines, standard information forms can have some use, but are no substitute for proper information to a patient. Under the requirements of the High Court decision, the information to be given to a patient must be tailored to the particular patient. It must take into account 'the particular circumstances of the patient, and the particular requirements of the patient'.

Similarly, a simple form signed by a patient is not conclusive proof that valid consent has been obtained. Indeed, in many other legal cases involving guarantees and contracts, the simple signature of the party involved has never been a deterrent to action being taken to contest the guarantee or contract, or to the Courts accepting that the plaintiff should not be bound.

Prepared consent forms and prepared information sheets certainly can have their place and can be used as a prompt or checklist for the discussion that must take place between doctor and patient. The forms are also useful for the patient to take away after the discussion as a reminder of some of the issues that had been considered. However, they are not, in themselves, adequate to ensure that informed consent has been obtained.

Conclusion

The ramifications for doctors are significant:

1. Since *Rogers v. Whittaker*, doctors must have revised the way they communicate with their patients, particularly in explaining the risks of procedures and treatment.
2. Doctors must consider the particular circumstances of each patient, and ensure that, as much as possible, adequate opportunity is given for the pre-treatment discussion.
3. Doctors should keep detailed notes and records, not just of the treatment, but of the advice and information conveyed to the patient prior to treatment.

The guidelines issued by the NH&MRC provide a good guide to the issues with which doctors should be concerned. They provide a general outline of the type of material that should be discussed with patients.

REFERENCE
1. Pickard. *Legal Liability of Doctors and Hospitals in Canada.* 1994; 66–67.

Professional obligations

L. ATKINSON

Introduction

Continuing medical education is a mandatory requirement for current standards of professional accountability with the Royal Australasian College of Surgeons. It is focused on ensuring the best standards of patient care. Increasingly, in Australian States and New Zealand, it is linked with the Annual Registration Certification. The Surgical Diploma awarded on completing the Fellowship training is becoming an historical document. It is not a 'blue chip' entry into lifelong surgical activity. Registration Boards, in response to community expectations, are seeking new ways to measure professional competency.

We live in times in which all levels of the community are challenged by change. We face the new Information Age, one driven by an explosion of ideas, innovations, new technology and new expectations. This calls for a new approach to handling medical information. Medical education based on memorising pages of anatomy and physiology is part of a bygone era. Problem-solving techniques have moved medical education up another gear.

The economist Sam Ferraro refers to 'the increasing rate of obsolescence in human capital'.[1] He observes that 'the implications for skills atrophy have given rise to an increasing sense of anxiety about job security. The rapid speed and nature of technical change has raised the demand for skills that are highly industry specific'. Generic skills are the ones we learn at school and university. They teach us about analysis and criticism. Specific skills are the ones we learn on the job, as in surgery.

The College and most education authorities doubt that re-examination provides an appropriate way of measuring competency in the specific skills of the practising surgeon. While the question of assessing competency remains an unresolved problem, there is evidence that there is a decay in one's intellectual capital over 6–10 years. Continuing Medical Education (CME) provides part of the solution to constantly upgrading the practising surgeon's skills so that each patient receives the benefit of current standards of care.

Again, to meet community expectations and modern education standards, the College must evaluate the continuing education of each Fellow. The Recertification Process was established and at 3-yearly cycles each Fellow must reach the standards laid down, in order to gain a Certificate of Continuing Professional Standards.[2,3] Increasingly, this evidence will be regulated by registration boards, medical indemnity groups and hospital accreditation committees.

The Royal Australasian College of Surgeons (RACS) has developed historically as an educational institution for young doctors aspiring to surgery and as an institution fostering research in academic surgical units. In association with the specialty sections and societies, the College must expand its vision rapidly so as to provide each Fellow with programs that maintain surgical skills and competency. This will require a change in focus, from the advanced trainee and the research academic, to the body of Fellows who need this protective mantle.

History

A formal CME program for Australasian surgeons was established in 1991. There was a gestation period that commenced at the turn of the century when the thoughtful William Oesler emphasised, in a 1904 lecture 'The Importance of Post-Graduate Study',[4] that 'education is a lifelong process'. He said 'daily contact with the bright young minds of our associates and assistants, the mental friction of medical societies and travel are important aids'. Oesler reminded us that 'the hospital was a place for continuing intellectual refurbishment for practising physicians'. By the 1930s university departments were setting up postgraduate refresher courses in the USA, based on the needs of practising surgeons.[5]

With the end of World War II, medical research and the expansion of the biological sciences created a need for specialisation. The specialist surgical societies and the universities responded with educational courses. By the 1960s, medical educators were applying new principles of adult learning. Youmans opened up new horizons in education with the postgraduate 'fellowship courses'.[6] Increasingly, programs were established with a formal content, objectives based on established needs of the surgeon, and an evaluation of the results. Previous emphasis on the memorisation of factual information was being transformed by the huge expansion in scientific information. 'Problem solving was to become the core of the new learning.'[6]

By 1962, the Joint Study Committee on Continuing Medical Education in the USA stated: (i) that the continuing education of physicians is the most important problem facing medical education today; (ii) there is a serious gap between available knowledge and application in medical practices; and (iii) that the continuing medical education of the physician is a nationwide problem for which a nationwide plan is a solution.

While the USA medical system was moving towards formal postgraduate medical education in response to the expanding information and the available communication technology, Australasian medicine was moving more conservatively. Hewson observed in 1986 that the Australasian Colleges 'always stopped short of making an obligatory commitment to continuing medical education'.[7] The President of the Royal Australasian College of Surgeons in 1976, ESR Hughes,[6] noted that 11 of the 22 Boards of the American Board of Medical Specialties had recertification programs in 1976.

The American Board of Surgery began a recertification program on a voluntary basis in 1980 and it became mandatory in 1985. In the UK, some discussion on recertification arose at the Merrison Committee's Report[7] and a report on competence to practise set up by the profession itself.[8] Both committees came to the similar conclusion that continuing competence to practise should be dealt with by continuing education rather than by statute.

ESR Hughes confirmed that the RACS 'has accepted in principle recertification and has re-affirmed this'. A report by the Queensland State Committee on Recertification[9] examined the question but felt that 'recertification for Fellows of the Royal Australasian College of Surgeons is neither necessary nor desirable'. They concluded that 'there was no need for recertification at present nor will it be desirable in the future provided the present standards of practice are maintained'. Still, by 1987 there was increasing concern within the College, expressed at a Sydney meeting of senior surgeons, that the assessment of competence of surgeons might be taken over by outside bodies. They called on the RACS Council to move more actively in this area.

Pressures and reaction

The rapid expansion of scientific information and associated surgical innovations began to ring alarm bells in the late 1980s. For the first 60 years of the College, the emphasis and focus had been on educating the advanced trainee and fostering research activities for the academic. Now, the practising surgeon was being faced with obsolescence unless he/she could upgrade his/her intellectual capital. Once again, the American medical education system was showing the way.

The senior surgeons' meeting in Sydney in 1987 sent back a strong message to the College, calling for improved standards of patient care and more attention to the competency of surgeons. Meanwhile, academics and senior surgeons on the Council also felt it was time to have a more uniform approach to continuing improvement in patient care.

Hospital Boards, awakened by the accreditation process of the Australian Council on Health Care Standards, began to credential their surgeons and clinicians.[12] They began to look at outcome measures and saw the need for encouraging and reviewing CME programs of their medical staff. Third party payers, medical benefit funds, insurance companies and workers' compensation boards also became more interested in patient care and adverse events.

The universities and postgraduate medical education bodies were sensing an opportunity to take over post-diploma educational activities from the clinical colleges. They were thirsty for funds and such educational opportunities were very promising. The community also had rising expectations of the surgical profession. It was known that domestic and international pilots had to show their skills and competency repeatedly through testing and evaluation. What was happening to surgeons as they faced up to new technology in their operating theatres? Governments and bureaucrats became a little more vocal about surgical competency. Their interest certainly was being driven by economics and rationalisation procedures. They tended to confuse utilisation results with health-care outcomes. Nevertheless, the message to the College suggested that they may intervene if we did not take more care and action. Meanwhile, there was a rising cost of medical indemnity for surgeons, particularly for orthopaedic surgeons, plastic surgeons and neurosurgeons, who were becoming much more defensive. Litigation against surgeons and hospitals was rapidly gaining the attention of lawyers starved of other areas of activity. Registration boards, particularly in New Zealand, were examining the link between annual registration of the surgeon and evidence of recertification. The registration boards were seeking confirmation from the College that individual surgeons were taking part in educational courses and maintaining their competence. A further stimulus was provided in the paper by Wilson *et al.* which suggested that 'each year 50 000 Australians suffer permanent disability and 18 000 die, at least in part as a result of their health care'.[10] It was estimated that the major categories of human error accounted for 70% of adverse outcomes and these particularly focused on 'failure in technical performance and failure to decide or act on available information'.[14] In summary, all of these pressures called for evidence that the practising surgeon was keeping up to date with the evolution of surgical practices and information. The College needed to document that each Fellow had evidence of CME, evidence of updated skills and evidence that the surgeons were achieving appropriate surgical outcomes.

While there were compelling pressures for the introduction of CME, there was an interesting ambivalence on the Council and through the College. Some surgeons resented change and they felt that they already worked hard enough to improve patient care. Others saw this as the first move towards cyclical examinations. Geographically isolated and older surgeons phasing out felt more threatened. There were some who saw this as a potential government takeover. The lack of medical educators within Australia and New Zealand and the fear that such educators would take over was yet a further concern. Lastly, new changes could be costly, as the Royal Australian College of Obstetricians and Gynaecologists had already discovered. Such costs would impact on established programs and established staffing.

The College wanted CME programs but enthusiasm was somewhat muted.

Specialist societies

In the development of CME, there were some contributions by the Specialist Societies and Divisions. During the 1980s, the specialist groups recognised the need to provide their members with increasingly sophisticated courses, workshops, seminars and self-assessment programs. In this respect the urologists, the orthopaedic surgeons and the ophthalmologists were the most outstanding groups. As a result of these services many Fellows questioned the value of the College to their professional development. It was the Sydney Presidents, Douglas Tracey, Thomas Reeve and Bruce Barraclough who recognised this danger most acutely, and moved to attract the specialties back to the College. The specialist groups were co-opted to the Council during the presidency of Professor Thomas Reeve and the societies were encouraged to work with the College on CME programs and recertification.

The program

The recertification program established for each Fellow the requirement to meet minimal standards in CME.[5,6] There was the additional need to be credentialled to an approved hospital or day surgery unit and a requirement to carry out an annual surgical audit with a peer review of the outcomes. The mandatory program commenced in 1994 under the supervision of the Board of Continuing Medical Education and Recertification. Recertification was defined as a process conducted by the College which requires that Fellows demonstrate their maintenance of professional standards of knowledge and performance. The initial 10-year cycle was reduced to a 3-year cycle in 1997. The program applied to all surgeons in the clinical care of patients. Some of the older Fellows who were reducing their case load found this difficult to accept. Still, as the medical educationalist Nancy Bennett had observed, 'adults of all ages can learn'.[15]

The Council had difficulty accepting a more objective evaluation process, but this was eventually introduced in 1997.[16] Each Fellow was then required to complete 225 hours of CME over a 3-year period. This had to be achieved in four categories. At the hospital and day surgery unit level, each surgeon had to include 10 hours of active involvement each year in hospital and committee meetings. These included specialty unit meetings, clinical outcome meetings including grand rounds, and involvement in such committees as infection control, quality assurance, clinical indicators, ethics, appointments, radiology, pathology and operating theatre committees. It was considered essential that each Fellow should be active in education at the hospital or day surgery unit level. Category 2 involvement was a level that could be more accurately evaluated. Here, each Fellow was required to average a minimum requirement of 25 hours per annum attending meetings such as the Annual Scientific Congress, State and New Zealand Annual Scientific Meetings, annual meetings of specialist surgical societies or approved meetings of international surgical societies. Attendance at workshops and seminars directed to improvements in patient care were also accepted. Again, it was recognised that in adult learning different surgeons learn differently. Also learning is best achieved when it is related to one's daily practice.[15] Therefore, categories 3 and 4 introduced more flexible options for self-education activities (e.g. arranged visits to special units, Internet activities related to clinical practice, preparation of and participation in self-assessment tests, acquisition of new skills related to surgical practice and the study of journals, tapes and videos). Category 4 activities also allowed great flexibility and acknowledged the value of a review of one's practice by peers, the refereeing of journals, participation in research, publication in refereed journals and the teaching of undergraduates and postgraduates. Here, in categories 3 and 4, a total of 40 hours annually was required. There was the requirement to show evidence of credentialling to an approved hospital or day surgery unit and to carry out a peer-reviewed surgical audit of some area of the practice annually.

The program was introduced with surprisingly few frustrations. Initially the compliance rate was 30% but by 1997 this had improved to 90%, 2% being exempt, 2% non-compliant and 6% non-returns out of the 2439 surgeons involved. The CME results showed 92% compliance, the surgical audit 86% and hospital credentialling 89%. In the CME area, the important category 1 compliance was 87%, with category 2 compliance 86%.

Once the foundations of the program were established, the Board worked to improve the registration of each Fellow's annual return and to evaluate compliance more accurately. In addition, counselling and the appeals process were put in place.

Evaluation

By 1995, it was time to evaluate the progress of the College's CME and recertification program. There was some reluctance to accept the expertise of an outside body. The Queensland Medical Education Centre[9] had the professional background to carry out this review. In addition, 10% of the practising surgeons within the College lived in Queensland, which provided probably the most decentralised health services.

The project team was directed by Dr Peter Livingstone, the Director of the Centre and past Director-General of the Health Department in Queensland. He was assisted by Mrs Barbara Mills as the Chief Investigator, and there was a reference group of surgeons from the College including Tony Green, Peter Woodruff, David Robertson, Andrew Bell, Leigh Atkinson and Ruth Windeler (the Head of the Department of Continuing Medical Education and Recertification at the College).

The terms of reference were: (i) to provide substantive evidence to the RACS and its agencies on the nature of participation in CME in Queensland, and (ii) to make recommendations, based on the evidence, to enhance the quality participation rate in CME activities.

The study was carried out during 1995. A cohort of 553 surgeons was contacted by mail. Replies were received from 58%. The professional distribution was 56% in the metropolitan area, 39% in provincial cities and 5% in towns of less than 20 000. Twenty surgeons were selected at random for more detailed personal interviews.

As a result of this study there were six recommendations from the review.

1. There was a need for the College to review category 1, the attendance at hospital meetings or its equivalent. Sub-specialists, the geographically isolated and those in metropolitan surgical practice were disadvantaged by the current requirements. Subspecialty surgcons did not find the old-style grand rounds of any value. In response to that recommendation, category 1 was expanded. Attendance at unit specialty meetings was included and the time spent working on hospital committees such as the theatre, patient care and infection control were recognised as educational opportunities.

2. It was recommended that the College review its communications with the Fellows regarding CME and recertification. There was a need to reach out to all Fellows about this new activity in the College. In response to this, printed material was distributed. Staff at the College also responded quickly to telephoned queries from Fellows, and the Department took a larger profile at the Annual Scientific Meeting.

3. It was recommended that the College develop ways to improve the identification of the learning needs of its Fellows. This included encouraging Fellows to improve self-assessment and peer review, developing self-examination materials, developing structured analysis of the recertification data forms, and regular monitoring and participation evaluation of CME activities. The study identified substantial evidence of individual differences in participation and preferences. The Fellows required access to computer-based learning packages and access to centralised resources. Fellows sought an ability to access efficiently the latest of any aspect of surgery via the Internet. Finally, it was recognised that the needs of the Fellows changed constantly as Fellows moved through different stages of their careers.

4. It was recommended that 'the College develop ways of meeting the needs of Fellows in accessing leading-edge knowledge and skills development'. This was to be done by: (i) encouraging and supporting further workshop-styled activities, both independently and in relation to major meetings in various locations; (ii) advertising methods for consulting with Fellows about the content structure, style and timing of these meetings; (iii) developing distant learning modes including computer-based education; and (iv) preparing Fellows for the use of computer-based instruction.

The study unearthed a perception of neglect. This was evident in those surgeons who were geographically isolated and also in surgeons in private metropolitan practice. These Fellows complained about the additional costs, the loss of income and the absence from their families that were necessary to comply with the education activities available to surgeons in the teaching hospitals.

5. It was recommended that the College develop ways to facilitate access to leading-edge knowledge and skills development for geographically and/or professionally isolated Fellows (Table 4). It was suggested that extra assistance should be provided for these Fellows. Locum relief services or exchange programs might

be set up. Some surgeons wanted evidence that the CME program was seen to be 'improving knowledge and skills'.

6. It was recommended that the College review the role of and the place of CME in the College recertification process. There was a suggestion that this could include 'collaborative research, e.g. with other Colleges and academic institutions, in assessing the outcome of CME in terms of desired effects on the practice of surgery'.

The Queensland Medical Education Study completed in 1996 caused a complete review of the CME program for Fellows. The plan of the four compulsory CME requirements was changed. The College recognised that most surgeons over the age of 40 years were certainly uneasy with computer-based programs, and often incompetent. It was necessary for the College to develop rapidly educational programs, particularly at Annual Scientific Meetings, to upgrade the skills and confidence of surgeons in the use of

Table 4. Ratings of factors most to least likely to attract participation in CME (response categories 4 and 5 combined)

Most to least likely to attract participation in continuing medical education	%
Presenters who are leaders in their field	86.8
Fits in readily with busy practice	82.1
Hands-on skill development	70.9
Allows a choice of activities	70.6
Workshop style, interactive learning	66.7
Can do it in own time	59.8
One-on-one interactions	54.3
Short duration with continuing support	49.1
Close to home	48.6
Provides effective follow-up	48.3
Held in interesting locations	48.3
Audio-visual instruction (e.g. videotapes etc.)	47.6
Self-paced material	40.0
Work-based interactions/audit	34.9
Large group, lecture style	22.3
Computer-based instruction	14.9
Material delivered by Internet	12.6

computers. Through the expertise of Ms Nancy Emmanuel, the new Head of the Department of Continuing Medical Education and Recertification, the College also set up a website on the Internet, one innovation being 'a virtual congress'.

Skills laboratories

The technology and excitement of films and the printed media have built up new expectations in our community. Today, many patients are surprised if they are not having 'laser surgery'. The rapid change in information and technology over the past 15 years has been challenging to the practising surgeon. This was highlighted by the introduction of laparoscopic cholecystectomy into Australia in 1986. The long-practised techniques of the general surgeon suddenly changed with the introduction of minimally invasive surgery. Before hospital boards and governments could assess the technology, surgeons and 'the industry' had embraced it with enthusiasm. The rate of bile duct injuries increased and it became evident that some surgeons may not have the capacity to use the technology.

Economics, reduced numbers of hospital beds and reduced lengths of stay have driven the need for minimally invasive techniques in all surgical specialties. Laparoscopy, hysteroscopy, endoscopy, vascular stents, arterial grafts and intra-luminal prostheses, together with computer-assisted surgery and robotics, have meant that the surgeon has had to learn new skills. Skills laboratories (S Deane, pers. comm., 1999) have presented an important learning opportunity for all specialties in developing techniques for training surgeons.

'See one, do one, teach one' has become an outdated philosophy, as the Colleges, the hospitals and the Australian Council on Health Care Standards call for credentialling of surgeons with the introduction of new technology to hospitals.

The Quality in Australian Health Care study had indicated that one of the major causes of adverse events in surgery was considered to be human error due to 'failure in technical performance'.[10]

It became evident that competency, performance and outcomes were under increasing scrutiny. Continuing medical education and enhancement of specific skills were new priorities.

In the Queensland Medical Education Centre Report in 1996 (see Table 25 of the Report) 66% of surgeons indicated an interest in advanced skills courses.[16] In comparison to the English College, RACS was slow in developing these facilities for practising surgeons although, again, some specialties such as orthopaedics had moved earlier.

The development of skills laboratories is now a priority within the College. It is an important facility for developing specific surgical skills. They can be applied to master classes for surgeons as well as to basic surgical training, advanced surgical training and training for nurses and surgical assistants. They can provide learning experiences with synthetic tissue substitutes, body-part simulators, animal tissues, cadavers and anaesthetised animals — in time, virtual reality simulators will be available. All specialties of surgeons will find valuable opportunities in these laboratories. They can be used to develop surgeons as educators, to select applicants for surgery and to carry out examinations. They allow surgeons to assess new technology and to learn new techniques. In a time of cost and time constraints we can now reach community expectations. We can possibly standardise methods of assessing performance and new technology.

Conclusion

In recent years the culture of change has accelerated globally but the medical profession seems to be able to accommodate. The healthcare system and surgeons are now confronted with more serious implications of change. Each practising surgeon is threatened by an expanding pool of information, new technology, a need for new skills and by possible obsolescence. Increasingly, the surgeon must turn to the College and the specialist societies to provide continuing education, upgraded skills and a recertification of professional standards. While the objective measurement of competency remains unresolved, the ultimate aim is to ensure continuing improvements in patient care and outcomes.

The historical emphasis has focused on training young surgeons and in supporting academic research. The culture of the past must change. Resources, energy and staffing need to be redirected into providing educational programs supported by competent medical educators well versed in techniques of adult education. If the College is to maintain its relevance, it is time for a commitment to support each practising Fellow.

REFERENCES
1. Ferraro S. Looking through the production prism: J.B. Were, Australian Research Report, 1999.
2. McGovern IP, Roland GS, Oesler W. *Continuing Education.* Springfield, Illinois: Thomas, 1969.
3. Uhl HSM. A Brief History. In: Brosof A, Fetch WC (eds). *Continuing Medical Education: A Primer*, 2nd edn. New York: Prager, 1992.
4. Youmans JD. Experience with a course for practitioners: evaluation of results: 1. *Assoc. Am. Med. Coll.* 1935; **10**: 154–173.
5. Hewson A. The development of obligatory education and certification program of the Royal Australian College of Obstetricians & Gynaecologists: A practical response to the increasing challenges of modern surgery. *Medical Teacher* Vol. II, No.1, 1989.
6. Hughes ESR. FRACS Report to Council 'Recertification', No. 6, 1976; 19–24.
7. A Report of the Committee of Inquiry into the Regulation of the Medical Profession, AMND 6018 HMSO, Merrison Committee, 1978.
8. Report of a Committee of Inquiry Set Up for the Medical Profession in the United Kingdom.
9. Recertification: A Report to the Council of the Royal Australasian College of Surgeons by the Queensland State Committee. Brisbane: Queensland Medical Education Centre; University of Queensland, 1977.
10. Wilson RM, Runciman N, Gibberd RW *et al*. The quality in the Australian health. *Med. J. Aust.* 1995; **163**: 458–471.
11. Charles AV. The human element of adverse events (Editorial). *Med. J. Aust.* 1999; **170**: 404–405.
12. *RACS Recertification Manual* 1994.
13. RACS Continuing Medical Education & Recertification Program: Information Manual and Diary. Melbourne: Royal Australasian College of Surgeons, 1998.
14. Recertification: Department Report to Council on Statistical Analysis. Melbourne: Royal Australasian College of Surgeons, 1999.
15. Bennett N. Adult learning: Uses in C.M.E. In: Brosof A, Fetch WC (eds). *Continuing Medical Education - A Primer*, 2nd edn. New York: Prager. 1992; 31–34.

16. Miflin B. Queensland Medical Centre Report on an Analysis of the CME Needs of Fellows of the College: January 1996.

Why medical boards?

P.C. ARNOLD

Introduction

This chapter does not describe the structure and function of Australian medical boards. This information is readily available from each board. Instead, it explores the origins of medical boards, the trust placed in the profession to be self-regulating, and public confidence that medical boards will always put public safety ahead of professional self-interest. The principles discussed apply equally to doctors in all fields of practice.

Private trust and public confidence

Trust is the key to understanding the role of boards. Surgeons expect patients to rely on their professional judgment. This dependence encompasses management of the presenting problem, diagnosis of the underlying disease, its treatment and the follow-up. Without this confidence, surgical intervention would, other than in emergencies, be impossible.

But this trust is not unconditional. In the aftermath of the Nuremberg trials after World War II, which revealed atrocities committed by doctors, it became apparent that doctors have the potential for evil as well as their assumed Hippocratic commitment. Their responsibility to individual patients could be, and had been, subsumed by a duty to a greater political ideology. Even since

Nuremberg, doctors have been involved in torture[1] and other atrocities.[2] Stephen Biko, founder of the Black Consciousness Movement in South Africa, died at the age of 31 years, of head injuries sustained in police custody. Two white doctors had declared him fit to travel, naked and handcuffed, in the back of a police van, over a journey of some 1000 km, when he was already unconscious.

The doctors' behaviour was exonerated by the then South African Medical and Dental Council. *Post*-Mandela, this decision was reversed. Surgeons are as capable as anyone else of seeing fellow men and women as means, rather than ends in themselves,[3] especially if we follow an ideology which categorises people who are like ourselves as normal, and others who differ racially, socially or politically, as being less than human.

At the same time, the public has become aware that some doctors, for reasons of vainglory, have falsified research, only to have their behaviour eventually exposed. The exposure by ABC science reporter, Dr Norman Swan, of Dr William McBride's fraudulent research into the alleged teratogenic effects of Debendox eventually led to Dr McBride's name being struck off the Medical Register in NSW. The public has also learned, through the efforts of a few whistleblowers, of attempts by the profession to hide the substandard work of some colleagues. Because surgeons' failures are generally more obvious than those of other doctors, their failures have received most attention, such as the excessive number of deaths of children undergoing cardiothoracic surgery at the Bristol Royal Infirmary. This was noted and reported by one of the anaesthetists, but ignored. The senior surgeon concerned and the chief executive of the Trust that ran the hospital were eventually struck off by the General Medical Council in London in 1998.

The public has come to realise that it is possible for a surgeon's advice to be coloured by concerns other than the patient's medical wellbeing. Early in the 20th century, before the introduction of health insurance in most Western countries, the doctor's dilemma lay in deciding whether to undertake a cheaper or a more expensive operation.[4] Adherents to the Hippocratic Oath took care not to let this influence them. Today, patients want to know much more about their surgeon's reasons for wishing to perform a particular procedure. In a Medicare-type environment, cost to the patient is now not the major issue. More important is the patient's concern about the surgeon's success and complication rates, and how these compare with those of his colleagues. Is this procedure the most suitable for that patient? Is the surgeon using a tried technique or experimenting with one that happens to be in vogue?

Adequately informing patients about the significance of the diagnosis, alternative methods of treatment, and the risks of encountering side-effects, is now part of the surgeon's clinical repertoire. Informing patients is discussed by B.J. Dooley and M.R. Fearnside, on pages 75–80 and on pages 81–88 by M.W. Gorton,[5] and touched upon by others. At a time when the consumerist movement is demanding a shift from medical paternalism, based on trust in the doctor, to a doctor–patient partnership in decision-making, the task is more difficult. Parallel with the decline in the trust exhibited by patients is a decline in society's confidence in the profession as a whole. 'All changed, changed utterly: British medicine will be transformed by the Bristol case' wrote Dr Richard Smith, editor of *BMJ*.[6] To understand how Australian society came to place its overall faith in our profession, and the doubts that have recently disturbed that relationship, a short historical look at the recognition of doctors is needed.

The world's first medical board

Most Australian doctors would probably be surprised to know that the world's first medical board, in a form we would recognise, was established in Hobart in 1837.[7] The Governor wanted to know which medical men could be relied upon to give scientific evidence at inquests. An Act of Parliament established a Board of suitably qualified men with British degrees, to distinguish between trained practitioners and charlatans. In the following year, and for the same reasons, the NSW Medical Board was created. Gradually, boards were appointed in all the colonies, and also in the ex-colonies in the USA. In England, the body now known as the General Medical Council was formed in 1958.

What distinguished the Tasmanian Board from other methods of licensing medical practitioners was that it was self-regulating. Doctors decided who possessed appropriate qualifications; this philosophy has continued. In most Australian jurisdictions today, the Governor (on the advice of the Minister for Health) appoints doctors to the medical boards. In NSW, the Minister's trust in the profession is reflected in his acceptance of doctors specifically nominated by individual royal colleges and the Australian Medical Association (AMA).

By contrast, across continental Europe and throughout the countries once colonised by the European Empires, the licensing of doctors is an administrative function of the Department of Health. The profession plays no role. Matters of discipline progress through standard public administrative law. Appeals lie with higher administrative bodies, with the final say often in the hands of the Minister. In the Netherlands, disciplinary matters relating to technical proficiency may be handled through the criminal courts.

The functions of medical boards

While medical boards were originally established to recognise trained doctors, their roles have changed over the past 150 years, and continue to evolve.

Registration

Having initially registered on graduation, doctors have a lifelong legal obligation to notify their board of any change to their current address. Doctors remain on the Register by paying an annual roll fee. Unregistered doctors are not recognised by hospitals, pharmacies, coroners, Medicare, health insurers and other bodies required to deal only with registered practitioners.

The early boards' registration of persons appropriately trained in the UK extended, with the inauguration of medical schools in Australia, to local graduates. Prior to the formation of the Australian Medical Council (AMC) and the commencement of its examination for foreign doctors, the boards were required to register doctors who had qualified in certain countries. The countries recognised in different jurisdictions varied through the 20th century, often at the political whim of governments. Interstate uniformity and mutual recognition were not achieved until the 1990s. Today, because all Australian and New Zealand medical schools undergo regular accreditation by the AMC, their graduates are *prima facie* entitled to registration. Graduates of other medical schools must either pass the AMC examination (in order to enter general practice or to undertake further training) or, if they were specialists in their home country, must meet the requirements of the corresponding Australian College.

Discipline

All medical boards are empowered to act on complaints about doctors. Board involvement in each jurisdiction varies. In most, the Board conducts the investigation, holds a hearing and imposes any sanctions needed to protect the public. In others, the Board acts as a conduit to an independent Ombudsman or Complaints Commissioner, who is legally empowered to investigate complaints. In NSW, the Board's role is restricted to consultation with the Commission about the manner in which complaints are handled, and to coordinating the panels which conduct the hearings.

With the rise of consumerism, the Medical Practice (Practitioners) Act (MPA) in each jurisdiction has been amended to enable the Minister to appoint public (i.e. non-medical) persons to medical boards. Membership of adjudicatory bodies has also been amended to include public members. This ensures that matters are not swept under the carpet because the respondent doctor has high standing in the profession, and that doctors are not made scapegoats because of some singularity of their personality or conduct.

In all jurisdictions, doctors found guilty of unsatisfactory professional conduct or of the more serious charge of professional misconduct (these terms and their precise meanings vary among jurisdictions) have a right of appeal. In some jurisdictions, the appeal lies with the Supreme Court, while in others it lies with an Administrative Appeals Tribunal.

Impairment

During the late 1980s, it became apparent that a number of doctors against whom complaints had been made were, in fact cognitively or physically impaired, rather than guilty of wilful misconduct. The causes included dementia, drug and alcohol abuse, psychosis, and uncontrolled organic diseases such as Parkinson's disease and diabetes mellitus. The NSW MPA was amended in 1992 to provide an alternative, non-punitive pathway for assisting these doctors, where possible, to practise safely, while restoring themselves to health. Impairment matters are handled as confidential notifications, without the involvement of the Complaints Commission, rather than as complaints, which by their nature imply misconduct. In time, other jurisdictions adopted similar therapeutic, non-disciplinary approaches, and the process has been adopted by boards registering other health professionals.

The problems of many impaired doctors date back to medical school. Accordingly, the NSW MPA was amended to provide, in respect only of impairment, for the registration of medical students. The Board has since encouraged the universities to co-operate in the management of impaired students.

Performance assessment

The experience of the NSW Board with complaints against doctors and of notifications of impaired doctors has led to a realisation that the overall practice of medicine by some doctors is seriously substandard. While the investigation of a specific complaint leads to the formulation of detailed allegations about a doctor's management of one or a few patients, the MPA does not provide an avenue for the Board to look at the doctor's overall standard of practice. Furthermore, there has been a steadily increasing public concern that the profession does nothing to *prevent* substandard practice. Put another way, the boards act as gateways through which all graduates must pass, but nothing is done by the boards to ensure that they retain and maintain their knowledge and skills throughout their careers. The boards act only following a complaint that a patient has been harmed or put at risk.

Awareness of medical misadventures elsewhere, such as the Bristol case, has also contributed to the decision by the NSW Board to investigate a further alternative to the disciplinary and impairment pathways. The Board has, in consultation with the Colleges, the AMA, the NSW Department of Health and other relevant medical bodies, prepared a discussion paper on a performance assessment pathway, based on the Board's proven methods of handling impairment. Although most of the Colleges have programs for the maintenance of professional standards, they can rely only on their powers of persuasion, as no College has effective legal backing to enforce compliance with their standards.

Doctors whose overall performance is judged by colleagues in the same field of practice to be unsatisfactory will, with the assistance of the Colleges and the hospitals, be helped to raise their standards. The NSW experience with student registration and with performance assessment is being closely watched by other Australian boards.

What medical boards do not do

As the Boards have evolved into new areas of activity, old areas have been relinquished. With the advent of uniform competition policy across Australia, boards now have little or no interest in advertising, or in persons purporting to be medical practitioners. While ethical doctors frequently object to the excesses of advertising in newspapers, magazines, telephone directories and even on radio and television, these matters are properly the domain of the Federal or State bodies enforcing the Trade Practices or Fair Trading Acts.

Similarly, boards are moving away from concern about the size and content of doctors' brass plates, and about whether or not they are practising in premises in association with pharmacies or other health-care practitioners. These, and other activities which would once have been perceived as unethical, have been overtaken by consumer and competition law. Now legitimate, such activities cannot be acted upon by the boards.

You and your medical board

Apart from notifying any change of address and paying your annual roll fee, you are unlikely to have much contact with your Board. However, if you are one of the few who is told by your Board about a complaint, always a distressing event, you would be wise to contact your medical defence organisation immediately, and to cooperate fully and promptly in the investigation. Cooperation should facilitate a speedier resolution, minimising your anxiety. Of the approximate 1000 complaints made each year in NSW, fewer than 40 reach a hearing, an experience mirrored in all jurisdictions. Delay in responding to a notice from the medical board or from the Health Complaints Commission only prolongs the ordeal.

The NSW Board receives approximately one notification weekly of a possibly impaired doctor. Doctors are often loath to acknowledge that we are as liable as our patients to 'suffer the slings and arrows of outrageous fortune' and that we, too, are at risk of abuse of opiates and other substances. We are slow to recognise impairment in our colleagues, and most reluctant to acknowledge it in ourselves.

A surgeon's dilemma

Following the publicity given to the Bristol case, it behoves all doctors to consider what action is open to them should they form an honest opinion that a colleague, whether senior or junior, is performing at a generally unsatisfactory standard. The poor performance might be due to impairment or to lack of skills. If you become aware of a colleague's poor performance, you will probably be reluctant to 'dob in'. However, a legal precedent was set in the UK when a senior anaesthetist at the East Yorkshire Hospitals, Dr Sean Dunn, was found by the General Medical Council to be guilty of unsatisfactory professional conduct. He had failed to take action in 1992 about a colleague, Dr Behrooz Irani, whom he knew to be practising dangerously as a locum anaesthetist. Dr Irani was subsequently struck off in 1993.

Awareness of a colleague's poor performance faces you, as the hypothetical informer, with a dilemma: to tell or not to tell. You may fear being accused of holding some unacceptable motivation, of wishing to harm a competing colleague's career, or of harbouring some personal malice. Human nature is such that you may not want to become involved but, merely through your having made an honest assessment of a colleague's unsatisfactory performance, you are involved. Should that poor performance lead to a catastrophe, as in Bristol, and should it become known that you were aware of it beforehand, you could be held responsible for not having acted on your honestly formed professional opinion.

More important, perhaps, is the question of whom to tell ? Passing on your concerns to someone in your own hospital could, for many of the above reasons, be potentially embarrassing for you, and perhaps leave you exposed to the criticisms and vituperation commonly levelled at whistleblowers.[8-10] It might be wise, therefore, if you do find yourself in this difficult predicament, to take your concerns in the first instance to a senior colleague at another hospital or to a State or Federal office-bearer of the RACS. Alternatively, you might approach the President of your State or Territory Medical Board, unless, of course, he works in your hospital, in which case you could approach the Deputy President, the Registrar or another member of your Board. Having passed your concerns on to a senior colleague who is neither directly involved nor affected by your information, but who is in a position to initiate some action, you have largely discharged any professional obligation which could reasonably be expected of you.

Conclusion

If our profession is to maintain its independence of clinical judgment and ethical practice of medicine, it is essential that we retain the trust of the public. To do that, we must demonstrate that we are willing and able to control those few colleagues whose behaviour is unacceptable. Whether they are evil or misguided, impaired or simply slack, we have a collective responsibility to find methods of ensuring that they are brought to account, and that the public is protected from them.[11,12] The public's trust is crucial to the maintenance of self-regulation. This confidence is strained if we appear not to be keeping our house in order, or when we seem to be abusing our privileged status to preserve financial self-interest.[13]

To the extent that the public loses confidence in our ability to self-regulate, it will turn to the State to control us. The challenge for us is to demonstrate to the public that we deserve their confidence. Should we fail, we risk losing our self-regulating capacity and may find ourselves, instead, under the control of a European-style, government-directed, bureaucracy which is unlikely to share our ethical and professional outlook.[14]

REFERENCES

1. Parameshvara V. Doctors and torture. *J. World Med. Assoc.* 1998; May/June 33–37.
2. Roy and Zhores Medvedev, historian and biologist, respectively, described the abuses of Soviet psychiatry for political purposes in *A Question of Madness*, published in 1971.
3. Italian novelist, Alberto Moravia's essay, *Man as an End*, published in 1941 at the height of European fascism, defended the essential humanness of each person and argued against the use of human beings as means to other people's ends.
4. Satirically portrayed by George Bernard Shaw in *The Doctor's Dilemma*.
5. In 1993, the NHMRC published its general guidelines for medical practitioners on providing information to patients.
6. Smith R. All changed, changed utterly. British Medicine will be transformed by the Bristol case. *BMJ* 1998; **316**: 1917–1918.
7. Anno Primo Vittoriae Reginae, No. 17. *The Hobart Town Gazette* 8 December 1837.
8. Dr Stephen Bolsin, the whistleblower in the Bristol case, has described the events, in Professional misconduct: the Bristol case. *Med. J. Aust.* 1998; **169**: 369–372.
9. Lennane J, de Maria W. The downside of whistleblowing. *Med. J. Aust.* 1998; **169**: 351.
10. Van Der Weyden MB. The Bristol case: the medical profession and trust. *Med. J. Aust.* 1998; **169**: 352–353.
11. Arnold PC. Wayward doctors: We have effective ways of dealing with impaired and incompetent doctors. *Med. J. Aust.* 1995; **162**: 453–454.
12. Arnold PC. Problem doctors and Medical Boards. *Med. J. Aust.* 1999; **171**: 399–400.
13. Dahrendorf R. In defence of the English professions. *Journ. Royal Soc. Med.* 1984; **77**: 178–185.
14. This topic is covered more fully in my contribution to the Oxford Companion to Medicine, in press.

Disciplinary and appeal processes

L. WALLER

Introduction

The Articles of Association of the Royal Australasian College of Surgeons, as published on 28 June 1996, create the framework for the relationship between the Fellows and the College. They contain a number of provisions for the discipline of Fellows, and for regulating the training and examination of medical practitioners who seek admission as Fellows by examination.

Termination and suspension of Fellows

Article 24 provides that a Fellow shall cease to be a member of the College in a number of instances. Two of these instances are not concerned with matters of discipline. A Fellow who is delinquent in the payment of her or his annual subscription ceases to be a member pursuant to the provisions of Article 23. Death or the submission of a written resignation ends a Fellowship: Article 24(a).

If a Fellow is removed from any register of medical practitioners, such as that established under the terms of the *Medical Practice Acts*, however entitled in any Australian state or territory 'on grounds of malpractice, misconduct, ethical or other similar grounds', her or his membership of the College ceases. The subject of the statutory registration of medical practitioners is described and reviewed in Chapter 7 of Breen, Pleuckhahn and Cordner's *Ethics, Law and*

Medical Practice.[1] Surgeons, like all medical practitioners, are subject to the provisions of those statutes, all of which contain detailed sections for the receipt, the investigation, and the determination of complaints, from their patients or from others, against doctors. The medical boards that are established under the terms of these enactments are empowered to conduct disciplinary hearings of various kinds. In most parts of Australia these may be either informal or formal. In the first, allegations of a less serious nature are tried, and the range of sanctions which the Board may impose is strictly limited. The second deals with all serious complaints, in a framework which has many resemblances to the structure and operations of a legal tribunal (or to a military disciplinary body). Here, the Board may impose the ultimate sanction of removal from the register for an indefinite period, which may be characterised as a sentence of professional death. The impugned behaviour may be described as unprofessional conduct, professional misconduct, or infamous conduct in a professional respect. In some States these hearings are before panels presided over by judges or lawyers. In most, they are now open to the public, so that proceedings are sometimes extensively reported. There are provisions for the review of, or an appeal against, an adverse decision, either to a superior court or to an administrative appeals body such as the Victorian Civil and Administrative Tribunal.

Expulsion

Article 24(d) states that a Fellow may be expelled from the College. The grounds upon which such action may be effected are found in Article 30. The grounds are a breach of the Constitution of the College, the division of fees, or 'conduct contrary or derogatory to or inconsistent with the principles, ethics, dignity, standards or purposes of the College' (all encompassed by the general expression 'derogatory conduct').

These grounds are not further defined in the Articles, and consideration for the purpose of characterisation of impugned behaviour may, of course, include the examination of and argument on decisions of courts in England and in Australia, in hearing appeals in this connection. It is important to emphasise that, given the nature of these proceedings and the severity of the penalties which may be imposed, the standard of proof used by such disciplinary bodies must be not simply the law's civil standard of the balance of probabilities. The standard is the degree of satisfaction enunciated by the High Court of Australia in *Briginshaw v. Briginshaw* (1938) 60 CLR 336; it should be firm, and based on convincing evidence.

Expulsion may occur only after the Council of the College has considered the particular allegation or allegations, and also considered any oral response made by the Fellow concerned, and any written submission tendered by her or him: (Article 30(b)).

Complaints

The Articles provide a detailed framework for the consideration of complaints or allegations of derogatory conduct. Articles 27, 28 and 29 provide for the making of complaints against any Fellow, and the establishment of Regional Complaints Committees and a Complaints Committee of the Council. All complaints must be in writing. The Secretary of the College may refer a complaint to a Regional Committee, or to the Complaints Committee Council, or to the Censor in Chief: (Article 27(b)). Any Regional Committee to which a complaint is referred must first decide whether there is a *prima facie* case to answer in that allegation. The Fellow concerned must then be given notice of the complaint, and invited to respond in writing within 14 days of the giving of notice: (Article 28(c), (d), and (e)). Thereafter, the Regional Committee may take any one of five decisions: (i) it may take no action; (ii) it may dismiss the complaint and exonerate the Fellow concerned; (iii) it may counsel the Fellow; (iv) it may censure the Fellow; or (v) it may refer the complaint to the Complaints Committee-Council: (see Article 28(t)).

The Council's Committee must give any Fellow against whom a complaint is made 30 days' written notice of its intention to consider the allegation, together with all particulars, and invite that Fellow to be present and to tender oral or written submissions in respect of the matter. The Committee must give 'due consideration' to any such submission.

If the matter is then brought before the Council, Article 30(a) provides for the same notice to be given to the Fellow accused, and for that Fellow to be entitled to be present and 'to make submissions to the Council in his defence'. In the alternative, the Fellow accused may make written submissions 'in his defence which shall be read at the meeting'. Article 30(a) empowers the Council itself to charge a Fellow with derogatory conduct. No member of Council who has already been a member of a Complaints Committee seized of the allegation or complaint may participate in the Council's consideration and determination of it.

If the Council finds the Fellow guilty of the charge, it may impose one of a number of penalties, which include censure, suspension of the Fellowship, or expulsion. Article 30(d) requires a majority of three-quarters of the members of Council present and eligible to vote to permit the penalty of suspension to be imposed.[a] The Council must ensure that the adverse finding is made known to the Fellow. It may publish the finding and the penalty imposed not only to the Fellowship but also to professional medical bodies, and to the public at large.

A Fellow suspended or expelled may seek to have that adverse decision reviewed in the courts. The conduct of the proceedings by Council must be such that natural justice is accorded to the accused Fellow. The specific provisions in the Articles which deal with the giving of notice, with the opportunity to be heard, and with the consideration of responses, address some of the most significant strands in the fabric of natural justice. The provision excluding from the deliberations of the Council any Fellow who has already been involved in the examination or the adjudication of the Fellow's conduct satisfies, substantially, the requirement that the tribunal be free of bias. Nonetheless, the right to seek judicial review remains an important legal safeguard in what is a, or for some, *the*, most serious of professional misadventures.

The College Appeals process

The College is one of the bodies responsible for advanced training,

---

[a] The special majority needed for the imposition of the penalty of suspension should clearly apply to the more severe penalty of expulsion as well. The present form of Article 30(d) may be the result of a slip in drafting the most recent version of the Articles.

examination and accreditation in the quaternary level of education in Australia. Members of the medical profession who wish to practise in the specialty of surgery as surgeons recognised by their peers, and by the profession as a whole, must undertake the courses of training the College prescribes, undergo the supervision it mandates, and pass the examinations it sets. Those doctors who do are awarded the accolade of Fellowship of the College. The College reviews and refreshes the education and the expertise of its Fellows through its continuing education and its re-assessment programs.

There is no doubt that in light of these powers and these responsibilities the College is bound to accord what is today called 'procedural fairness' in the conduct of its education, training, examination and accreditation programs. In particular circumstances, the College's actions in these connections may be scrutinised and evaluated in the courts or in other, quasi-judicial, tribunals, at the suit of an aggrieved person. The high importance and the critical consequences of decisions made in relation to admission to training, exclusion or dismissal from training, failure in examinations and associated matters justify this conclusion. Superior courts in Australia, including the High Court of Australia, the final appellate tribunal, would decide, in my opinion, that the rules Australian courts have enunciated under the current rubric of 'procedural fairness in administrative law' apply to the College's activities in the areas mentioned. The rules of natural justice (an older but still used expression) apply to the College's work in these connections. The College is obliged 'to act fairly, in the sense of according procedural fairness, in the making of administrative decisions which affect rights, interests and legitimate expectations ...' of those people to whom I have already referred.

Fundamentally this means that, in this context as in that already covered, there must be impartiality and non-partisanship in the administration of the College's rules, and in the application of its standards in the admission of trainees, in the review of their progress, in the dismissal of trainees, and in their examination.

Those standards, and the specific criteria used in selection and in evaluation, must be clearly stated and be readily accessible to applicants and to trainees. There must be due notice where adverse action is proposed. The communication of an adverse decision to an applicant for a training program should be effected in a way that not only sets it out clearly, but also explains why it has happened. An applicant must be told whether there may be opportunities to apply again, and what conditions may be applied or considered in relation to any further applications. There must be an opportunity to seek review of any such action which so seriously affects the expectations, or the current career, of a doctor who would be a surgeon.

That is why the appeals mechanism of the College is of such significance. The College instituted its own appeals process in 1992, which has been considered and revised, most recently in late 1997. This mechanism has been devised and implemented by the College itself; it is not an external imposition. It draws very considerable strength from its origin as a result. Any person who considers that she or he has been adversely affected by a decision of any Board or any Committee of the College with responsibilities for training, accreditation, examination or related matters may lodge an appeal. That appeal, provided it is made in writing and is timely, will be heard and determined by the Appeals Committee which the College has established. The Appeals Committee is so constituted that while there is a core of surgical knowledge and great experience in its membership, there is the substantial leavening of the lay. The composition of the Committee is two Fellows and two lay members. The two Fellows who sit on any Appeals Committee shall not be drawn from that specialty in which either the appellant, or any respondent, is or are involved.

Since late 1997, the Committee must be chaired by one of the lay members. The Chairman may exercise a casting vote and a deliberative vote. The Committee has the benefit of advice from the Secretary of the College, from the College's Honorary Solicitor, and from the Chairman of the relevant Surgical Board or her or his nominee, or some senior Fellow drawn from that specialty in the context of which the appeal sits. But the appeal is determined only by the members of the Appeals Committee.

The grounds for appeal are threefold. The appellant may claim that there has been an error in law or process; specifically, in this context, in relation to the failure of a person to be selected for a training program, or in relation to her or his dismissal from a training program. (The complete list of decisions that may be the subject of review by the Appeals Committee is set out in the Appendix.) The appellant may claim that she or he has additional information in relation to the issues, which was not before the original decision-maker. The appellant may claim that the adverse decision was clearly contrary to the weight of the evidence, or the arguments, before the Committee or body which made it.

The Appeals Committee must hear the appellant, if she or he desires to be heard, rather than relying upon, or in addition to, the submission of written materials. The Appeals Committee may allow an appellant to be represented before it by counsel or by a solicitor. The Appeals Committee may dismiss the appeal, and affirm the original decision. It may allow the appeal, and revoke the original decision absolutely, or allow the appeal and replace the original decision with whatever decision the Committee considers is appropriate in all the circumstances. It may refer the decision under appeal to a Board or a Committee of the College for reconsideration, upon such terms and conditions as it thinks appropriate.

The Appeals Committee first met in 1993. Since then, it has considered and determined a number of appeals in relation to applications for selection and the removal of trainees from training programs. In my opinion (and I declare, as a member of the Committee, an interest in its operations and their outcomes), the conduct of those appeals has been undertaken with scrupulous care and with complete fairness. In addition, recommendations made by the Appeals Committee, as a result of particular appeals, have been considered, and implemented by the Council and by appropriate training committees.

REFERENCE
1. In: Breen, Pleuckhahn and Cordner (eds). *Ethics, Law and Medical Practice*. Allen & Unwin, 1997.

Appendix 1. The decisions that may be reviewed by the Appeals Committee are:

1. Decisions of the Censor-in-Chief's Committee, Court of Examiners, Board of Examiners, Surgical Boards, Regional Subcommittee of Surgical Boards or Supervisors of Surgical Training, in relation to the assessment of progress of trainees of the College (including admission, dismissal or recognition of training).
2. Decisions of boards and committees in relation to applications for admission to Fellowship.
3. Decisions of the Censor-in-Chief and Surgical Board Chairmen in relation to applications from overseas-trained doctors for assessment for recognition on behalf of the Australian Medical Council, or the New Zealand Medical Council, or any applicable State or Territory medical board (or for other appropriate purposes).
4. Decisions of the Censor-in-Chief and Surgical Board Chairmen in relation to examinations or training required to be undertaken by overseas-trained doctors for assessment as set out above.
5. Decisions of the Board of Continuing Medical Education and Recertification in relation to participation in the recertification program, and awarding of the Certificate of Continuing Professional Standards.
6. Decisions of the Council and Executive Committee of the College on the advice of the Censor-in-Chief's Committee in relation to accreditation for training of hospitals, units, teaching centres or supervisors.
7. Decisions of Complaints Committees Council and Regional in relation to their requirements that complainants be counselled, censured or have the complaint against them referred to Council pursuant to Article 30 of the Articles of Association.
8. Decisions of the Honorary Treasurer in relation to the financial status of Fellows, trainees, or other persons. Such other decisions of the College, its Boards or Committees as the Council may determine from time to time.

Impaired surgeons

J. PHILLIPS

Surgeons are, be they male or female, young or old, along with all other members of the medical community, vulnerable to psychological disturbances of every kind. This is a fact which is often forgotten by surgeons and medical practitioners in general. Yet, strangely, there has been only modest interest in the psychological problems of doctors, both in Australia and elsewhere. In preparing for this chapter I carried out a search of Medline and psychINFO, producing relatively few papers of direct relevance to my task. I will be calling largely on my clinical experience as psychiatrist with special interest in the diseases of doctors and on two addresses given by me in recent years: The Graham Coupland Oration in 1993 and the Harry Harris Lecture in 1996.

There may be a number of factors that place surgeons and other doctors at risk for psychological illness beyond the statistical chance of becoming ill as an ordinary member of the community.

First, surgeons and other doctors often hoodwink themselves into believing they will not become ill. In psychological jargon, surgeons deny the likelihood of illness. Surgeons were all taught to be tough at medical school and the legacy continues. In keeping with the process of denial, the ill surgeon will come to recognise his/her symptoms only at a relatively late stage in the development of the disorder, whatever form it may take.

Second, surgeons not uncommonly have personalities marked by obsessional traits. In some ways this is a professional advantage, allowing for hard work, good time management and close attention to detail. However, obsessional traits can be a liability as there is an accepted link between obsessionality and vulnerability to anxiety and/or depression.

Third, surgeons have the task of balancing long and often unpredictable professional hours with their family lives. It has been said, perhaps correctly, that doctors are married twice, to their spouse and to their profession. The psychological tension arising from this hardly needs to be laboured.

Fourth, surgeons face major stressors in their professional lives in keeping with the type of work undertaken. The pressure of intra-operative decision-making should not be underestimated and stress elsewhere in their day-to-day occupation is of importance also.

Some would say that it is the surgeon in mid-career who will be at greatest risk for psychiatric disorder. Our younger colleagues, across the spectrum of medicine, are beginning to challenge the pathological work ethic of the profession. Our interns and registrars still work hard, but rarely work the inhumane and dangerous hours that were once the norm. Additionally, many younger practitioners are making lifestyle decisions which emphasise time with their families rather than their unending devotion to their professional career.

Fifth, surgeons are working in an increasingly difficult environment. The standards demanded of medical practitioners are ever higher and are now being determined by the courts rather than within the profession itself. Litigation is on the march and many surgeons have experienced terrifying ordeals when a complaint has been made against them. Whether it is a good thing or not, there is an increasing tendency to practise defensive medicine, with the spectre of litigation never far away.

Sixth, surgeons live in a professional world in which they often cannot succeed. Much of the illness treated is chronic in nature and, despite the best efforts of the doctor, the patient will fail to improve and may become worse and die. Disability and death are often difficult to accept.

However, before we rationalise the psychological problems of doctors as being consequences of a tough career, other factors including family history of psychiatric disorder, life experiences and personality factors will need to be explored.

What we do know is that doctors have at least the same risk for developing psychological disorders as others in the general population and some would say the risk is greater. However, illness is often not identified and is sometimes harder to treat. Women within the profession are particularly likely to develop psychological disorders, perhaps as a result of irreconcilable role strain.

We propose to consider the 'big ticket' diseases of doctors before addressing the practical issue, in particular how we might help ourselves and our colleagues who are in trouble.

Many would say that alcohol and drug dependence are the most common psychological diseases of doctors. The experiences of medical boards would tend to support the contention.

There is good Australian evidence to suggest that approximately 8% of doctors abuse alcohol at some time in their lives and approximately 1% abuse narcotic drugs. Furthermore, there is evidence that alcohol and drug abuse commences early in the medical career of the affected doctor and not uncommonly at medical school. The major problem is to have the abusing doctor recognise that he/she has a problem that requires treatment.

It has been accepted wisdom that doctors become addicted to narcotic agents because of their ability to obtain drugs. Doctor addicts, in contrast to addicts elsewhere in the community, almost always abuse opiate agents available on prescription. In keeping with other addicts, the affected doctor will often have had a disturbed childhood and/or troubled early adult life.

Arguably, disturbance of mood is the most worrying psychological problem faced by doctors. Depression is a major problem in the general community with possibly one in four women experiencing a substantive depressive disorder at some time in the lifecycle and men being affected at nearly the same rate. There is international evidence to suggest that doctors, overall, have at least a one in four chance of experiencing depression and female doctors are 10 times more likely to become depressed than their male counterparts. There is a tendency for depression to emerge as a problem relatively early in the career of the doctor, often during the period of postgraduate study. It is worrying that relatively few depressed doctors feel comfortable about seeking treatment.

Why are doctors prone to depression? The bent twig hypothesis suggests that certain individuals are predisposed to depression, with the disorder appearing as an inevitability. The job strain hypothesis suggests that long hours, the rigours of tough decision-making and the stress of postgraduate training push the doctor in the direction of depression. Female doctors still experience prejudice within some craft groups, may lack role models and have special difficulties balancing career and family commitment. We do not think that the two hypotheses are mutually exclusive.

Anxiety, when occurring in medical practitioners, can exist alone or, more commonly, will coexist with depression. Undoubtedly there are doctors who are genetically prone to anxiety. However, the overwhelming number of doctors who present with anxiety will identify stressors that trigger their various symptoms, generally without any evidence of anxiety in the more distant past. Underlying depression, often unrecognised, is very common. Indeed it has been said that any person who becomes anxious for the first time when over 30 years of age is depressed until proven otherwise.

Co-morbid physical disease and psychological disorder is something always to be considered. It is sometimes impossible to continue to practise medicine in the context of physical disease. The doctor may find himself/herself struggling to continue in mainline medicine where the average non-medical person in the community who is in the same position can continue in employment. Physical illness, particularly when chronic or of an advancing type, might become a particular issue for a doctor. Not surprisingly, co-morbid psychological problems, specifically depression and/or anxiety, are likely to emerge in this situation.

It is not possible to consider the doctor experiencing depression, depression with co-morbid anxiety, or depression with co-morbid physical disease, without considering suicide. While male doctors do not have a suicide rate greater than matched groups in the general population, female doctors have a higher than expected suicide rate. Every loss of a person by suicide is a tragedy. We need not dwell on the magnitude of the tragedy when one of our younger colleagues dies in this manner.

While not a psychological disorder, this is the place to mention medical marriages. There is strong evidence that approximately 50% of doctors have problematic marriages. Doctors have a higher divorce rate than similar groups in the population. There are numerous reasons why doctors make unsatisfactory marital partners. The obvious causes stand out, such as workaholic ways, the general pressure of a medical career and split loyalties. More subtle, but perhaps of greater importance, might be the poor communication skills of many doctors, particularly in the non-work environment. Well known, also, is the capacity of the doctor or their spouse to live in substantial pain. Clearly, this is no solution to a relationship problem.

The message is simple. Doctors in general, and surgeons among them, are vulnerable to a variety of psychological disorders. Furthermore, psychological disorders are far more common than the average doctor would believe.

Recognition of psychological problems is not always a simple task. As mentioned already, surgeons and other doctors are notoriously bad at noting the early signs of emotional disturbance in themselves. There are a few simple pointers which might assist:

1. Never believe that you are unlikely to experience a psychological disorder.
2. Consider any increase in the amount you drink as an early warning sign.
3. Take seriously the onset of anxiety, pervasive despondency or a disturbance of sleep.

4. Never prescribe psychotropic medication to yourself. If you think you require a benzodiazepine tranquilliser or an anti-depressant, it is time to seek consultation.

Similarly, doctors are poor at recognising when a colleague is under stress and even worse at doing something about it when the signs become obvious. There are simple rules in this area:

1. If you are concerned about a colleague, speak directly with that person or if this is not possible confer with someone who may be able to assist.
2. Offer to arrange assessment if your distressed colleague feels unable to do so. Additionally, offer to accompany your colleague to the assessment if it is his/her wish.
3. Make sure you follow up on how your colleague is managing.

The medical profession as a whole is slowly establishing systems to assist doctors who have psychological problems. The Doctors Health Advisory Service (DHAS) has been active in some States for many years. The medical boards are beginning to establish panels for the support of ill doctors, this being separate from their disciplinary function. The Committee of Medical Presidents (CPMC) has identified the health of doctors as an area of priority.

Closer to home, the Royal Australasian College of Surgeons (RACS) has probably gone further than any other medical college with the development of a health line and associated mechanisms to assist a member of the fraternity to obtain appropriate care. The mechanism established by the RACS could be used readily by other medical colleges.

Essentially, the medical profession is trying in various ways to break down the unfortunate stigma attached to doctors who have psychological problems. Substantial gains have been made so far, but further developments are needed.

A particularly thorny issue is the connection between psychological impairment and professional competence. Generally, a doctor with a psychological disorder will be competent to remain in medical practice, other than when he/she suffers from acute, serious or chronic symptoms. The impaired doctor is not in a situation to make a rational decision about whether to continue to practise medicine. This is a task for the treating doctor who should assess the situation in an objective manner.

There are occasions, particularly when a doctor has a problem of substance abuse, where it becomes necessary to place controls on that person. This might be done by agreement between the doctor patient and his therapist or where appropriate by the medical board. The usual controls mandated by a medical board will include revocation of prescribing rights for opioid agents, with doctor patient to submit to routine or random urine testing and the doctor patient to attend an appropriate therapist on a regular basis. While the impaired doctor may initially resist such restrictions, they are ultimately for his/her protection and also for the protection of the public.

A particular issue arises when a surgeon requires psychotropic medication. There may be risks where a surgeon operates after taking more than minimal amounts of benzodiazepine tranquillisers, older anti-depressant agents or major tranquillising drugs. The risks are much reduced where the doctor is medicated with one of the newer anti-depressant agents or when the doctor takes lithium carbonate. We doubt that any hard-and-fast rule can be set regarding a surgeon continuing in medical practice when taking medication. Clearly, it is not the responsibility of the doctor patient to make judgment in this area, the matter resting with his/her therapist.

Psychological illness can visit any of us today, tomorrow or in the future. We need to appreciate our personal risks, to recognise when we are in trouble and to know how best to seek assistance. Furthermore, we need to be able to protect our peers and particularly our younger colleagues. We must hold firmly in our minds the necessary steps that we will take if someone we know and respect becomes ill.

FURTHER READING

Cantrella M. Physician addiction and impairment: Current thinking. A review. *Addictive Dis.1994;* **13**: 91–105.

Gabbard G, Menninger R. *Medical Marriages*. American Psychiatric Press Inc. 1988.

Quadrio C. Sex and gender and the impaired therapist. *Aust. NZ. J. Psych.* 1992; **26**: 346–363.

Serry N, Ball J, Block S. Substance abuse among medical practitioners. *Drug Alcohol Rev.* 1991; **10**: 331–338.

Simon W. Suicide among physicians. Prevention and postvention. *Crisis* 1986; **7**: 1–13.

Stimson G. Recent developments in professional control: The impaired physician movement in the USA. *Sociology Health Illness* 1985; **7**: 141–146.

Legal liability of doctors

B.J. DOOLEY, M.W. GORTON

The practice of medicine is not perfect. Many patients suffer from disease or conditions for which there may be no, or no adequate, treatment. Nonetheless, patients have come to expect perfect results.

Much has been stated of the 'adverse medical outcomes' which patients may suffer within the health system. These more often are a result of the natural outcome from the disease or condition which they suffer, the inherent risks and side-effects of a procedure or administration (i.e. drug) or some other systemic error which is unrelated to the doctor's care and attention.

The health-care system is a cumbersome, sophisticated and technical system, which operates under great pressure and stress. Patients may not obtain perfect results for reasons that have nothing to do with the negligence or lack of care of doctors.

At law, doctors are responsible for their own want of care, or the failure to apply the proper standard of skill and attention that might be expected in the circumstances. Doctors are vicariously responsible also for the negligence of their servants (employees), e.g. negligence of a surgery nurse or secretary.

Examples of obvious negligence are death or injury resulting from: (i) administration of the wrong drug or an excess of a normal drug being administered; (ii) administration of a drug in the wrong area of the body; (iii) the wrong limb being operated on; (iv) tourniquet remaining too long, with vascular complications; and (v) pressure areas or burns or other injuries to an anaesthetised patient.

Liability can arise under different causes of action.

Negligence

In addition to a failure by the doctor to exercise proper care and attention, the doctor could also in some circumstances be negligent in failing to obtain informed consent (informing the patients of all material risks relevant to the procedure).

Assault/trespass

If a doctor treats a patient without proper consent, the doctor is technically committing a trespass or assault on the patient.

Breach of fiduciary duty

In rare cases, the courts have recognised a fiduciary duty arising from the 'special relationship' between the patient and the doctor. Where a doctor fails to act in the best interests of the patient, and fails to disclose any conflict of interest, it is sometimes argued that this fiduciary duty is breached.

Breach of contract

In common with a negligence claim, it is sometimes argued that failure by the doctor to exercise due care is also a breach of the contract between the patient and the doctor.

In a negligence claim, the courts will usually assess three elements: (i) the duty of the doctor to take reasonable care of the patient; (ii) whether there has been a breach of duty by the doctor; and (iii) whether the damage that the patient has suffered is a result of the doctor's failure of care.

Doctors are generally asked to exercise the standard care expected of doctors of good quality and standing, and with the requisite degree of skill and experience in the relevant specialty of the doctor.

A specialist practitioner in a certain field is required to have that skill 'of the ordinary skilled person exercising and professing to have that skill'. Previously, if a responsible body of medical practitioners would have acted as the defendant did, then the defendant was not negligent. The law recognises the variability of individual practitioner's skills and does not demand that doctors always perform at the highest standard of their peers. However, in *Naxakis v. Western General Hospital* (1999) 73 ALJR 782, the High Court has explained that it is the court, not the medical profession, which is the ultimate arbiter in deciding whether the requisite standard of care has been reached. Evidence of medical experts will have an important role in aiding the court to decide whether a medical practitioner has been negligent.

The standard of care to be observed by a person with some special skill or competence is that of the ordinary skilled person exercising and professing to have that special skill. The courts will determine whether that standard has been met. While the court may have regard to the practices and procedures of other doctors in similar circumstances, the court will determine whether the standard has been met, having regard to the skills of the doctor, general practices in the profession, the level of knowledge and research available and the other relevant factors.

A doctor may also owe a duty of care to rescue a person in danger even though they have never treated the person previously (see Doctors to the Rescue). A hospital may have a duty to guard the mentally depressed from suicide and the public from dangerous patients who may escape to commit crimes.

Negligence can arise from positive conduct, but can also apply where the doctor has failed to undertake any action.

Compensation

Patients will be entitled to claim compensation for loss or damage that they suffer as a consequence of the negligence of a doctor.

Patients have always been able to claim for physical injury. It is more difficult to maintain an action for mental injuries. Such claims relate to 'nervous shock'. Nervous shock is not grief or depression. It is often limited to sudden psychiatric illness that results from an extremely distressing sight, or hearing or reading distressing news, rather than an accumulated effect. For secondary victims (i.e. persons not physically injured), the injury must be foreseeable. Doctors must, therefore, be careful to pass on correct information to patients or relatives.

The patient must show that the loss or damage would not otherwise have arisen if the doctor had not been negligent. This distinguishes between negligence and merely an adverse outcome.

As the High Court of Australia has recently said:

> 'The onus is upon the plaintiff to prove that the breach alleged was the cause of the damage shown....
>
> If the damage of which the plaintiff complains could have occurred without the intervention of the negligent behaviour, it will often be possible to conclude that the negligent behaviour was not a cause of that damage....
>
> If, however, the damage of which the plaintiff complains would not have happened without the intervention of the negligent behaviour, it will often be possible to conclude that the negligent behaviour was a cause of that damage.'

Trainees

Training or junior doctors, like other professionals, are required to exercise the skill of the 'ordinary skilled person exercising and professing to have that skill'. This test is satisfactory for patients who choose their physicians, but public hospital patients cannot choose their practitioners. A junior doctor is required only to fulfil the skill required of his/her position. However, this junior will be liable, if he/she negligently performs a duty outside his/her range of skill or fails to refer a question beyond their capabilities to another practitioner. (The hospital may be directly liable under its non-delegable duty of care if the junior doctor escapes liability by referring a situation to a superior and the negligent treatment is not dealt with soon enough.)

The state of medical knowledge

Other factors may affect whether the requisite standard of care has been reached in diagnosis and treatment. A medical practitioner is expected only to have the knowledge of an 'ordinary skilled' person in his/her field. If the state of medical knowledge means that a failure of equipment could not be predicted, preventative measures such as were required to prevent injury were not regularly taken at the relevant time, or the dangers of a type of treatment were unknown, there may not be a breach of duty.

The law accepts that, in order for medicine to progress, new techniques must be tested. However, if such techniques are used, there is a very high standard of disclosure required that demands patients be informed of alternative forms of treatment. For example, after the AIDS virus broke out, there was much litigation over injuries arising from infections that arose from blood transfusions. Now, if certain procedures are followed, legislation protects the Red Cross Society and hospitals from liability arising from transfusions.

Res ipsa loquitur

Res ipsa loquitur means 'the event speaks for itself'. In such a situation, the events themselves which led to an injury may imply that the incident could not occur without negligence on the part of a defendant. For example, in the case of *Mahon v. Osborne* (1939) 1 A11ER 535, a swab was left in the stomach of a patient. It was held more likely than not, that the swab was there because of the negligence of the surgeon or staff who performed the operation.

Failure to disclose risks

Doctors must exercise reasonable care and skill in providing advice and treatment to patients. The standard of care and skill required is that of the ordinary skilled person exercising the particular specialist skills of the doctor involved.

However, included in the care of the patient, the law also recognises that a doctor has a duty to warn a patient of a material risk which is inherent in any proposed procedure or treatment.

The High Court of Australia has formulated:

> 'A risk will be considered material if in the circumstances of the particular case, a reasonable person in the position of the patient, if warned of the risk, would be likely to attach significance to it, or if the medical doctor is, or should reasonably be, aware that the particular patient, if warned of the risk, would be likely to attach significance to it'

The doctor must therefore consider two separate matters:

1. Would a reasonable person in the position of the patient be likely to attach significance to the risk?
2. Is the doctor aware, or should the doctor reasonably be aware, that this particular patient would be likely to attach significance to that risk?

Doctors must warn of risks that meet these criteria.

Failure to diagnose or follow up tests

One of the obvious areas for negligence is failure to diagnose accurately or properly the particular disease or condition of the patient. Many celebrated cases involving the diagnosis of cancer (either the failure to diagnose or delayed diagnosis) highlight the issues.

These cases are an application of the simple test of negligence, requiring the doctor to exercise care and skill of the 'ordinary skilled doctor, exercising the particular specialist skills of that doctor'.

A recent case in South Australia has also highlighted the responsibility doctors have to ensure appropriate follow up on tests ordered or reports requested. It confirms that doctors must have appropriate systems in place to ensure that, when tests are ordered or reports requested, there is a follow up to ensure that any adverse outcomes are detected within time. Reports and test results can often go astray. The courts have now confirmed that 'it is unreasonable for a professional medical specialist to base his whole follow-up system, which can mean the difference between death or cure, on the patient taking the next step'. Doctors cannot rely on patients contacting them again for follow up, and doctors must therefore have their own systems to ensure that follow up occurs.

Doctors, therefore, when undertaking tests or requesting reports, should keep detailed notes of the tests undertaken and the reports requested, and have a follow-up system to ensure that the results are received, the results are seen by the doctor and any further necessary action taken. The doctor has the prime responsibility for these matters. An administrative system is necessary to ensure that follow up occurs.

The system should be relatively sophisticated to cope with a range of exigencies, including changeover in staff, computer failure, facsimile machine failure, holiday periods and all of the other administrative errors to which any office may be prone.

Doctors should also emphasise to patients, to a much greater extent, the need for the patient to call back to ascertain the results of tests, and should advise the patient, in detailed terms, of the implications of failing to follow up or failing to keep an appointment made.

Vicarious liability

At law, an employer may be held responsible for the negligence of its employee, acting in the course of his or her employment. Accordingly, hospitals and other health institutions are responsible for and will be liable for the acts or omissions of their staff.

The staff member nonetheless remains liable for his/her own negligence.

Additionally, doctors will be liable for the actions of their own employees (e.g. locums, administrative staff, office staff, etc.). These issues are important in considering whether an insurance policy maintained by the employer will cover particular staff members. For example, in Victorian public hospitals, the common health insurance policy includes all relevant medical and other staff. In New South Wales, it is not always the case that hospitals will cover medical staff specialists (if they are not employees).

These issues highlight the need for medical practitioners to ensure that they have adequate and appropriate insurance for themselves, their practice, and for their employees (for whom they may be liable).

Law reform

Many doctors have expressed concern at the increase in recent years in the value and number of negligence claims made by patients against their doctors.

There has been a corresponding rapid escalation in the cost of medical defence premiums, now ranging from $15 000 to over $30 000 per year.

Concerns have also been expressed about the litigation process, which is generally protracted, costly, uncertain in its outcome, and stressful on participants.

Some recent suggestions for reform of this area include: (i) compulsory conciliation, by extending the role of Health Services Commissioners (or similar bodies); (ii) preliminary screening of claims; and (iii) arbitration panels.

Most surgeons would agree that early discussions before a Health Services Commissioner or arbitrator (without the public glare of the courts) may well settle many cases. Expert medical reports could be provided by both sides. Vexatious or frivolous complaints would be detected at an early stage.

Many recognise the need for lawyers appearing for plaintiffs and defendants in medical negligence claims to be expert, and specifically accredited in personal injury law.

There is strong support for courts having a more interventionist role, allowing judges to access 'independent' medical reports, rather than simply relying on the medical reports supplied by each side. Greater use by the courts of mediation or arbitrators could assist early resolution of complaints.

Doctors are rightly concerned by the impact of publicity which can greatly affect reputations, even where the ultimate findings may be in the doctor's favour. There is a need for courts to have the ability to prevent publication of case details, particularly the names of parties, before a final decision is made.

Additionally, there is great concern in relation to cases which proceed on a lawyer-assisted 'no win/no fee' basis, or with Legal Aid or other assistance, where the plaintiff has no means to pay the doctor's legal costs in the event of the doctor being successful. The cost of litigation in any case could amount to as much as over $200 000, and the doctor or his or her medical defence organisation may have no recovery for those legal costs against the plaintiff in such cases.

It may, therefore, be appropriate in some cases to ensure that either the plaintiff or the solicitors involved (who are effectively funding the action and have a financial interest in the outcome) provide some security for the costs of the defendant.

The Law Reform Committee in Victoria has recommended that a party to a claim for negligence arising out of the provision of health services should be able to choose conciliation before the Health Services Commissioner, prior to the issuing of proceedings, as an alternative to court-run pre-trial conferences. A further recommendation is that, despite a complaint being referred to the Medical Practitioners Board, the Health Services Commissioner should still be able to provide conciliation services to the parties involved.

In most States, the State Government is ultimately responsible for medical negligence claims by public patients. The State is vicariously liable for the actions of doctors within its system. An obvious advantage in these cases is that all health service providers and the hospitals themselves are covered, in effect, by one insurer. However, one insurer, covering all parties, does not necessarily ensure that the interests of each party are covered adequately in the course of the defence.

The case for law reform is great. Several suggestions have been made over the years, and there is a real need for governments to act.

ACKNOWLEDGEMENT

The authors acknowledge the assistance of Patrick Joyce of Russell Kennedy, Solicitors, in the preparation of this chapter.

Risk management

R. DICKENS

Risk management is the continuous pro-active process of determining risk factors, with the primary objective of prevention or reduction of all types of risk. It is similar to the process one undertakes in a quality assurance program.

It is not surprising that the incidence of claims reported by medical defence organisations has increased dramatically over the last decade. The current social environment has created a community with an increasing propensity to litigate. The educational standards of the community have risen and the attitude to the medical profession has changed to one of less trust.

Court procedure has become more familiar to the community in general; various popular television programs have reduced the fear of court action. The legal environment has changed and there is an increased number of legal professionals in the community.

Core activity

The core activity of any medical practice is the role of the doctor.

The medical profession must have, as a primary concern, the wellbeing of the patient, keeping in mind the need to do no harm. Academic and technical skills must be developed to a high standard and maintained through an ongoing program of re-education, peer review and practice audit.

A practitioner must maintain good relations with patients. This attribute, not well-taught during training, entails good communication with the patient and family, not just in taking a history and conducting an examination, but in learning to deal with the disappointing outcomes that inevitably occur in any practice, to deal with patient complaints and to deal with peers.

As part of their education, practitioners must be aware of the common malpractice problems that arise, and develop procedures to reduce the risk of these adverse events occurring in their own practices.

The clinical problems that arise for the practitioner in the core activity are wrong diagnosis, incorrect treatment, complications of treatment, failure to achieve an expected or desired result and failure of communication, especially with regard to informed consent (Table 5).

The path to legal action usually follows the occurrence of an adverse event or an unexpected outcome in which no satisfactory answer is given to the patient as to causation.

To manage this outcome, the clinician should avoid creating unrealistic expectations. More time must be spent with patients, and all questions answered fully.

If the patient sustains an outcome which is regarded as adverse, or if the outcome has an influence on the capacity of the patient to earn a living, or if he/she is left with a continuing disability, it is likely that blame will be laid. Because of lack of knowledge, the

Table 5. Medical malpractice: Characteristics of claims closed in 1984. (United States General Accounting Office, April 1987)

The cause of malpractice claims	Percentage of claims (%)
Surgical mishaps	25.4
Failure to diagnose	23.6
Incorrect treatment	19.9
Medication errors	7.8
Obstetrical mishaps	7.5
Other causes	5.8

patient may blame the doctor for the outcome, becoming angry and seeking compensation or retribution.

If an adverse outcome or complication arises, the practitioner must (i) deal directly with the patient and allow the patient to have a full understanding; (ii) be sympathetic to the possible anger that may be expressed by the patient about the result; and (iii) give a full explanation of the likely outcome and how the problem can be dealt with so that the patient is fully informed and anxiety is reduced. Poor communication skills by the practitioner underlie nearly all malpractice action.

Communication

It would seem inappropriate to suggest that doctors should listen to their patients but, more importantly, a doctor must become very aware of other non-verbal signs in dealing with their patients. They must show interest, maintain eye contact, and control their emotional response to what the patient is telling them. The doctor should take the opportunity to repeat certain comments and seek clarification wherever appropriate, so that there is no doubt as to what the patient is saying. All communications must take place in an environment where confidentiality can be maintained without distraction or interruption (e.g. extraneous telephone calls).

In recent years, a number of medico-legal publications have emphasised that the best form of protection against litigation is good communication with patients, both before and after treatment. This is particularly so in the event of an adverse outcome (whether through negligence or not).

Studies in America and Australia confirm that in only a small percentage of treatments involving an adverse outcome do patients consider, and ultimately initiate, litigation. There is now a strong suggestion that one factor influencing some patients to choose to litigate is the communication and aftercare explanation given by the doctor after an adverse event has occurred.

This should not be surprising. Our common experience suggests that we are prepared to take matters further when the other party has been rude, inconsiderate or indifferent. A patient in the unfortunate circumstances of having an unexpected adverse event, and not having the training and experience of the doctor, will be partly suspicious, partly ignorant and partly just seeking an explanation. How the doctor handles the patient's concerns and fears may have a significant impact on any future claim, including whether a claim is made at all.

Studies of patients' complaints, and the reasons why they complain, indicate that some of the following factors are relevant:

1. They have not received an explanation that they can understand and accept.
2. They believe their treatment has been negligent or below standard (whether, in fact, it has or not).
3. They have not been treated with consideration, sympathy or courtesy.
4. They have sought information but have not received any explanation, or their reasonable requests have not been met.
5. They have been discharged before they have fully recovered (or before they thought they had fully recovered), or discharged without proper explanation or follow up.
6. They are chronic complainers.

The proper handling of patients and their families can be an important part of the doctor's armoury against litigious claims.

As has previously been noted in the *Australasian Journal of the Medical Defence Union*:

> 'The patient is entitled to a prompt, sympathetic and above all truthful account of what has occurred. This should be given either by the practitioner concerned or, if appropriate, by a senior colleague such as the consultant in charge. It is plain that for a patient to hear of such an event from a third party, such as a porter or receptionist, is the worst of all possible options. It is very important that a sincere and honest apology is made. Any patient who has had the misfortune to suffer through an error of whatever nature

should receive a proper expression of regret. To apologise that such an instance should have occurred is, after all, only common courtesy and should not be confused with a formal admission of legal liability.'[1]

Of course, a friendly smile and courteous demeanour are no replacement for competent treatment and professionalism in practice. However, they can be an important part of the overall doctor–patient relationship, and may help avoid the distress and cost of litigation in the future.

The process of informed consent should be dealt with in great detail. The National Health and Medical Research Council has produced guidelines on informed consent and these should be observed whenever giving patient advice (see Informed Consent: Patient Communication).

Prevention

In any consultation, there must be a diagnosis or provisional diagnosis. There must be discussion covering the natural history (where known), advised treatment, and the consequence of not treating the condition.

The patient should be made aware of the anticipated outcomes of the treatment and any risks or side effects that may result from the treatment.

There should be an open discussion on any other matters. In particular, the costs of the treatment and the costs of hospitalisation should be discussed. Time lost from work is of major concern to patients.

There should be an opportunity for the patient to ask questions and, if there is ongoing concern, there should be an opportunity for the patient to have a second opinion — a process which should be encouraged by all clinicians involved in patient care.

If the treatment being recommended is of an experimental nature, the patient must be informed of this fact. Approval for such activities should be obtained through an ethics committee appropriately approved by either the hospital or College.

Clinicians must be continually aware of their responsibility to their patients, and of their patients' rights. At no time is it appropriate to test patients for conditions without first discussing this with the patient and obtaining his/her consent (e.g. HIV testing).

In defence of an allegation of failure to provide informed consent, it is not sufficient to resort to the defence that it is your usual practice always to inform a patient of a certain risk. In a court, this is unlikely to be accepted.

Informed consent is a process which includes personal communication and provision of information. It can include handouts, if deemed appropriate.

Record-keeping

The practitioner must record in the medical notes any advice that has been given, including negative advice. The patient must be given the opportunity of review to discuss the issues in more detail and/or be offered another opinion.

A handout outlining the risks of any treatment is not a substitute for direct communication with the patient. All information provided to the patient should be noted in the medical record. Records should not be altered retrospectively.

Perceived services

Having dealt with the basic services provided by the clinician, one must then look at measures to reduce risk in those areas of service which are perceived by the patient to be significant.

Facilities

The physical surroundings that the practitioner provides, and the services and impressions that a patient receives from those facilities, are important factors in the patient's attitude towards the doctor.

The office waiting area is an important and often disregarded area of service to the patient, and must be carefully monitored. It is inappropriate to have reading material that is old and in poor condition. The waiting room and office area should be a clean and comfortable environment for the patient.

Personnel

The presentation of the staff and the manner in which they deal with the patient is a vital factor in determining the patient's level of respect for the care being received. The office set-up should be such that the patient has true confidentiality when dealing with the doctor. Equally important, when dealing with the staff, the patient should be allowed to have confidentiality from other people in the waiting area, particularly if there is a discussion about financial issues.

Efficiency

The services within the practice should be efficient. The impression the patient receives when informed that their records cannot be found or their X-rays are missing is always an adverse impression which impacts on their total perception of the doctor's performance.

Waiting time

If the doctor is delayed for any reason, attempts should be made to explain to the waiting patient the reasons and the likely length of delay that will be necessary. Many patients have other major and significant activities with which they must deal, and are equally as disrupted by the delay as is the practitioner.

Length of consultation

A patient who has experienced a very cursory history-taking and examination often remarks upon this when an adverse event occurs. This is perceived as an inappropriate or inadequate assessment. In some cases that may well be true.

Records

Inadequacy of records is a major area of concern to patients. They are unimpressed if the doctor is unable to recall their previous consultation and the problems presented. If these are not recorded in the history, this does create a bad impact on the consultative process.

Access to records

It is likely that patients soon will have access to their records in the private sector (see Medical Records and Confidentiality). Clinicians would be well-advised to record only factual and appropriate details.

Reports and follow up

In the current legal climate it is no longer appropriate for the doctor to expect the patient to follow up tests that have been performed. The profession is of the view that failure of the patient to do this is a contributory factor in any adverse event that may arise. In a court this defence of contribution would almost certainly fail. There are examples of this already in case law.

This puts a very significant responsibility on the clinician. On the one hand, he/she is being criticised by the community for being paternalistic and on the other, criticised for not being so.

All practitioners involved in testing of patients, for either pathological or radiological investigations, must have a system within their office that alerts the doctor to the fact that tests have been performed and that the results have or have not returned and have or have not been reported to the patient.

No pathology test result should be allowed to enter the patient's records without first being seen and signed off by the clinician. Staff protocols must be developed to prevent this from occurring.

Appointment reminders

The responsibility of the doctor to follow up patients who fail to attend appointments is a difficult issue. If one is over-zealous, particularly in the general practice area, there is the potential for accusations of touting for business and over-servicing. However, where patients have a significant and serious condition, and it is deemed important that ongoing follow up occurs, the practitioner has a responsibility to check his appointment book and detect such cases and send a reminder where appropriate.

Summary

The core activity of a practitioner, medical skill, is accepted by patients and taken for granted.

They assume the practitioner's qualifications and competence. It is up to the practitioner to maintain that level of expertise through continuing education, audit and peer review.

The perceived services, many of which are staff-related, must always be kept in mind. Efficient and appropriate practice management is an important aspect of a risk management program.

The physical facilities provided to patients are of equal importance.

> *'The evil that men do lives after them, the good is oft interred with their bones.'*
>
> Mark Antony (*Julius Caesar*)

REFERENCE

1. Allsopp. *Aust. J. Med. Defence Union* **1988**.

Court proceedings and subpoenas

M.W. GORTON

A doctor's interaction with the court system can be quite varied.

Medical practitioners have an important role to play in coronial proceedings. Doctors are also important expert witnesses in civil proceedings particularly where personal injuries are involved. In the worst case, some doctors may find themselves involved in court proceedings in which disciplinary actions are warranted.

In the main, our courts have two major jurisdictions: criminal, and civil.

The criminal jurisdiction arises from various crimes that either exist at common law, or have been created by statute (legislation of our State and Federal Parliaments).

Civil jurisdiction largely arises from breaches of contract or general negligence. Other chapters in this book deal with many of the issues of civil liability which may arise for doctors.

In addition to the courts, each State has an array of tribunals or boards which may deal with specific matters. These include: Administrative Appeals Tribunal, Medical Board, Small Claims Tribunal, and Crimes Compensation Tribunal.

Traditionally, tribunals tend to operate on more flexible and less formal rules, and tend to be specifically directed to particular issues.

For example, in many tribunals the strict rules of evidence applicable in the courts are not rigidly observed.

In most of the Australian courts and tribunals, proceedings are based upon the 'adversary system', in which a party makes a claim and another party, or parties, seek to defend that claim. The judge acts as the independent umpire, applying the court rules and applying the law. A jury may be involved, to determine which facts of the case it accepts as being accurate or truthful. If a jury is not involved, the judge will be the determinator of both the law and the facts.

In criminal cases, the prosecutor commences the action. In civil cases, a plaintiff (the claimant) initiates the case.

In a normal hearing, the plaintiff has the first opportunity to present the facts and opinions to support their claim (evidence in chief). This may consist of a series of documents or records, and witnesses and expert witnesses giving evidence. Where a witness gives evidence at the hearing, the defendant has an opportunity to cross-examine, to clarify information, or to obtain from the witness information which might otherwise support the defendant's case.

In the courts, strict rules of evidence apply to ensure that the evidence being presented is first hand, relevant and objective. Witnesses are not usually entitled to give opinions, unless they have particular qualifications to enable them to give an expert opinion. Many doctors will experience the court system in this role, as an expert witness, where their observations and opinions are presented to assist one side or the other.

A doctor might also receive a summons either to attend a court hearing or present his or her medical records for the purposes of the hearing. This is by way of subpoena. A subpoena is a court order to either attend at the court or produce records to the court. A subpoena must be answered. Failure to act upon a subpoena may constitute a contempt of court, and sanctions may apply. Any doctor receiving a subpoena should immediately consult his/her medical defence organisation or legal adviser.

Subpoenas

Notwithstanding that medical records may now be regarded as being owned by the doctor, with no automatic right of access by a patient, medical records are still documents which may be producible in court proceedings.

In all types of legal proceedings, medical records may form part of the evidence produced to the court. The proceedings may include: (i) personal injuries claims (civil proceedings); (ii) criminal proceedings and applications for compensation to victims; (iii) custody or access issues in relation to children in family law matters, or proceedings relating to care of children under State child protection legislation; and (iv) administrative proceedings, which may involve decisions taken by hospitals, government departments, etc.

In the course of the proceedings, a party may have the court issue a subpoena to the doctor requiring the doctor to produce certain medical records to a court. Because the subpoena represents a decision or order of the court, the doctor has an onus to comply, and to produce the relevant documents to the court by the required date. Failure to comply may result in contempt of court proceedings against the doctor.

A subpoena is a court document and should have official recognition, stamping or other information signifying that it has been issued by a particular court. If in doubt, ring the court to ensure that the subpoena has been issued validly.

The subpoena must set out details or a description of the documents that are to be produced. Only documents in existence can, of course, be produced. A subpoena cannot require a doctor to create new documents that are not in existence.

Only documents as described in the subpoena should be produced. Any documents that do not meet the requirements of the subpoena should be removed (to preserve privacy and prevent a potential breach of doctor–patient confidentiality). Some careful consideration will be required to establish which documents are relevant and which are not.

There is always the possibility that the information contained in the records could embarrass the patient, the doctor or a third party. In issues relating to mental health in particular, some sensitivity may be required. It is appropriate, under these circumstances, to forward documents to the court in a sealed envelope, labelled 'Confidential' or 'Judge Only'. In such circumstances, it is worthwhile forwarding a covering letter addressed to the court or the judge explaining the reasons for the confidentiality and why the material is sensitive.

In such circumstances, it is also recommended that the parties in the proceedings be advised that sensitive material has been sent to the court.

For obvious reasons, a patient should be notified if their records or documents have been sent to a court, particularly where they are a third party and not the party initiating the request for the information.

It is strongly recommended that photocopies are retained in all cases when original documents are sent.

In some cases, it may be sufficient that copies of documents are sent to the court. The solicitors issuing the subpoena can be contacted to establish whether originals or copies should be sent.

Doctors should be aware that the information being sent could, unless handled properly, amount to a breach of patient–doctor confidentiality. Accordingly, documents should be couriered directly to the court or sent or transported in such a way as to ensure that confidentiality is preserved. While it is sometimes difficult to do so, the doctor should also attempt to get a receipt or acknowledgement from the court to confirm that the documents have been received, in accordance with the subpoena.

It should be noted that the subpoena requires that the document be produced before the court (or tribunal) involved. It does not require that the documents be produced to a particular party or solicitor. The subpoena will set out the address of the court or tribunal for the delivery of documents.

The subpoena may also require that the doctor attend court. Each subpoena should be checked to establish exactly what is required. If the subpoena also requires the doctor to attend court, some contact with the issuing solicitor will be required, in order to establish appropriate times of convenience to give evidence, etc.

If in any doubt, contact your legal adviser or medical defence organisation.

Medical records and confidentiality

M.W. GORTON

Ownership

It remains generally recognised that records made by a doctor in the course of a patient's treatment are owned by the doctor. The records are created for the doctor's purposes to assist in treating the patient and are therefore the doctor's property and are not 'owned' by the patient. However, under certain circumstances, discussed below, the patient may have a right of access to such records.[1]

This general principle differs in the case of reports obtained by the doctor on a patient's behalf (e.g. pathology, radiology, etc.), especially where the costs of the reports are met by the patient or his or her relevant health fund. In circumstances where a report is obtained by the treating doctor at the cost of the patient, it is generally regarded that such reports are 'owned' by the patient. In Victoria, for example, there is a legislative requirement for a patient to receive a copy of any radiograph upon written request to the owner of an ionising radiation apparatus used for radiological purposes.[1]

In September 1996, in the decision of *Breen v. Williams* (1996) 186 CLR 71, the High Court of Australia accepted that doctors owned their own medical records, and that there was no automatic right of access by patients.

The *Breen* decision was intended as a test case on this issue. There was some concern that the High Court might follow Canadian decisions, which determined that it was part of a doctor's duty to permit his or her patient to have access to medical records kept and maintained by the doctor. The implications for Australian doctors of the Canadian decision would have been that doctors would be much more careful about the records they keep and the comments they make in their records. It had potential to hinder proper medical practice and a doctor's freedom to keep records in a way meaningful to him/her, as well as increasing administrative burdens.

The High Court has specifically rejected the Canadian authority. While the High Court recognised that there was some community feeling that patients should have access to doctors' medical records, it suggested that this was a matter for parliaments to legislate, and not for the High Court to determine.

However, there are other legal and ethical requirements to ensure that patients have access to important information regarding their health. Doctors acting in public hospitals will be subject to Freedom of Information legislation, which requires that medical records of patients be available. Both the Australian Medical Association (AMA) and many medical boards also regard it as an ethical duty of doctors to ensure that information regarding a patient is available and transmitted to other consultants or representatives, as necessary, for the patient's health.

AMA policy is summarised as follows:

> *'AMA policy remains therefore that a patient has a right to be informed of all relevant factual information contained in the medical record, but all deductive opinion therein remains the intellectual property of the doctor maintaining the record. On request, a patient should be informed of all or any content of the following sections of the medical record:*

- *History*
- *Findings on physical examinations*
- *Results of investigations*
- *Diagnosis or diagnoses*
- *Any proposed plan of management.*

The patient should be allowed access to other contents of the medical record, such as reports by specialists, beyond the materials above specified, only at the discretion of the doctor or doctors who completed such additional section, or sections, or as a result of a legal requirement. Doctors are entitled to recoup their reasonable costs of providing information contained in the medical record from the patient or other legally authorised requester of the information.'

It should be noted, however, that the *Breen* decision may amount to a pyrrhic victory. There is increasing pressure for the Australian Government to legislate in relation to a patient's access to medical records. Extensions of privacy legislation have been foreshadowed and are currently the subject of government review. Legislation in other jurisdictions, notably the Australian Capital Territory, New Zealand and the UK, already extend these rights. It is assumed that, in the event of any legislation, it will be prospective, and not retrospective, so that past medical records will not be subject to the legislation. This does, however, depend on the nature of the legislation.

Doctors should, therefore, be free to maintain medical records meaningful to them, but mindful that they may ultimately be subject to scrutiny (whether by way of legal compulsion as the subject of legal proceedings, or by legislation) and, accordingly, adverse personal comments, etc. should be avoided.

The principle that a doctor has ownership of medical records produces complications for doctors practising through public and private hospitals and doctors practising in partnership or through private companies. Records created within a public or private hospital, in most circumstances, are likely to be the medical records of the hospital and therefore, 'owned' by the institution. Similarly, with records created by doctors in partnership or where a doctor is the notional employee or contractor of an incorporated medical practice, it may be found that the medical records created are in fact owned by the partnership as a whole or owned by the private company. While this is unlikely to produce problems in most circumstances, in the event of a partnership dispute or a falling out between the doctors engaged jointly through an incorporated medical practice, a dispute as to ownership of medical records may produce unwanted results. The retiring doctor in a dispute may find the medical records remain with the partnership/incorporated practice. This may produce difficulty for the doctor seeking to continue treatment for his or her former patients. These are certainly matters which should be dealt with in the terms of any partnership agreement or agreement in relation to an incorporated practice.

Access by patients and others

As noted above, notwithstanding a doctor's ownership of medical records, a patient may be entitled in a number of circumstances to access to those records and to take copies.

Freedom of Information legislation

At present, no State or Federal law (other than the Australian Capital Territory) obliges private doctors to provide patients with access to medical records regarding their private treatment, particularly in relation to records created by the doctor at their own practice or rooms (other than in Victoria in respect of radiographs). However, Freedom of Information legislation of the Federal Government and most State and Territory Governments now provides a general right of access to patients' medical records in public institutions (*Queensland Freedom of Information Act 1993, Hospital Records and The Freedom of Information Act 1991*).[1] The provisions of the various Federal and State laws are not uniform and some issues remain as to: (i) whether it is the patient solely or the patient's guardian or legal representative who may seek access; (ii) precisely what information a public institution may be required to provide (and whether a summary is sufficient); and (iii) whether the public institution is required to provide any follow-up information in the event of any queries which may arise.

In some States, even access to records in private hospitals may, under certain circumstances, be provided to patients. For example, in New South Wales a licensee of a private health establishment may be required to provide access to patients' or residents' records.

Most Freedom of Information legislation contains an exception for the disclosure of information or records which may be prejudicial to the health or wellbeing of the patient (e.g. *Victorian Freedom of Information Act 1982, Tasmanian Freedom of Information Act 1991*).[1]

Litigation

Medical records may be accessed pursuant to a court order in the course of litigation. The access may be obtained by the patient or, in some cases, by a third party who is participating in the litigation, seeking details of the patient's medical history and records. In some States the privilege of a doctor's confidential relationship with a patient is protected at law, particularly in relation to civil rather than criminal proceedings.[a]

Research/quality assurance activities

There is no general right of access to patient records for those conducting bona fide medical research.[1] Clearly, this would be a breach of patient confidentiality unless the express or implied consent of the patient has been provided. Some doctors may be surprised at this conclusion, since they may have been obtaining patient information for medical or clinical studies without the consent of the patient. Doctors should, therefore, be wary and acknowledge that obtaining such information without the consent of the patient may give rise to litigation for breach of confidentiality. Certainly doctors should avoid publishing any information or results which may identify a particular patient.

In addition, the Federal Government and some State Governments have enacted quality assurance legislation which permits approved quality assurance activities to have access to information regarding patients (and doctors) on a confidential basis, and usually under the strict proviso that no information is used or revealed which may identify a particular patient (*Health Insurance (Quality Assurance Confidentiality) Amendment Act 1992* (Cwlth)).

Consent

As noted above, access to patient records by researchers, other treating doctors or the particular institutions in which treatment

[a] *Australian Product Liability Reporter* (1993) 4 APLA 73.

may take place can be given freely with the express or implied consent of the patient. For example, it is generally recognised that there is an implied consent for medical records to be communicated to other doctors or health specialists who may be involved in the course of a patient's treatment.[2]

Medical reports of deceased patients

Sometimes doctors may be requested to provide information about the health, particularly mental health, of a patient who has died. This may particularly apply in situations where the patient may have made a Will shortly before death.

The duty of confidentiality owed by a doctor to a patient continues after the death of the patient.

The doctor must, therefore, ensure that confidentiality is maintained, particularly in circumstances where there may be some dispute concerning the mental capacity of the patient making the Will.

In such circumstances, the doctor must maintain confidentiality, but may be required to provide evidence to a court as to the capacity and status of the patient. Evidence under oath in court will be protected, even where a breach of confidentiality may be involved.

There may be some information which a doctor can reveal to the parties involved in any dispute, or to the executor of the deceased patient's estate. However, such information will be limited and legal advice should be obtained.

Confidentiality

All doctors will be aware of their general duty to maintain patient information in the strictest confidence. The Hippocratic Oath, as developed in the common law of the UK and Australia, recognises the professional duty to maintain medical confidence as a fundamental legal principle, with legal liability attaching to any unauthorised breach.

Furthermore, in Victoria, Tasmania and the Northern Territory the general legal position has been modified to some extent by legislation to protect the privilege attachment to medical confidentiality.[3] Under certain circumstances a doctor cannot be compelled in civil proceedings to disclose information which may breach the doctor's duty of confidentiality.

Accordingly, any doctor who proposes to disclose confidential information regarding a patient, must consider seriously the ethical and legal implications that may arise. While there are some clear exceptions to the duty of confidentiality, the legal liability that may attach to any breach would suggest that the doctor should always obtain proper advice in such circumstances.

In general terms there are exceptions to the principle of confidentiality. These are discussed below.

Legislative requirements

A doctor may be compelled to provide information under legislative provisions such as Freedom of Information legislation and other health-related legislation.

In addition, some States have now adopted a mandatory reporting regime for child abuse and other circumstances. There is a general duty on doctors to report such circumstances which would override the doctor's duty of confidentiality.

In some States it is a requirement for doctors, in the practice of their professional duties, to report episodes of physical or sexual abuse of children or minors. If a doctor has a belief on reasonable grounds that a child requires protection because he or she has suffered or may suffer significant harm as a result of physical or sexual abuse, the doctor must notify the relevant Government department or Authority. For example, in November 1993 amendments to the *Child and Young Persons Act (Vic)* required certain groups of professionals (including doctors) to report cases of abuse or suspected abuse of children.

By court order

In the course of litigation, doctors may, by court order, be required to disclose confidential information. This is subject to those legislative provisions in some States where the privilege of confidentiality is protected in civil proceedings.

By consent

The express or implied consent of a patient will permit a doctor to reveal confidential information. Consent will be implied in the case of information provided by a referring doctor or where information would generally be required by other treating doctors in the course of the patient's treatment.

Possible harm to the patient

There is some support for the conclusion that where disclosure is required to prevent harm to a patient, the disclosure is permitted notwithstanding the fact that the patient has not given any consent.[2] This is particularly so in the area of mental health where the disclosure of confidential information may be necessary to ensure that a patient receives proper treatment or where the possibility of further harm may arise without such disclosure (e.g. in the case of a suicidal patient). This general exception is tempered nonetheless by the doctor having to be satisfied that the disclosure of the information is necessary to prevent further harm to the patient.

This exception is sometimes categorised as 'permitting disclosure in the public interest', including circumstances where it is not necessarily further harm to the patient, but harm to others which may arise.[2] In the New Zealand case of *Furniss v. Fitchett* (1958) NZLR 396, there was acknowledgement that in some circumstances disclosure of confidential information may be necessary in the public interest where the possibility of harm to the patient or to others arose. Similar issues arose in circumstances surrounding the Victorian 'Queen Street killings' in 1987, where a counsellor/ psychologist of the gunman may have been aware of a psychiatric disorder. The coroner in that case suggested formal mechanisms for referral of such information where harm to the individual or others was possible.

There have also been cases where it has been suggested that a doctor may have a possible duty to warn of information, provided on a confidential basis, regarding the possibility of harm to others. In the USA case of *Tarasoff v. Regents of the University of California* (1976) 551 PZd 334, 118 Cal Reporter 129; 131 Cal Reporter 14A a psychologist became aware of a threat by a patient to kill the patient's girlfriend.[3] The psychologist issued no warning regarding this intention and the Court determined that the public interest required disclosure, which was not outweighed by the importance of preserving the confidentiality of the doctor–patient relationship. Similarly, the English decision of *W v. Egdell* (1989)2 WLR 689, involved disclosure by a doctor without the patient's consent of information regarding the psychological state of a patient.[2] The English Court agreed that although the doctor owed a duty of confidence to the patient, the doctor had an overriding duty to the public to put before proper authorities the doctor's opinions and reports in the public interest.

Again, if the trends in these cases are followed in Australia, a general duty of disclosure may arise. A duty may be imposed on doctors to disclose confidential information where the public interest requires it. How a doctor is to determine what the public interest may require, what the full ramifications of the information may be and what other issues may be involved will no doubt produce further headaches for doctors!

Retention and destruction of medical records

There are few statutory requirements for the length of time medical records should be retained. However, it is advisable that records be retained for at least the length of time any claims or legal proceedings may arise. Of course, records should be retained where they may be relevant to the ongoing care of patients.

It is generally regarded that medical records should be retained as follows: (i) for at least 7 years in all cases; (ii) for at least 25 years in relation to obstetric cases, after the birth of the last child; and (iii) for at least 7 years after children have reached the age of 18 years, where treated as a minor under the age of 18.

As noted above, medical records are either owned by the doctor, or may be owned by the company or partnership where a doctor works in a joint venture or collective with others.

In the event of the death of a doctor, medical records should still be retained for the periods referred to above, in case a claim is lodged against the Estate of the doctor.

Some suggestions for dealing with the medical records of a retiring or a deceased practitioner include: (i) having another doctor take care of the records and arrange to notify patients of this position; (ii) notifying patients and asking them to take their own records to their new doctor; (iii) inviting patients to nominate another doctor to whom the records can be sent.

It may be critical, where there is ongoing treatment of patients that, following the death of a doctor, the records are reviewed and matters appropriately referred to another doctor to continue the ongoing treatment and care.

If medical records are to be destroyed, it is essential that confidentiality be maintained. The use of shredders or commercial services to destroy medical records should be considered. Dumping of medical records through public methods is not advised.

Access to medical records in the Australian Capital Territory

New legislation in the Australian Capital Territory now requires that doctors create and maintain records in a manner which ensures the privacy of health information, but also requires that consumers have adequate opportunities to access the information held in those records, in relation to information that concerns them.

The *Australian Capital Territory Health Records (Privacy and Access) Act 1997* applies to records maintained by doctors and health services both public and private in the ACT, as well as personal information which may be contained in documents kept by other organisations, not necessarily health services organisations. Accordingly, local medical centres, municipal health services and/or contractors to health services may all be responsible for certain obligations under the legislation.

Privacy principles

A doctor who maintains personal health information in the ACT must observe the 'privacy principles' set out in the legislation.

MEDICAL RECORDS AND CONFIDENTIALITY

In summary these are:

1. The personal health information recorded must be relevant to the health services provided.
2. The patient should know why the information has been recorded and who will have access to it.
3. The information recorded must be accurate and relevant to the purpose for which it is collected (and not intrusive).
4. The information must be safely and securely maintained.
5. Upon request by a patient, the doctor must advise whether he/she possesses personal health information on the patient, and how the information may be accessed.
6. Personal health information may be accessed only by the patient, treating doctors and health professionals, relevant management/administration personnel, or others with specific legal authority.
7. Personal health information cannot be altered, but accurate information may be added (including to correct any inaccurate information). Statements by patients can be added where they disagree with information in the records. Incorrect or misleading information can be kept separately from day-to-day information.
8. Doctors should ensure that information is up to date and accurate.
9. The personal health information can be used only for treatment purposes, unless the patient has otherwise consented to other uses, the use is necessary to avoid risk to the patient's health, or the other use is authorised by law.
10. Personal health information can be disclosed only to the patient or other treating health professionals if the patient has consented, the disclosure is necessary to avoid risk to the patient's health, the disclosure is authorised by law, or an immediate family member needs to be consulted in an emergency situation.
11. If the doctor's practice is sold or discontinued, patients must be given an opportunity to nominate another practice to which

records may be sent, and remaining records must nonetheless be stored safely. Ultimately, records may be destroyed as part of normal archive destruction.

12. A current treating doctor must have access to the patient's records.

Access

The legislation now contains a statutory obligation for a doctor in the ACT to provide access for patients to personal health information and records maintained by the doctor.

While access arrangements clearly can be negotiated between the patient and the doctor, and access given in any manner and on such terms as the patient and doctor agree, the legislation can require that the doctor allow access: (i) by permitting the patient an opportunity to inspect records (and, if in electronic form, a printout of the records), and take notes of the contents; (ii) by providing the patient with a copy of the record (or printout); and (iii) by providing the patient an opportunity to inspect the records and have the contents explained by the doctor.

Accordingly, even though doctors will often maintain records in shorthand form, with technical information, abbreviations, etc., there will now be an obligation on the doctor to provide an explanation of the record, its meaning, import and implications.

Where a written request for access to documents has been made, the legislation requires the doctor to respond within 14 days, and in most cases, access must actually be provided within 30 days.

The doctor can charge a reasonable fee for photocopying.

It is not clear whether the discussion of contents of the information may actually amount to a 'consultation'. If the discussion amounts to a consultation, the usual consultation fee may be charged.

The doctor is entitled to require proof of identity before disclosing personal health information.

It is also possible for patients to authorise other people to seek access to medical information. A patient can specifically authorise another person to obtain a record on their behalf. Parents and legal guardians can also make requests in relation to children or people under their control. People with Enduring Powers of Attorney and legal representatives of deceased people may also make requests.

The right of access does not apply to opinions recorded before the legislation commenced (1 February, 1998).

Exemptions

The legislation contains three broad exemptions where a doctor may not be required to disclose personal health information: (i) if the doctor believes on reasonable grounds that the provision of the information would constitute a significant risk to the life or health of the patient; (ii) where the provision of the information may constitute a significant risk to the life and health of another person; and (iii) where provision of the information, or access to the information, may constitute a breach of confidence.

If a doctor refuses access based on these exemptions, the patient can ask for a review of the decision by another medical practitioner. Ultimately, a patient could request a review of any exemption by the Australian Capital Territory Community and Health Services Complaints Commissioner.

The legislation also contains provisions for offences (with penalties) for doctors who destroy personal health information, or take it out of the ACT, in order to avoid providing access, as required under the legislation. Failure to comply with the privacy principles can be the basis of a complaint to the Community and Health Services Complaints Commissioner. It is also an offence for a person to request or obtain health information by threat or false representation.

Privacy

While our general law has no legal right of privacy, the enactment of the *Privacy Act 1988* in Australia and the *Privacy Act 1993* in New Zealand has created some limited forms of a right to privacy in particular circumstances. For example, information regarding employment and credit of individuals now has some legislative protection.

The *Australian Privacy Act* 1988 also empowers the Privacy Commissioner to approve the creation of guidelines for the protection of privacy in the conduct of medical research, so long as the Commissioner is satisfied that the public interest in the promotion of the research is greater than the public interest in maintaining the right to privacy.

ACKNOWLEDGEMENTS

The author acknowledges information supplied by the Australian Capital Territory Department of Health and Community Care, *The Australian Capital Territory Health Records (Privacy and Access) Act 1997*, Information for Consumers and Providers of Health Services.

REFERENCES

1. *CCH Australian Health & Medical Law Reporter*. The Law Book Company Ltd.
2. Otlowski. Confidentiality of Medical Records. *Alternative Law J.* 1992; **17**: 235.
3. Mendelson. "Mr Cruel" and the medical duty of confidentiality. *J. Law Med.* 1993; **1**: 124.

Medical reports

K.W. MILLS

Surgeons are often requested to provide medico-legal reports to insurance companies, government bodies or solicitors, regarding patients, either under their care or under the care of other medical practitioners. It is a surgeon's duty to comply with these requests and, for an agreed fee, to supply such medical reports. No doctor has the authority to supply information on any patient to a third party without the patient's written consent. Most requests relate to injuries sustained at work, or in transport or other accidents. Occasionally, there may be a request to examine a patient and supply a report concerning injuries alleged to be the result of medical negligence. The majority of these cases are actually the result of an adverse medical outcome, where there is no apparent breach of standards. Thus, in this area, only surgeons who are accepted as being experts in the particular area of specialty expertise would consider providing such reports and, again, only when they have obtained all the facts and have 'walked a distance in their colleague's shoes and those of the plaintiff'.

Medico-legal consultations

These differ from normal consultations. The Health Services Commissioner, in collaboration with the medical profession, has developed a code for conducting medico-legal examinations. Essentially, this is as follows:

1. People coming solely for such assessment, and not for medical diagnosis and management, are treated with the same courtesy and attention as others.

2. The surgeon should advise the patient of his/her particular area of professional expertise.

3. The surgeon should reassure the patient of his/her impartiality and independent consultant status, at the same time stressing that he/she is not the treating doctor or, indeed, the person who decides the patient's claim, and that he/she is there only to obtain and judge the medical facts.

4. If the patient asks about the purpose or relevance of any questions or procedures, clear answers should be given.

5. The patient should be advised that the clinical examination may cause discomfort, an explanation given regarding its necessity, and the patient given assurance that it will not worsen the condition.

6. As with every patient, a separate area should be provided for examination and appropriate gowning. For certain patients, it is advisable to have a witness present during the examination.

7. The surgeon should avoid making value judgments or personal comments regarding others, particularly medical colleagues, when such are not based on direct clinical observation.

The medical report

Medical reports are generally prepared at the request of solicitors. In general terms, doctors should consider including the following in their medical reports: (i) identification of the doctor and his/her qualifications and experience most relevant to the report; (ii) identification of the patient's name, address, age and occupation; (iii) reference to the solicitor's engagement letter, or details of the contact requesting the report, together with a list of all materials and records supplied, upon which the report is to be based; (iv) details of the history of the patient, particularly those most relevant to the injuries suffered, and the incident from which they are alleged to have arisen; (v) details of the observed injuries, illness and condition of the patient at present; (vi) details of the examination conducted, and the results and opinions arising; (vii) details of any special examinations, diagnostic investigations or reports; (viii) the doctor's opinion and diagnosis of the patient's condition; (ix) the doctor's opinion of the likely outcome for the patient and the patient's future condition; and (x) consideration of any particular items or questions raised by the solicitor or contact requesting the report.

Relevant past history is necessary, as it may have a bearing on the patient's current disability and impairment. In the final analysis, the important considerations are what effects the current injury has on the patient's disability and impairment. Thus, it is important to obtain all the facts. This may require communication with the treating hospital and/or surgeons, and also seeing the relevant X-rays or imagings.

Most importantly, the diagnosis should be a pathological diagnosis, with clinical impressions. The surgeon should also establish whether the pathology and abnormal physical findings relate to the specific accident or injury, and establish what part may be due to pre-existing injury or disease and, in giving a prognosis, also ascertain whether any future complications would relate to the natural progression of the pathology, and what part of such future complications would be considered as related to the accident or injury in question.

Disability and impairment

It is important to answer the specific questions posed by the solicitor or third party. These will include whether the condition has stabilised, how the condition affects the patient's work capability and activities of daily living and, commonly, giving an impairment assessment. The surgeon must understand that there is a difference between impairment and disability. Disability is any restriction in or lack of ability to perform an activity in the manner or within the range considered normal for a human being, taking into account the social environment, education and training of that individual. Because it relates to an inability to perform specific activities, disability should not be quantified in percentage terms. The medical practitioner may formulate an opinion on disability for particular activities, such as work duties, recreational activities (e.g. sports and hobbies), activities of daily living and social activities, etc. These are best expressed in descriptive terms, and finally, may be a judgment of the Court or others to assess. The doctor's main duty in this area is to give an objective impairment assessment (i.e. any loss or abnormality of psychological, physiological or anatomical structure or function). It is necessary to quantify an impairment using schedules and guidelines (i.e. the American Medical Association Guides to Impairment, or separate Commonwealth Schedules).

Most medical reports are straightforward. The most difficult reports concern chronic pain, particularly when such pain develops into a chronic pain syndrome, with apparent abnormal illness behaviour. It is important for the surgeon, as far as is possible, to make an objective physical assessment and, if there are clearly clinical features of abnormal illness behaviour, to describe these and the reasons for such assessment, and to point out the extent to which these affect the physical impairment assessment. The area in which this is most difficult relates to spinal soft tissue injuries where, in the absence of fracture, dislocations or obvious neurological abnormalities, there are few if any parameters by which a surgeon can judge the exact impairment. However, this must be done, to the surgeon's best ability.

In summary, then, a good medical report is a brief for the solicitor or barrister. In effect, it is addressed to the mediator, conciliator or judge. It must be factual, unbiased, and contain a full diagnosis, prognosis and opinion, amplified and expressed clearly with logical reasoning, by which most cases can be settled without delay or need to proceed in a protracted way to an adversarial court hearing. Great skill and expertise is required on the part of the surgeon to separate facts from non-facts and decide what part the original injury or accident plays in the plaintiff's final impairment and disability, and what part the injury may contribute to these in the future. While the surgeon supplies valuable medical opinion and assessment, the final judgment is made by the arbitrator or judge, and sometimes a jury. In making their final decision, lay people depend heavily on the expert medical report and witness, and they take most note of the medical expert whom they perceive as giving a balanced, accurate and well-reasoned assessment.

In addition to the reports obtained by both parties, a judge or conciliator can seek an independent medical report which, combined with the others, again can lead to early dispute resolution mechanisms, allowing satisfactory and fair settlement for all parties.

Expert evidence by surgeons

H. SELBY

Introduction

The expert evidence of surgeons includes both the written reports and the spoken evidence given in a court or tribunal. Although the popular excitement belongs to the courtroom, most of the work is done in preparing the written report.

Surgeons may prepare reports that are later used in litigation for such reasons as reporting to the referring physician about a patient; intra-operative and postoperative report on surgery for the hospital records, medico-legal assessment of an applicant in a personal injury claim following referral by an insurer or a lawyer, or responding to a claim of professional negligence by reporting to a medical defence fund about what was done and why.

Thus, sometimes surgeons are reporting about what they did, and sometimes they are commenting upon what other surgeons have done or not done. In all cases the writer is expected to demonstrate competence, thoroughness, civility and detachment.

However, the capacity of the reading audience to understand properly what the surgeon has written is quite variable; in descending order of immediate understanding one might expect colleagues in the same specialty to be followed by allied specialties, general medical practitioners, and only then intelligent lay people among whom must be numbered judges, lawyers, and then jurors.

Similarly, when surgeons enter the witness box to talk about their report by explaining their opinions, they are far removed from the sort of discussion they can have at a conference, or even with keen medical students. The surgeon giving expert evidence, whether it be written, spoken, or a combination of the two, must be a teacher who can capture and keep the interest of lay people.

We look first at what the courts expect from an expert. Lawyers are expected to present their witnesses and their evidence in line with those expectations. However, the adversarial system provides significant opportunities for the more skilled litigation team to triumph over the less experienced.

This chapter discusses some aspects of case preparation and courtroom technique which influence how the expert performs in the courtroom, and how to give evidence so as to capture and keep the interest of lay people.

What the courts are looking for

A recent study of the Australian judiciary examined their attitude to expert evidence and expert witnesses.[1] While more than 80% of respondent judges often or always found expert evidence useful, there were some significant reservations about those who presented it and their opinions.

Less than 5% of judges had never encountered bias on the part of the expert. Almost 35% identified bias on the part of the expert as the single most serious problem encountered with expert evidence; this figure is almost three times that of any other category of problem with expert evidence. Some 70% of judges noted that the same expert witnesses regularly appeared before them for the same side. Almost 88% had encountered partisanship in the expert witnesses appearing before them. The most well-known expression of frustration with such partisanship is found in a late 1980s NSW case where the trial judge could contain himself no longer and referred to, 'that unholy trinity ... the usual panel of doctors who think you can do a full week's work without any arms or legs'. The judge went on to refer to one doctor's evidence, 'as negative as it always seems to be—and based on his usual non-acceptance of the genuineness of any plaintiff's complaints of pain' (*Vakauta v. Kelly* (1989) 167 CLR 568: 87 ALR 633).

After impartiality, it is clarity of explanation that judges most want. Such clarity entails that the complex will be presented intelligibly. Asked to rank their comprehension problems with various professional groups, judges ranked expert medical evidence as easier to comprehend than that from science, accounting or engineering and on par with psychological evidence. Intelligible, persuasive written and spoken evidence will have a clear structure, a vocabulary that lay people can follow, and explanations that encompass all that the lay person needs to know in order to both understand and evaluate what the expert is presenting.

And then the judges are wary of those experts who, for whatever reason, stray beyond their expertise. About 12% noted that experts often failed to stay within the parameters of their expertise; however, 80% saw this happen occasionally. Judges are best assisted by the expert stating frankly that the question raises a topic which is not within his/her area of expertise.

It is clear that our judges want experts to be impartial, to give clear explanations, to have prior experience in the field, and to be familiar with the facts about which they are expressing opinions.

In late 1998, the Federal Court of Australia published expert witness guidelines. These reshape the reception of expert evidence in Australia. In place of an *ad hoc* approach to experts and their evidence, there is now a set of principles against which all expert preparation and performance can be evaluated. Although these guidelines have not yet been adopted by many other courts, they can and will be used by advocates in any court or tribunal to test the value of any expert and their opinions.

Hence, it is useful for any surgeon preparing a report or expecting to give spoken evidence to be familiar with the guidelines. First, the general duty that the surgeon offering opinions owes to the court is explained. In particular, the surgeon's overriding duty is to assist the court.The surgeon is not there to present a point of view for the party who has retained him or her; the surgeon is neither an advocate nor a partisan.

Second, the guidelines address how surgeons demonstrate in the body of the report that the court or tribunal can rely upon them and then upon their opinions. The status of the opinion giver is determined by such factors as their training, their qualifications, their experience, their familiarity with current trends, and the esteem in which they are held by other members of their profession. Of course, the evaluation of training and experience is not merely a function of length of time. Quality and quantity are both relevant: some institutions are renowned, others are not.

The surgeon must always remember that, because the court is looking to adopt an explanation for something that is beyond its own experience and training, the court's first task is to determine that there is someone with the necessary reputation to proffer a reliable opinion.

An excellent reputation, however, is not enough to warrant a court preferring one opinion over another. It is essential that the process of fact gathering and analysis used by the surgeon is clearly set out in any report. There are two good reasons for this:

1. It must be possible for a third party to track through the report and replicate or test everything within it. Therefore, any textbooks or articles referred to must be listed, as must any assumptions that are made. If test results done by others are applied then those tests must be specifically identified.

2. The report should be a statement of reasons that can be understood by others who will rely upon it. While the person or party commissioning the report obviously needs such clarity, so too does the court during the hearing, and so too do the parties, and especially the losing party, when they read the judgment which will include why the court preferred one view of the surgical evidence to another.

To help the court in its quest for a reliable report, the guidelines also impose new disclosure requirements on the parties and their experts. In our adversarial system, the parties and their advocates are often not equal. Sometimes there is a great disparity between the parties in terms of their financial and skilled litigation resources.

The court needs an adversarial process which, through competent case preparation and good questioning skills, will expose poor opinions.

However, that same adversarial process is intended to produce a winner and a loser. When the stakes are high, whether it be because of the likely dollar amount of damages or because of injury to professional reputation, there is an inevitable wish by one or more parties to fashion the evidence so that some relevant issues are highlighted while other, also relevant, issues are downplayed or even suppressed.

As a means of balancing the adversarial quest for accountability with the adversarial desire to exploit any opportunity to secure victory, the guidelines require that the surgeon's medico-legal report must attach (i) all instructions (written and spoken) given to the surgeon which define the scope of the report; and (ii) the documents and other materials which the surgeon has been instructed to consider.

As well, the surgeon is required to set out any qualifications upon their opinion, such as insufficient data available, or some issue addressed in the report which falls outside the surgeon's specialist knowledge.

While these requirements will help the court to assess the value of the surgeon's written and spoken evidence, they are primarily intended to ensure that the parties to the litigation focus upon the expert issues *before* trial. Surgeons' reports are lodged with the court and exchanged with the other parties well before the hearing date. Hence, there is opportunity for each party to consider the full range of expert opinions that are being presented in the case. Along with the reports, each party must provide all other parties with any additional materials that complement their reports, such as photographs, diagrams and video.

It follows that any surgeon who has been asked to prepare a report for litigation should require that they be provided promptly with any other relevant reports that are commissioned or received by the party who has approached them.

Sometimes additional information or a differing approach found in another expert's report will persuade an expert that their opinion must change. The court requires that, when there is a change of view, the new opinion be provided to each entity to whom the earlier report has been delivered. It is the expert's task to set out the new opinion and the reasons for it. It is the lawyers' task to make sure that every other party and the court are promptly informed of the change.

The adversarial approach

Properly prepared litigation requires the lawyers to develop a theory about the facts and legal principles in the case which explains not only their own side's views but also those of any other party. Hence, a good case theory must both advance its proponent and anticipate and rebut the case of opponents.

The theory must then be tied to a tactical plan. This is the plan by which the lawyers will persuade the court that their theory is to be preferred. The plan and its implementation begins a long time before the court hearing. It includes the selecting of experts, identifying which issues require expert opinion, determining the ideal mix of written and spoken evidence from the expert, preparing any visual aids (such as diagrams, photos or transparencies) which will assist explanations and reduce misunderstandings, identifying likely ways in which the expert could be cross-examined by opponents and taking steps to neutralise such attacks, and preparing the expert for giving evidence in court.

The point of both the theory and the tactical plan is to persuade the opponent and the court that the party should win the case. That persuasion begins with the documents that are filed with the court and passed among the parties long before any formal hearing. Most cases are settled before the date for trial. A good many more settle at the door of the court as the parties focus upon the real strengths and weaknesses of their case.

The high rate of out of court settlement means that the authors of expert reports may write many such reports and never face cross-examination. Consequently, it is something of a shock to be confronted one day with cross-examination questions suggesting poor history taking, reference to out of date texts, failure to quote the latest authoritative literature, a propensity always to make the same findings, a willingness to stray outside of the practice specialty and make remarks which should be made by others, and an expertise that is inferior to that of experts called by the other side.

Each criticism can be avoided by complying with the guidelines. In other words, the expert surgeon witness should always assume that a case will not settle, that they will be required to give spoken evidence, and that their written report, therefore, should advance their opinion, rather than be exposed as their Achilles heel.

Because the Federal Court guidelines are such a significant step towards more efficient, helpful and accountable expert evidence, this chapter has been based upon their application. There are, however, important and very busy 'personal injury' jurisdictions where the prevailing conventions discourage prehearing contact between the advocate and the expert and where the written reports are not put into evidence. Instead, the advocate is expected, with one eye on a copy of the written report, to ask the expert questions so that the spoken answers amount to the content of the report.

Clearly, this system must fail if the report does not give the advocate all the clues and explanation that the lay advocate needs in order to understand the expert's last answer and pose the next relevant question.

Advocates also need to bear in mind that less than 10% of judges have never experienced difficulty in evaluating opinions expressed by one expert as against those expressed by another. Some 70% have occasionally had problems and an alarming 20% often have such problems.

Necessarily, this means that there has been a failure in case theory, in preparation and in communication. The quest to persuade has failed. This is borne out by the judges indicating that the difficulty in evaluation was, in more than half of all cases, the result of a fundamental irreconcilability of views; in another 20% of cases it reflected the complexity of the expert evidence.

More than 50% of judges identified clarity of explanation as the single most important factor when an expert is giving spoken evidence. Such evidence these days is often given by telephone or video link. The surgeon can remain in his/her office with a copy of the report and all the references at hand. However, whether the surgeon is in the office or in the witness box, it is important that the advocate for his/her party asks sufficient questions to settle the surgeon, establish some rapport with the court, ensure that the most important points are understood by the court, and neutralise likely cross-examination before the expert is turned over for questioning by other parties.

It is quite common, after the expert has been identified to the court, to hear the following inadequate introduction:

Advocate: You prepared a report for my solicitors which is dated 'x' and has 'y' pages?

Surgeon: Yes.

[The report is tendered as evidence.]

Advocate: And you still hold to the opinion expressed on page 'z' of that report?

Surgeon: Yes.

Advocate: No further questions, but please wait as my learned colleague wishes to question you.

A better prepared, and more competent, advocate will have taken some time to prepare the surgeon to give spoken evidence. For example, if evidence has been given for the other side which conflicts with your position, then the advocate should have discussed with you how to respond to that other opinion. Early in your examination in chief by the advocate for your party, an exchange like the following should occur:

Advocate: Now, you have read the report of Mr Smith?

Surgeon: Yes.

Advocate: And, you have heard his spoken evidence today too?

Surgeon: Yes.

Advocate: That's both his spoken evidence in chief and when I cross-examined him?

Surgeon: Yes.

Advocate: Before I cross-examined Mr Smith, you and I discussed his report and his spoken evidence, didn't we?

Surgeon: We did.

Advocate: There are a number of matters where you and Mr Smith differ, aren't there?

Surgeon: Yes.

Advocate: I am now going to ask you some questions about the differences between your opinion and that of Mr Smith. We'll start with the history as given by the plaintiff......

Note that in this better 'settling' question series the advocate has brought out that his earlier cross-examination of Mr Smith was informed by his discussion with his expert surgeon. Furthermore, the surgeon has been in court to hear the evidence of another expert with whose opinion he disagrees. Experts are an exception to the rule that witnesses remain outside of court until it is their turn to give evidence. Courts will give permission for experts to hear other evidence, both lay and expert, before their own is taken. Some 80% of judges consider that it is helpful to have expert witnesses in court to hear the evidence of other experts. Finally, the advocate has clearly indicated to both the court and the witness what is going to happen during his examination in chief of the expert—in particular that the expert will explain the differences in expert opinion.

As your spoken evidence will be in addition to your earlier written report, the importance of ease of access becomes obvious as soon as others are trying to find a particular passage. Whether you are in the witness box, or in your office and giving evidence by phone or video link, it is not very persuasive to be taken to 'about line 29, on the 4th or is it the 5th paragraph of page 9' of your report. As the judge, the jurors, and the various counsel all find different places and varying levels of irritation it is far better for everyone to be directed to paragraph 46 point 3.

You can then be asked such questions as:

Advocate: Since writing that opinion have you received any new information?

Surgeon: I have.

Advocate: What is that information?

Surgeon: (describes)

Advocate: How does that information affect the opinion given at paragraph 46?

Surgeon: It means (describes).

Similarly, whether you are in the courtroom or in your rooms, it is often much easier to explain when the listeners are looking at photos or diagrams or transparencies that you have included with your report.

There is a sting in the tail to the new guidelines. The Federal Court requires that experts should declare at the end of their report that, '[the expert] has made all the inquiries which [the expert] believes are desirable and appropriate and that no matters of significance which [the expert] regards as relevant have, to [the expert's] knowledge, been withheld from the Court'.

What could be fairer or more dangerous than that? Consider the possibilities in a medico-legal assessment report when the surgeon is being cross examined:

Advocate: Now you still perform surgery don't you?

Surgeon: Yes.

Advocate: So, naturally, you keep up to date?

Surgeon: Of course.

Advocate: And in preparation for 'x' procedure it is usual to do 'y' isn't it?

Surgeon: Yes.

Advocate: And you follow that usual practice don't you?

Surgeon: Usually.

Surgeon: You weren't provided with a report on the outcome of 'y' in this case were you?

Surgeon: No.

Advocate: And you prepared your report about 'x' without any reference to 'y' didn't you?

Surgeon: Yes.

Advocate: And you declared at the end of your report that you had made all inquiries which you believed to be desirable, didn't you?

Surgeon: Yes.

Advocate: Naturally, you thought about the meaning of that declaration before you signed it?

Surgeon: I did.

Advocate: Your usual practice shows that 'y' is desirable doesn't it?

Surgeon: Yes.

Advocate: But 'y' is not mentioned in your report is it?

Surgeon: No.

Advocate: Nothing further.

REFERENCE

1. Freckleton IR, Reddy P, Selby HM. *Judicial Perspectives on Expert Evidence: An Empirical Study.* Melbourne: Australian Institute of Judicial Administration, 1999.

FURTHER READING

Freckleton IR, Selby HM. *Expert Evidence*, Vol.1. Sydney: LBC Information Services, 1993–2000.

Freckleton IR, Selby HM. *The Law of Expert Evidence*. Sydney: LBC Information Services, 1999.

Doctors to the rescue

M.W. GORTON

Liabilities in emergencies

Doctors are often concerned about the liability of doctors who attend emergencies or who 'come to the rescue'. With the increased risk and fear of litigation and willingness of patients to initiate proceedings, doctors are becoming more worried about their legal liability in situations where they are asked to act in an emergency.

A situation arose in Queensland which highlighted the situation where a doctor assisted in an acute asthma attack, having to resuscitate a patient 20 times in the course of travel to hospital. The doctor was painted as a Good Samaritan and the patient survived. However, it was subsequently revealed that the doctor may have been impaired by alcohol after being charged with a drink driving offence relating to the same evening.

The Brisbane *Courier Mail* (16 July 1998) commented:

> *'However the realisation that it could have been a different story points to the dilemma faced by off-duty doctors enjoying a few drinks when they are called to act in a medical emergency at a sporting event or dinner party or maybe in a plane.'*[1]

A recent report of the Law Reform Committee of the Victorian Parliament confirmed that there has been no reported Australian case where a doctor has been held liable for providing assistance in good faith in an emergency situation or accident.[2] However, the Committee also noted that it had been told 'that the fear of malpractice causes medical practitioners to avoid offering medical attention to people at the scene of an accident or in an emergency'.

Two questions arise:

1. Must doctors render assistance at the scene of an emergency?
2. If a doctor attends an emergency, what is his or her liability?

Must doctors render assistance?

There is no general requirement at law for anyone to provide assistance in an emergency or accident, even where it may be clear or foreseeable that the failure to act may result in death or injury. The liability of a rescuer in such circumstances is much reduced from the ordinary liability for negligence. The duty in such cases is simply to ensure that the conduct of the rescuer does not increase the risk or peril of the person in danger.

There is a general duty for a person coming to the rescue to act reasonably, but this is interpreted at a reduced level, given the context of the emergency situation.

Additionally, at law, there is no legal obligation for doctors to give assistance at the scene of an accident or emergency. However, a positive duty to act does exist where the doctor is in a particular role or part of a system, part of which is to deal with accidents or emergency situations. For example, a doctor in an emergency department clearly has a role to play in dealing with emergencies as they arise. However, even in these cases, even where a doctor is in a casualty department, the English courts have found that there was not a general obligation to examine all patients who came to the department. The overriding determination by the courts, is whether a doctor has acted reasonably in all of the circumstances.

The courts also recognise the ability of doctors to carry out procedures, without informed consent if necessary, where treatment is reasonably necessary in the particular emergency situation. Clearly where treatment is necessary in an emergency to save life or prevent serious injury a doctor is entitled to act.

Apart from the law, the doctors might have a responsibility to attend an accident or emergency under ethical or professional obligations. General professional 'moral' obligations certainly recognise the requirement for doctors to render assistance where they are available to do so and such assistance is within their competence.

In New South Wales, for example, the *Medical Practice Act* 1992 contains a specific ethical duty. It may amount to 'professional misconduct' if a doctor refuses or fails, without reasonable cause, to attend within a reasonable time after being requested to do so to render professional services, in any case where the doctor has reasonable cause to believe that the patient is in need of urgent attention by a doctor.

The decision in New South Wales of *Lowns v. Woods* (1996) A. Torts Reports 63 confirmed that, if a doctor fails to respond to an emergency request for help, even if the victim is not an existing patient, the doctor will have responsibility if: (i) the request for assistance is made in a professional context; (ii) the doctor and the patient are in close physical proximity (such that the doctor could attend): (iii) the doctor is aware of the need for emergency treatment or attention for a serious medical case; and/or (iv) the doctor is appropriately qualified to provide the treatment, has the equipment which may be necessary and is not otherwise at physical risk.

Obviously, any requirement to attend will depend on a range of circumstances:

1. Is the doctor able to attend?
2. Are there other patients requiring his attention?
3. Are ambulance or other medical services readily available?
4. Are the doctor's skills sufficient to deal with this situation?
5. Is he/she competent in the area of treatment or procedure that may be required?
6. What is the nature of the illness or remedy required?
7. Is it a real emergency or merely perceived by those around to be an emergency?

8. What are the circumstances of the emergency (i.e. is it a road accident in the bush or a heart attack of a visitor in a hospital?).
9. What are the resources available?
10. These principles obviously apply differently to other professionals such as nurses, paramedics, teachers, etc.

The medical legislation in other States is similarly broad enough to encompass a professional obligation on doctors to attend. For example, in Victoria the *Medical Practice Act* 1994 defines 'unprofessional conduct' to include conduct which is of a lesser standard than that which the public might reasonably expect, or conduct which is of a lesser standard than that which might reasonably be expected of a doctor by his or her peers. In the Northern Territory, Section 155 of the Criminal Code provides that any person who, being able to provide rescue or treatment to a person urgently in need of it and whose life may be endangered if it is not provided, and who callously fails to do so is guilty of a crime and liable to imprisonment for 7 years. The Northern Territory legislation has been particularly applied in hit-and-run accident situations, where the driver fails to render assistance to the victim.

What is the liability of doctors who render assistance?

As noted previously, the law recognises a lesser onus or duty on doctors who render assistance in an accident or emergency situation. The law merely requires that a rescuer, particularly a doctor, acts reasonably, in accordance with the circumstances. Those circumstances include the fact that the usual medical equipment and supplies may not be available and that the doctor is acting under extreme, stressful situations. The law will require a doctor to conduct only procedures that are reasonably necessary in the emergency situation. Of course, the doctor may be liable where his or her own actions contribute to or exacerbate injuries.

The position at law in some States has been modified by legislation.

Queensland

Queensland contains the most substantial legislation dealing with the situation of the Good Samaritan. Section 3 of the *Voluntary Aid in Emergency Act* 1973 provides that:

> *'Liability at law shall not attach to a medical practitioner or nurse in respect of an act done or omitted in the course of rendering medical care, aid or assistance to an injured person in cirumstances of emergency:*
>
> - *at or near the scene of the incident or other occurrence constituting the emergency;*
>
> - *while the injured person is being transported from the scene of the accident or other occurrence constituting the emergency to a hospital or other place at which adequate medical care is available*
>
> *if:*
>
> - *the act is done or omitted in good faith and without gross negligence; and*
>
> - *the services are performed without fee or reward or expectation of fee or reward.'*

To take advantage of this provision, the doctor must act without gross negligence, which goes beyond simple negligence or misadventure. The doctor would have to be so reckless or incompetent that it warranted the description of 'gross negligence'.

The doctor must also be acting in good faith. Clearly, if the doctor was acting under the influence of alcohol, it is arguable whether the doctor is acting in good faith. If the doctor is clearly under the influence of alcohol and acts incompetently, it may also be that the doctor is grossly negligent. This raises interesting situations where doctors are at social functions, where clearly they have had a few drinks, but may be asked to act in an emergency situation. On the one hand, society would want doctors to intervene and exercise the skills and specialist knowledge that they obviously possess. On the other hand, an impaired doctor may not be of assistance and may, in fact, exacerbate the situation.

Reform in other States?

Clearly, other States in Australia and New Zealand should consider the Queensland legislative model, to clarify and reassure doctors and health service providers, and to encourage them to act in the case of emergencies or accidents.

The Law Reform Committee of the Victorian Parliament recommended that the Victorian Government should enact legislation based on the Queensland model to provide a limited defence for medical practitioners and nurses who provide medical assistance at the scene of an accident or other emergency.

Approaches by the College in 1999 to other State governments have not been encouraging. Some other States rely on the fact that there is no evidence to indicate that their existing legal situation is inadequate, or evidence of the fact that doctors may be resisting providing their services in an emergency situations. This is not, however, an answer. Clearly, the profession is concerned about the matter. Anecdotal comments suggest that doctors do indeed think twice before responding to an accident or request for emergency treatment. The fears and concerns of potential liability and litigation are real. If parliaments wish to encourage doctors and other health-care professionals to provide their services in emergency situations, then legislation similar to that in Queensland should be considered.

REFERENCES
1. *Courier Mail*, 16 July 1998, Brisbane.
2. *Legal Liability of Health Service Providers*, Report of the Law Reform Committee, Parliament of Victoria, 1998.

Coronial inquests
and the medical profession

V. HARCOURT

Introduction

The obligation to report a reportable death is fundamental to the operation of the coronial system. In most of Australia, every person, including doctors, has a duty to report deaths which may attract the jurisdiction of the coroner. Failure to report deaths may result in a financial penalty.[a]

This obligation particularly affects the medical profession.

Reporting deaths

In Victoria, any person who has reasonable grounds to believe that a reportable death has not been reported must report it as soon as possible to a coroner or the officer in charge of a police station.[b] Doctors present at or after the death of a person are obliged to report the death if it is a reportable death, or if the doctor does not view the body or is unable to determine the cause of death.[c] The obligation to report a death falls upon the doctor present at or after the death

---

[a] See for example *Coroners Act 1985* (Vic) s13(1).

[b] *Coroners Act 1985* (Vic) s13(1). The obligation to report deaths in Western Australia, Tasmania, Northern Territory and Australian Capital Territory is comparable to Victoria. *See Coroners Act 1997* (ACT) s77; *Coroners Act* 1997 (NT) s12; *Coroners Act 1995* (Tas) s19; *Coroners Act 1996* (WA) s17

[c] *Coroners Act 1995 (Vic)* s13 (3).

if the cause of death cannot be determined from the deceased's immediate medical history and no doctor attended the deceased 14 days prior to his or her death.

In New South Wales, doctors cannot certify the cause of death in stipulated cases but must report it to the police who then report it to the coroner. Effectively, all deaths in health-care institutions are reported to the coroner. Otherwise, any person who has reasonable grounds to believe that a death or suspected death which would attract the jurisdiction of the coroner has not yet been reported must notify the police or the coroner.[d]

Queensland casts a similarly wide net, obliging any person who may have knowledge of a death into which the coroner has the jurisdiction to hold an inquest, to report it to the police. Doctors cannot provide a death certificate in such cases and must make a report of deaths which have, in the opinion of the doctor, occurred under suspicious circumstances.[e]

Reportable death

In Victoria, a coroner has jurisdiction to investigate a death if it appears to the coroner that it is or may be a reportable death.[f] The definition of a reportable death is comprised of two parts, the first relating to a territorial connection to the State, and the second prescribing the circumstances of the death.[g]

The territorial connection may be established by the presence of the body in Victoria, or by the fact that the death or cause of death occurred in Victoria, wherever the body may be. It can also exist by virtue of the deceased having been a resident of Victoria, wherever the death or cause of death occurred or the body is. The circumstances of the death include a death which appears to have been unexpected, unnatural or violent, or resulted from accident or injury. Relevantly, it also includes a death occurring during or as a result of an anaesthetic, or where the death certificate has not been signed.

[d]   *Coroners Act 1980* (NSW) s12A, 12B.
[e]   *Coroners Act 1958* (Qld) s11,12,13.
[f]   *Coroners Act 1985* (Vic) s15(1).
[g]   *Coroners Act 1985* (Vic) s3.

Where the coroner has the jurisdiction to investigate a death, an inquest may be held if it is desirable,[h] except where the Act requires an inquest. Examples of when an inquest must be held include where the coroner suspects homicide, or where the deceased was a person held in care. The latter refers, among others, to persons under the control, custody or care of the Secretary to the Department of Human Services or the custody of the Secretary of the Department of Justice, or the police.

New South Wales prescribes a range of circumstances in which the jurisdiction of the coroner is attracted.[i] There must first, however, be a territorial connection of the death to the State.[j] The connection is defined in much the same terms as in the Victorian Act but is wider in relation to deaths occurring outside the State. To attract the jurisdiction, the deceased must have had a 'sufficient connection' with NSW. This embraces the death of a person who was in the course of a journey either to or from NSW, or was last at a place in the State before the circumstances of the death arose.[k]

The range of circumstances in which the jurisdiction of the coroner is attracted includes when the person has died a violent or unnatural death, under suspicious or unusual circumstances or suddenly from an unknown cause. It also includes a death occurring during or as a result of an anaesthetic, but this is specified in terms more precise than in the Victorian Act. In other words, in NSW the person must have died while under, or as a result of, or within 24 hours of the administration of an anaesthetic administered in the course of a medical, surgical or dental operation or procedure, other than where it has been administered solely to facilitate resuscitation from apparent or impending death.[l] In such cases an inquest must be held if a relative of the deceased makes a request for an inquest.[m]

---

[h] *Coroners Act 1985* (Vic) s17(2). For the purposes of the Act, inquest is deemed to include a formal hearing. This is distinct from a coronial investigation and it is possible that findings can be made without an inquest being held.

[i] *Coroners Act 1980* (NSW) s13.

[j] *Coroners Act 1980* (NSW) s13C(1).

[k] *Coroners Act 1980* (NSW) s13C(2).

[l] *Coroners Act 1980* (NSW) s13(1)(f).

[m] *Coroners Act 1980* (NSW) s14C(2).

An inquest is mandatory where the identity, time or place of death has not been determined, or if it appears that there has been a homicide, or if the death occurred in custody or the manner or cause of death has not been sufficiently disclosed.

It is not within the scope of this book to examine the legislation in each State or Territory.[n] While it can be said that similar provisions exist in the other jurisdictions with varying degrees of difference, none makes mandatory an inquest where the death apparently occurred during or as a result of an anaesthetic. All Acts except for South Australia and the Northern Territory, make some provision for a request to be made of the coroner to hold an inquest, by, for example, the deceased's relatives.[o]

The medical profession and inquests

The modern Australian coroner is largely defined by legislation. As now would be apparent, the legislation is different in each State and Territory.[p] Although the jurisdiction, restrictions and powers prescribed in the statutes lack uniformity, each retains the fundamental role of the coroner to investigate deaths. The primary function [q] of the coroner is to make findings as to the identity of the deceased, how the death occurred, and the cause of death.[r] The coroner's powers of investigation are limited by what is relevant in the legal sense to the cause or circumstances of the death, and to making the findings required by the legislation.[s]

---

[n] For a comparative discussion of the legislation see CCH Australia Ltd, *Australian Health and Medical Law Reporter*, Chapter 33; *The Laws of Australia*, section 20.10. The Law Book Company Ltd.

[o] *Coroners Act 1997* (ACT) s64; *Coroners Act 1980* (NSW) s14C; *Coroners Act 1997* (NT) s16; *Coroners Act 1958* (Qld) s7B; *Coroners Act 1995* (Tas) s26; *Coroners Act 1985* (Vic) s18; *Coroners Act 1996* (WA) s24.

[p] *Coroners Act 1997* (ACT); *Coroners Act 1980* (NSW); *Coroners Act 1997* (NT); *Coroners Act 1958* (Qld); *Coroners Act 1975* (SA); *Coroners Act 1995* (Tas); *Coroners Act 1985* (Vic); *Coroners Act 1996* (WA).

[q] *Harmsworth v. The State Coroner (1989)* VR 989,996.

[r] *Coroners Act 1997* (ACT) s52; *Coroners Act 1980* (NSW) s22; *Coroners Act 1997* (NT) s34; *Coroners Act 1958* (Qld) s43; *Coroners Act 1975* (SA) s12; *Coroners Act 1995* (Tas) s28(1); *Coroners Act 1985* (Vic) s19(1); *Coroners Act 1996* (WA) s25.

[s] *Harmsworth v. The State Coroner (1989)* VR 989,995–6.

What is also common in each State and Territory is that a significant number of inquests involve an investigation of the conduct of the medical profession and health-care institutions relating to the death of a patient. Coronial inquests involving the medical profession and its institutions are more difficult than the average case[1] for a variety of reasons.

The difficulties do not present themselves so much in the task of determining the cause of death, but rather in the understanding of the complexities of the illness or injury the deceased may have been suffering prior to his or her death, and the examination, diagnosis and treatment of the patient. In Australia, the office of the coroner is held by a lawyer who is usually an appointed magistrate,[†] not a health professional. Hence, medical evidence must be presented in a way that will enable the coroner, and any other parties involved in the investigation, to comprehend the medical issues.

The family of the deceased may be present or have legal representation at the inquest. For family, relatives and friends of the deceased, an inquest can be a harrowing and traumatic experience. The grieving and sense of loss felt in relation to the death may be experienced again, particularly as inquests do not usually take place until many months or even years after the death. It may be the first opportunity for the family to obtain information about the death of the deceased or to test independently the explanations given by the health professionals. The emotion can spill over to the manner in which witnesses are cross-examined, and submissions are put, where the emphasis is upon finding someone to blame for the death.

What is often overlooked is that a coronial investigation may be similarly traumatic and distressing for health professionals. In addition, the focus is upon the professional conduct of the doctors, nurses or health-care providers. Did the standard of treatment fall below that reasonably expected and did their acts or omissions cause or contribute to the death of the deceased?

[†] *Coroners Act 1997* (ACT) s5; *Coroners Act 1980* (NSW) s4A; *Coroners Act 1997* (NT) s4; *Coroners Act 1958* (Qld) s6; *Coroners Act 1975* (SA) s7; *Coroners Act 1995* (Tas) s10; *Coroners Act 1985* (Vic) s6; *Coroners Act 1996* (WA) s6.

In Tasmania and until recently in Victoria, a coroner is required to name in the findings a person who is found to have contributed to the death.[u] In all other jurisdictions in Australia it is open to a coroner to identify a contributor, but it is not mandatory to name that person.[2] The primary function of coronial investigations is otherwise to make certain findings as to the identity of the deceased, how the death occurred, and the cause of death.[v]

A finding that a health professional caused or contributed to a death is not the equivalent of a determination of criminal or civil liability. The Victorian State Coroner, Mr Graeme Johnstone, has made this clear:

> '*A finding of civil and/or criminal liability is not part of the coroner's role. Moreover, such a finding should not be perceived in the public eye as being part of the coroner's reasoning when a finding of contribution is made.*'[w]

However, its impact upon the person concerned can be devastating, especially where the inquest attracts publicity.[3] It has been described as having an 'extremely deleterious effect' upon that person's character, reputation and employment prospects[x] and as a 'very serious allegation'[y] demanding a commensurate standard of proof. It has also been recognised by the High Court of Australia that the potential of an adverse finding upon the reputation of a person demands that a person against whom such a finding may be made should have the right to be heard.[z]

For these reasons, coronial inquests have often developed into hard-fought adversarial contests. A coronial investigation is

---

[u]   *Coroners Act 1995* (Tas) s28 (1)(f); *Coroners Act 1985* (Vic) s19(1)(e) now repealed.
[v]   In this chapter, we shall deal only with the jurisdiction of the coroner to investigate deaths. However, the relevant Acts variously empower the coroner to also investigate fires and other phenomena in certain instances. The legislation is not uniform.
[w]   *Inquest Findings, Comments and Recommendations into Fire and Nine Deaths at Kew Residential Services on 8 April 1996*. State Coroner, Victoria, 17 October 1997, 283.
[x]   *Anderson v. Blashki* (1993) 2 VR 89,96.
[y]   *The Secretary to the Department of Health & Community Services v. Gurvich* (1995) 2 VR 69,74.
[z]   *Annetts v. McCann* (1990) 170 CLR 596, 599 & 609.

essentially inquisitorial in nature. In other words, the coroner directs the investigation, gathering evidence on matters he or she considers relevant and informing him- or herself as they see fit. The requirements of natural justice dictate that interested parties be given the opportunity to participate, notably where an adverse finding may be made against that party. Otherwise, the parties should assist the coroner in his or her function.

Adversarial contests distract the coroner from what may be considered to be the more important functions of public education, understanding and prevention.[4] Ascertaining the cause of deaths enables the community to learn about problems which may exist, to agitate for change to remedy the risk and to prevent further injury or death. The recommendations made by the Victorian State Coroner in the Kew Residential Services Inquest in 1997 were implemented by the State Government, leading to considerable reform in managing fire risks in intellectual disability residential centres.

The investigation and making a statement

The investigation of reportable deaths by a coroner or the coronial investigators such as the police is facilitated by wide powers of entry onto premises, the inspection of documents and the possession of evidence. When a death occurs in a health-care facility or is related to the treatment provided by a medical practitioner, the investigator inevitably will seek access to and usually possession of the deceased's health file.

The health file is the primary and obvious source of information in a coronial investigation. While the coronial investigator's demand for the file normally cannot be resisted, a copy should be made for your reference. This may appear self-evident but it is not always arranged. Keeping a copy of the file enables you to refer to it if and when you are required to make a statement for the coroner. It also facilitates the cross-checking of its contents if the integrity of the original is corrupted over time by virtue of the number of times it is handled by other people.

The importance of accurate and appropriate record keeping for legal purposes cannot be understated. Where there is a conflict in the evidence, or even doubt as to the evidence given from memory alone, the existence of proper records may be invaluable in resolving the issue in your favour. When health file records are made, the principal objective may not be to assist in the recollection of events for the purposes of giving evidence. Nonetheless, file notes of observations and the treatment of patients must be adequate, legible and contemporaneous if they are to be of any reliable use in making statements or giving evidence. The quality of health records as a primary source of information depends very much on the care taken when making the entries.

Common mistakes made in the recording of events in the health files include: (i) file notes that do not record the observations or treatment in any meaningful or detailed way; (ii) no file note at all is made of relevant observations or treatment; (iii) the file note is made some time after the event, often from an imperfect recollection and sometimes from notes made on a scrap of paper at the time; (iv) the file note contains comments not relevant to the observation or treatment of the patient, but which may be offensive or insulting; (v) alteration to file notes, for whatever reason, which may later be attacked as an attempt to 'doctor' the record; (vi) illegible handwriting which either lends itself to misinterpretation, or worse, no reasonable interpretation; and (vii) the author of the file note is not disclosed from the record, nor can it be divined from the handwriting.

These problems are readily overcome if care is taken when the file notes are made, and make the task of meaningfully utilising them at a later point in time easier. Providing statements to the coronial investigator, who is usually a police officer, will be a simpler task with a file in front of you which contains comprehensive file notes.

The initial investigation of a reportable death will frequently be carried out by a police officer. The police officer will interview relevant witnesses and seek statements to be included in the Inquest Brief and produced at the inquest, if one is held. The statement will form part of the evidence tendered at the inquest. If you are called to give evidence, the statement will stand as your evidence in chief.

Evidence in chief is the evidence given when a witness first enters the witness box. Cross-examination will then follow.

The police may well be performing a dual function when investigating the death. They may be investigating the death as part of a criminal investigation and as part of a coronial investigation. If the statement is being obtained as part of a criminal investigation, the police must warn you at the outset.

In the context of a coronial investigation, there is usually no reason why a statement should not be provided to the police. However, prior to making a statement, you must familiarise yourself with the file relating to the deceased. Specific regard should be had to your entries and the progress notes or continuation sheets generally, discharge summaries, observation and medication charts, incident reports, and any communication relevant to the deceased, including medical reports or letters from family or friends. If asked to provide a statement you have the right to obtain legal advice, and you should contact your lawyer, defence union or insurer before making any statement. Obtaining proper legal advice at the outset may avoid unnecessary difficulties later in the investigation or inquest.

The statement must be accurate in every respect and based upon the file and your clear memory of events. It should not be a reconstruction of events, it should not be based on guesswork and it should not be based upon hearsay or a collaborative effort with other witnesses. The statement must reflect your understanding of events and be in your words. Usually, the police will allow you to prepare your own statement. If, however, the statement is prepared by the police at the time of the interview, you must be aware that the statement will reflect the perception of the police officer as to what is relevant, and will be in that officer's words, not yours. You must, therefore, not sign the statement unless you are satisfied that all relevant information is contained in the statement in a form with which you are comfortable.

The statement should be concise but thorough. An over-elaborate explanation of the facts runs the risk of delving into irrelevant areas and appearing defensive. Unless specifically requested to provide a critical analysis of the events that have unfolded, your statement should avoid making judgments of the acts or omissions of others. At the time of making the statement you will rarely be in the position of knowing all the facts, or the recollections of other witnesses. An honestly held opinion expressed in such circumstances may needlessly cause tremendous problems at the inquest. In the same spirit, the statement should not be emotive. There is nothing to be gained in expressing in a statement anything other than the facts in objective and neutral terms.

Giving evidence

If you are to appear in court as a witness you will probably receive a summons to give evidence.

Upon receipt of the summons, advice should be sought from your legal adviser. If you believe that you are not the appropriate person to attend to give evidence in a particular matter, this should be raised with your legal adviser. This will allow your legal adviser the opportunity to discuss the matter with the coroner's assistant. Often the coroner is simply concerned to ensure that the most relevant person gives evidence. If you are not the appropriate person, the coroner may excuse you from giving evidence.

Shortly prior to attending the inquest you should re-read your statement and be totally familiar with it. You should also thoroughly familiarise yourself with the file and your particular entries. An area of focus for coroners has been that directives and procedures are adequate and that they have been complied with by staff. You should refresh your memory of any relevant policies, procedures and guidelines.

If, by reason of the passage of time, you cannot now recall all that the statement deposes to, even after having re-read the statement, say so. If there are inaccuracies or omissions, remedy them. In a forum as highly charged as an inquest, ensure your evidence is given in a most compassionate manner, noting that family members and friends of the deceased are present and often reliving the evidence you are giving. Not uncommonly, the inquest is seen by grieving family members as the last step in the process and, equally, an important step in helping them get on with their lives.

Conclusion

Coronial inquests should be an opportunity to assist the community to prevent injury and death. It should not be a hunting ground to gather evidence to launch civil proceedings at a later stage. Nor should it be used by parties to push their own self-interest at the expense of others. However, having said that, the reality is that inquests are so used by potential litigants and other parties. The medical profession has, probably more than any other class of witness appearing at inquests, unnecessarily suffered more criticism from parties due to these factors.

The culture of parties appearing at inquests must change if inquests are to achieve their full potential. The removal in Victoria of the requirement for a coroner to name if possible any person who has contributed to the death will, it is to be hoped, assist in the change of culture. It would also help if parties took up the suggestion of the Victorian State Coroner and consider: (i) identifying and notifying the coroner of issues of concern on health and safety, and, in appropriate cases, requesting further investigation (this should be done as soon as possible); (ii) identifying similar cases (through requested searches of the National or local Information System); and (iii) suggesting areas where the coroner may make practical recommendations.[5]

Until this change takes place, coronial inquests will continue to cause some angst to the medical profession and so should not be treated lightly. If you are involved in an inquest, prepare thoroughly at all stages and seek legal advice at the outset.

REFERENCES

1. Waller K. *Coronial Law and Practice in New South Wales* 3rd edn. Sydney: Butterworths, 1994; 189.
2. Freckleton I. Inquest law In: Selby H (ed.). *The Inquest Handbook*. Sydney: Federation Press, 1998; 5.
3. Alsop C. Preparing for an inquest. In: Selby H (ed.). *The Aftermath of Death*. Sydney: Federation Press,1992; 29.

4. Hallenstein HR. *The Coroner's Investigation - A Social Catalyst*. 11 March 1992, State Coroner, Victoria, 2.
5. Johnstone G. Coroner's inquiries and recommendations. In: Selby H (ed.). *The Inquest Handbook*. Sydney: Federation Press, 1998; 43.

Medical manslaughter and other crimes

A. MERRY, M.W. GORTON

Introduction

Medical negligence is usually dealt with under the civil law or by means of disciplinary proceedings, but when a patient dies there has been an increased tendency, internationally, to resort to criminal prosecution of the health professional concerned. This tendency has been discernible in the UK and USA, but it has been strikingly obvious in New Zealand (a country of only 3 million inhabitants), where nine health professionals have faced criminal charges arising from unintentional errors during the normal medical or nursing practice in a period of less than 15 years.[1]

There are examples in which the criminal law has been used in non-fatal cases of iatrogenic harm, but these are rare. There is no rational justification for a prosecution policy which warrants the use of the criminal law on the basis that death, rather than injury, has occurred. The moral culpability associated with iatrogenic harm lies in the actions themselves, not in their outcome. Furthermore, the suffering associated with serious injury, such as paraplegia or brain damage, may equal or exceed that associated with death, particularly if the patient who dies is very old or has a terminal illness.

This is not to suggest that age or ill health negates the criminality of murder or manslaughter in general (although there is a fine line between killing someone, and failing to save his or her life). On the contrary, even with elderly or very ill patients, there will be circumstances in which it is entirely justifiable for a coroner to initiate criminal proceedings, after due consideration of the facts reported, as a matter of legal obligation by the medical practitioners concerned. However, a society is in deep trouble if its trust of the medical profession has diminished to the point where police, in the absence of specific reason to suspect foul play, feel called upon to pre-empt the normal processes by which medical practice is regulated by exercising their power to investigate any death. Unfortunately, this has been the case in New Zealand, where (until recently) the arrival of police on the scene has been almost the norm in the event of an unexpected death.

The position in New Zealand has changed substantially and is now consistent with that in Australia, the UK and Canada. In the USA, the absolute number of criminal prosecutions of doctors has been very small (given the size of the country), but use of the criminal law does seem to be increasing in cases which previously would have been confined to the civil courts.

The Harvard Medical Practice Study[2] and The Quality in Australian Health Care Study[3] have shown that unintended harm to patients is disconcertingly common in hospital practice, and may at times result in permanent injury or death. Acknowledgment of the extent of this problem may have contributed to a greater demand for accountability from health professionals. Given the extent of the problem of iatrogenic harm, there are those who would argue that the number of criminal prosecutions has, in fact, been relatively small, even in New Zealand, let alone in the USA.[1] However, there is a substantial difference between advocating more effective accountability and suggesting that criminal law is an appropriate means of achieving this. It is, therefore, worth understanding the issues at stake.[1,4-6] We review the legal principles underpinning the concept of criminal negligence, and illustrate the way in which the criminal law has been used in response to negligently caused deaths in Australia, New Zealand and other countries.

Some basic concepts

In the medical context, doctors are held to have a duty of care to their patients simply on the basis that they have accepted them as patients, and in some circumstances whether they wish to accept them or not. 'Negligence' is usually framed in reference to standard of care, and is taken to imply that the treatment given fell short of the standard expected by the law. This is usually defined in reference to the standard that could reasonably have been expected in the circumstances. 'Recklessness' is generally used to describe situations in which a person understood a risk, but determined nevertheless to run that risk. In other words, the state of mind in recklessness is culpable, while it is generally neutral or even commendable in negligence. It is important to distinguish between a lack of care and a deliberate intent to cause harm — recklessness does not imply malign objectives, just a disregard for the safety of others.

For the purposes of civil liability, all that is needed is so-called 'simple' negligence. For criminal liability, however, it is usual to require something more serious than simple negligence, often referred to as 'gross' negligence. During the Industrial Revolution, it was common to use the criminal law in circumstances in which injury was caused by little more than a mistake. However, more modern approaches tend to reserve the criminal law for the most serious cases. In practice, the precise level at which negligence is considered serious enough to justify criminal prosecutions has varied from country to country, and from one time to another.

In order for liability to be proved in respect of injury, it is also necessary to establish that the breach in the expected standard actually caused harm. In civil cases, it is enough to prove causation on the balance of probabilities, but for criminal purposes, proof beyond reasonable doubt is required.

Medical manslaughter in Australia

In Australia, civil suits against doctors and health professionals have increased dramatically in recent years, but there have been relatively few convictions of manslaughter arising out of negligent medical treatment. It is settled law in Australia that simple negligence is not sufficient to justify a finding of manslaughter. The distinction between simple and gross negligence is well recognised by the Australian courts (*R v. Holness & Banks* (1970) Tas SR 74).

This position is similar to that in the UK, and is the same in Australian States under the common law and in those which have codified criminal law.

The Common Law States: (Victoria, New South Wales and South Australia)

As in the UK, the common law in Australia is that simple negligence is insufficient to warrant conviction for manslaughter:

> 'Negligence which is essential before a man can be criminally convicted must be culpable, exhibiting a degree of recklessness beyond anything required to make a man liable for damages and civil action. It must be such a degree of culpable negligence as to amount to an absence of that care for the lives and persons of others which every law abiding man is expected to exhibit.' (*R v. Gunter* (1921) 21 SR (NSW) 282).

The Code States: (Queensland, Western Australia and Tasmania)

Queensland, Western Australia and Tasmania have provisions in their criminal codes that are virtually identical to the former Section 155 of the *New Zealand Crimes Act 1961* (see below). The Queensland and Western Australian provisions are as follows:

> 'It is the duty of every person who, except in a case of necessity, undertakes to administer surgical and medical treatment to any other person or to do any other lawful act which is or may be dangerous to human life or health to have reasonable skill and to use reasonable care in doing such act; and he is held to have caused any consequences which result to the life or health of any person by reason of any omission to observe or perform that duty.' (*Queensland s.288, Western Australia s.266*, see also *Tasmania s.149*)

However, in the leading Australian authority, the High Court case of *Callaghan v. The Queen* (1952) 87 CLR 115, it was determined that mere negligence, based on the civil standard, is not sufficient for a person to be convicted of manslaughter under these provisions. The High Court stated:

> *'It is in a criminal code dealing with major crimes involving grave moral guilt. Without in any way denying the difficulties created by the text of the criminal code, we think it would be wrong to suppose that it was intended by the code to make the degree of negligence punishable as manslaughter as low as the standard of fault sufficient to give rise to civil liability.'*

Australian cases involving breaches of the criminal code that have imposed a duty on persons in charge of dangerous things to use reasonable care and to take reasonable precautions to avoid such danger, have universally concluded that a breach of this duty could sustain a conviction for manslaughter only if it involved negligence of the degree required for manslaughter at common law (*R v. Scarth* (1945) ST R QD 38 and *Evgeniou v. The Queen* (1964) 37 ALJR 508*)*.

New Zealand

In New Zealand, the threshold needed to establish a breach of duty of care for negligent manslaughter is dealt with under one of several 'duty of care' sections of the *Crimes Act* 1961. This is usually Section 155 in medical cases, but Section 156 may apply. These sections are essentially similar to provisions in those States in Australia that have criminal codes, but the position in practice has differed substantially from that in Australia and the UK. Thus, until recently, the standard of negligence in New Zealand has been no greater than that needed for civil actions. Prosecution could and did result from failures to meet the required (civil) standard of 'reasonable knowledge skill and care' that were, in practice, indistinguishable from normal human errors. There is no doubt that the tragic consequences of these failures demanded some form of credible response, and this may well have influenced the development of the New Zealand position. Unlike Australia, New Zealand maintains a system of accident compensation which almost always precludes civil actions in negligence. Thus, the increase in such actions in Australia and elsewhere has not occurred in New Zealand, and lack of recourse to the civil law has been cited in justification of the former position in New Zealand by those who argue that more accountability is needed from the medical profession.

We know of no prosecutions of health professionals for manslaughter in New Zealand before 1980. In 1981, during his first anaesthetic in Greymouth, a British anaesthetist recruited from Australia administered carbon dioxide instead of oxygen to an 11-year-old undergoing an appendectomy, with a fatal result. He had taken the trouble to familiarise himself with the local equipment the night before, but in a different theatre. His colour blindness may also have been a contributory factor. The Judge instructed the jury that the required standard of care was not absolute perfection, but 'reasonable care and skill ... taking into account all of the circumstances of the case'. After almost 10 hours, the jury found the doctor guilty, but recommended leniency. He was fined $2500 and ordered to pay $2000 costs.

Perhaps the best-known New Zealand case is that of Te Kuiti anaesthetist, Dr Yogasakaran. Namsivayan Yogasakaran administered dopamine instead of doxapram to a high-risk patient at the end of a cholecystectomy, in response to a developing emergency in which the patient was biting the endotracheal tube, developing respiratory obstruction and becoming cyanosed. There were a number of contributory system-related factors, the most obvious of which was the fact that the dopamine had been placed in the compartment labelled doxapram by some other, unidentified, person. The patient suffered cardiac arrest, but Dr Yogasakaran managed to resuscitate her and transfer her to the intensive care unit in Waikato Hospital. On his return to Te Kuiti, he identified his error and drew the appropriate people's attention to what had happened. In consequence, he was charged with manslaughter.

The trial Judge summed up the case against Dr Yogasakaran:

> 'The Crown said [Dr Yogasakaran] is a highly trained, experienced, responsible man whom the Crown says made a mistake, through carelessness, on this one occasion'.

The jury found Dr Yogasakaran guilty and the Judge discharged him without sentence. The Court of Appeal upheld the verdict, and the Privy Council refused leave to appeal.

An 11-year-old patient died in Napier in 1990 following the administration of a sedative cocktail to facilitate the extraction of teeth by an oral and maxillo-facial surgeon. In the fourth day of the trial in the High Court at Napier in 1991, the Judge discharged the surgeon because of new evidence which revealed the possibility that the patient may have suffered from a rare heart disorder, and which left the Crown unable to establish beyond reasonable doubt that the death could have been prevented by the surgeon.

In 1991, a consultant radiologist pleaded guilty to manslaughter after the death of a young man undergoing a myelogram. The radiologist had been handed the wrong medium by an experienced radiographer, and had injected it into the patient's spinal canal. The Judge accepted that the mistake, 'was a matter of momentary carelessness in circumstances where he had no reason to be on guard'. He was convicted and discharged.[1]

A nurse was convicted and discharged after pleading guilty to manslaughter in 1994. She had reset an epidural infusion mistaking it for an intravenous infusion, with fatal consequences for an elderly patient recovering from surgery for lung cancer.[1]

By this time, considerable disquiet was being expressed, not only by members of the medical profession, and active debate had developed over the subject of so-called 'medical manslaughter'. The fundamental issue has, at times, been misunderstood. This issue was standard of negligence under which prosecutions were being brought, rather than the merits of bringing them in any particular case (notwithstanding the fact that many health professionals thought the prosecutions unjust). In other words, the question at stake was the threshold at which negligence would be considered criminal. The subject was considered by the Court of Appeal in *R v. Yogasakaran* (1990) 1 NZLR 399. The Court considered that the issue was well settled in New Zealand, by the previous cases of *R v. Dawe* (1911) 30 NZLR 673 and *R v. Storey* (1931) 1 NZLR 417, and did not think it appropriate to reconsider the view of the section, as stated so authoritatively in the two previous decisions.

The citation usually referred to is as follows:

> *'This term cannot be defined, but the standard must be set in each particular case by the jury by applying their common sense to the evidence as to the facts of the case and any admissible expert evidence that is adduced. The standard should be neither too high nor too low: it should be a 'reasonable' standard, the standard of skill and care which would be observed by a reasonable man. I desire, however, expressly to say that, while I think, having regard to Section 171, 43 of the* Crimes Act *and to what was said in Dawe's case, there is no distinction in New Zealand between negligence as the foundation of criminal liability and negligence as the foundation of civil liability. It follows that, under that section, as under Section 170, 44, a mere mistake or error of judgment which should in a civil action prevent an act or omission from being imputed as negligence is equally a good defence on a criminal charge involving negligence.' (Page 435, per Myers C J).*

This is clearly a description of simple negligence.

The matter was brought to a head in 1995, when a Hamilton anaesthetist was charged with manslaughter, in circumstances that most doctors (and many others) considered palpably inappropriate (*Long v. R*, T 43194, Hamilton Registry, 7 June 1995). It was alleged that the doctor had been negligent in that, having pressurised a bottle to speed up the rate of administration, he had not adequately monitored the rapid infusion of fluid into a patient. The patient concerned was elderly, and extremely high risk — a matter that had been discussed with the family, and with the staff of the intensive care unit, before agreeing to undertake the surgery. The patient was found, on opening the abdomen, to have dead gut. During an attempt to resect this, her blood pressure began to fall. It was as part of his response to this developing crisis that the doctor inadvertently allowed some air to enter the patient's vein. This air may have contributed to the patient's death, but expert evidence on this point changed to the degree that a jury could not properly have convicted the doctor. In a remarkable judgment, Hammond J, dismissed the charges under Section 347 of the *Crimes Act* 1961. The Judge cited three difficulties with the Crown's case:

1. On the evidence, the death could have been due to another cause.
2. The volume and composition of gas released at post-mortem was uncertain, and the Crown could not prove its case.
3. Because of the hopeless prognosis, resuscitation attempts had been deliberately truncated, in part, on the insistence of other practitioners present. The Judge felt that the accused doctor was entitled to say that the charge should be brought only where all reasonable resuscitation efforts had been carried through to fruition.

However, His Honour then went on to consider an alternative ground of discharge under Section 347. He said:

> *'This recital demonstrates that Mrs B was* in extremis *with an extremely complicated set of conditions, but that those attending her (including the doctor) were making every effort even before the events now complained of — right up to the edge of the Hippocratic Oath — to keep this woman alive. This was 'heroic' surgery in every sense of that term. The police's own consulting anaesthetist thought that the matter had got into a situation where the 'ethics' of keeping someone alive come into play in a very practical way ... surgeons and anaesthetists operate against the awesome complexity of human life itself and the wondrous but still largely inscrutable processes that sustain it.'*

The Court then said:

> *'A conviction for manslaughter is, of course, in and of itself a very harsh penalty for harm inadvertently caused. The ability to practice; and certainly the ability to practice overseas, are unquestionably compromised. The social stigma of a manslaughter conviction is very heavy. To inflict those sorts of consequences upon this doctor in the circumstances of this particular case would in my view be unwarranted. I would have been prepared to discharge this accused on this ground.'*

Partly in response to this development, the Minister of Justice, the Right Honourable (now Sir) Douglas Graham, appointed Sir Duncan McMullin, a retired Judge of the Court of Appeal, to report on Sections 155 and 156 of the *Crimes Act*. On the basis of this report, the Minister introduced a Bill to Parliament which, after consideration by a Parliamentary Select Committee, passed into law as the *Crimes Amendment Act* 1997.

This Act, at Sir Duncan's recommendation, adopted a threshold for criminal responsibility in respect of the relevant duties, defined as 'a major departure from standard of care expected of a reasonable person to whom that legal duty applies in those circumstances'.

It is important to understand that this provision applied to all people who fall within the ambit of the 'duty' sections of the *Crimes Act* 1961 — not just doctors. Key points accepted by the Select Committee included the fact that some human error is unavoidable and therefore cannot be prevented by deterrence. They accepted that the tragic consequences which may follow a normal human error do justify every effort to reduce recurrence, but do not (of themselves) mean that the error was a crime. The 'major departure' formulation provided a focus on behaviour rather than on outcome, and codified the principle that serious criminal charges should require something more than normal human error. This does not imply that errors of this type should carry no consequence for the person who has been the cause of harm, but rather that other statutory provisions are more appropriate in less culpable circumstances. Furthermore, it does not imply that doctors should never be charged with manslaughter, but rather that manslaughter (and other criminal charges) should be reserved for situations of clear moral culpability.

United Kingdom

In essence, the English common law requires that an accused must have caused the death of another through his or her 'gross' negligence or recklessness. Over the years, there has been extensive discussion of the English case law authorities. A pivotal case involved the injection of a cytotoxic drug intrathecally instead of intravenously by two junior doctors (Prentice and Sullman). The direction of Owen J, in *R v. Prentice* (1993) 4 AELR 935 (House of Lords) describes what amounts to objective recklessness. 'Objective recklessness' is a difficult concept for the medical mind to grasp, and, at first sight, appears to be an oxymoron. However, it can be understood in reference to the example of excessive speed on the road, in which the driver's belief in his/her skill is such that he/she has no insight into the risk he/she is creating to others, but in which that risk is real and obvious to (essentially) everyone else. It would imply, in effect, that a momentary lapse by doctors who believed themselves to be doing the right thing, might be sufficient to incur criminal liability — a position disconcertingly close to that applying in New Zealand at the time.

Obviously, junior doctors should check before they undertake dangerous procedures, but one of the difficulties of inexperience is that of knowing when a procedure is more dangerous than usual. It seems reasonable to expect that hospitals would have systems in place to ensure that dangerous injections were carried out by junior doctors only under proper supervision or after appropriate familiarisation with the risks. That this is a good example of a problem with the system, rather than the individuals concerned, is attested to by the fact that the mistake made by doctors Prentice and Sullman has now occurred at least 10 times in UK hospitals.[7]

The English Court of Appeal listed four states of mind, any one of which could be sufficient grounds for finding criminal negligence. These were: (i) indifference to an obvious risk of injury to health; (ii) actual foresight of the risk coupled with the determination nevertheless to run it; (iii) appreciation of the risk coupled with an intention to avoid it, but also coupled with such a high degree of negligence in the attempted avoidance as a jury may consider justified conviction; and (iv) inattention or failure to advert to a serious risk which went beyond mere inadvertence in respect of an obvious and important matter which the defendant's duty demanded he or she should address.

The House of Lords, considering *R v. Adomako* (1994) 3 WLR 288, confirmed that the appropriate test for cases of manslaughter by criminal negligence involving a breach of duty was the gross negligence test. Lord Mackay, commending the words of the trial Judge in *R v. Adomako* said: 'You should only convict a doctor of causing death by negligence if you think he did something which no reasonably skilled doctor should have done'.

The Law Lords made it very clear in *R v. Adomako* that gross negligence was the requirement. They stated further that it was unnecessary to refer to a test of 'recklessness', although it was open to a Judge to use the word 'reckless' in its ordinary meaning as part of his or her direction of the jury.

Canada

Under the Canadian criminal code, the requirement for criminal prosecution of negligence is 'wanton or reckless disregard'. The Supreme Court, in *R v. Baker* (1929) 2 DLR 282, took a similar view to that in the Callaghan case in Australia, and subsequent statutes expressly adopted the distinction of gross negligence.

The United States of America

The situation in the USA varies from State to State, but there seems to have been very little tendency to invoke the criminal law in cases of medical negligence until relatively recently. In general, the requirement seems to be for some formulation of the concept of gross negligence.

In 1996, a Denver anaesthesiologist was convicted of negligence after an 8-year-old died following ear surgery in 1993. The doctor was accused of having fallen asleep during the anaesthetic; he denied this, but admitted that he had been confronted with falling asleep during previous anaesthetics.[8] The jury concluded that the doctor's conduct amounted to 'an extreme deviation from generally accepted standards of medical practice', but was unable to reach a unanimous decision on whether this constituted criminally negligent homicide or reckless manslaughter. The doctor's medical licence was revoked in 1994 by the Colorado Board of Medical Examiners — a contrast to the situation in Australia and New Zealand in which Medical Council proceedings tend to follow the completion of criminal prosecutions. There have been several other recent criminal prosecutions of doctors in the USA.

Conclusions

There is no debate about whether the criminal law should be applied to doctors (or other health professionals) — of course it should. There is, in reality, no such thing as 'medical manslaughter' — just manslaughter arising from negligence. The proper place for the criminal law in medical practice is in dealing with deliberate and willful wrongdoing. The most obvious examples are those of fraud, sexual abuse of patients (especially children), and falsification of records with the intention of perverting the course of justice. There may often be an argument for holding organisations, rather than individuals, responsible for accidental harm, and this is nowhere more apparent than in the case of very junior doctors, who deserve better supervision than they are sometimes given. Charges of corporate manslaughter have succeeded in at least one (non-medical) UK case.

If a doctor charged with manslaughter is found not guilty, he or she is subsequently very likely to face a coroner's inquest, civil proceedings (perhaps for exemplary damages), disciplinary proceedings, and ongoing harassment by the media — the whole process taking years to complete. These protracted proceedings are typically just as harrowing for the patient's family and the outcome seldom seems to be satisfactory for either party. This is unconscionable. When patients are unexpectedly harmed, they deserve something better than is currently available, but if their doctors have been acting in good faith, the criminal law is seldom the answer. It is beyond the scope of this chapter, but there is a considerable body of knowledge concerning the relative ineffectiveness of draconian punishment in reducing the incidence of accidents in the context of well-motivated professionals working in a complex system, and demonstrating the importance of the design of systems in promoting safety.[4] It is gratifying that the Courts in the UK, Canada, New Zealand and Australia now seem to be taking a balanced and restrained approach to the legal response to accidental injury. It is equally gratifying, if overdue, that there is also a growing recognition within the medical profession of the urgent need for systematic initiatives to address the problem of iatrogenic harm in health-care.[9]

REFERENCES

1. Skegg PDG. Criminal prosecutions of negligent health professionals: The New Zealand experience. *Med. Law Rev.* 1998; **6**: 220–246.
2. Brennan TA, Leape LL, Laird NM *et al*. Incidence of adverse events and negligence in hospitalised patients. *N. Engl. J. Med.* 1991; **324**: 370–376.
3. Wilson RM, Runciman WB, Gibberd RW, Harrison BT, Newby L, Hamilton J. The quality in Australian health care study. *Med. J. Aust.* 1995; **163**: 458–471.
4. Smith AM, Merry A. Medical accountability and the criminal law. New Zealand v the World. *Health Care Anal.* 1996; **4**: 1–10.
5. Paterson R. Medical manslaughter law reform: A mistaken diagnosis. *Health Care Anal.* 1996; **4**: 170. 54–59.
6. Smith AM, Merry AF. Medical manslaughter: A reply to Paterson. *Health Care Anal.* 1996; **4**: 229–233.
7. Dyer C. Doctors cleared of manslaughter. *BMJ* 1999; **318**: 148.
8. Annas GJ. Medicine, death and the criminal law. *N. Engl. J. Med.* 1995; **333**: 527–530.
9. Berwick DM, Leape LL. Reducing errors in medicine. *BMJ* 1999; **319**: 136–137.

Ethical issues
in clinical research

M.R. FEARNSIDE

'The principle of medical and surgical morality consists in never performing on man an experiment which might be harmful to him to any extent, even though the result might be highly advantageous to science.'
                                        Claude Bernard (1813-1878)

If it is the goal of medicine, as defined by the World Health Organization, to promote the 'complete physical, mental and social wellbeing' of humankind, it is the goal of medical research to discover new methods to enable these ends to be achieved. Using directed investigation, the researcher aims to discover a verifiable fact or set of facts through the careful study of a subject. By virtue of the fact that human research involves human subjects, ethical issues and tensions arise, which are in every way as important as the scientific issues and which may bear heavily on the research question.

It is undeniable that medical research has been of immense benefit to humankind. The development of antibiotics for the treatment of bacterial infections and vaccinations to prevent them are but two powerful examples. Research findings, as a source of information when applied to the treatment of diseases, have enabled cure, the relief of suffering or the flourishing of meaningful life. Such knowledge has prevented public catastrophes that a society cannot allow, such as epidemics of infectious disease. Today, not only is there a general expectation of prevention of such harms, there is a further anticipation of active and continuing efforts to improve the various domains of health care.

In contrast, the acquisition of knowledge may expose other people, the research subjects, to risk or danger, sometimes in circumstances where there may be no direct benefit to themselves. This is the central tension around which ethical discussion about human research is conducted: the need to gain particular knowledge in order to improve the human condition and the requirement to protect the interests of those who are the subjects of the research project.

The ethical groundings for such an assessment of risks and benefits are found in the notions of beneficence, the requirement to increase good (applied knowledge gained through research) and non-maleficence, the requirement not to harm the research subjects. To these two notions, we add autonomy, where self-determination and informed consent should dictate whether an individual becomes involved in a research project, and justice, which includes fairness in the selection of the research subjects, the protection of vulnerable groups, transparent procedure and compensation for harm done.

Justification for using human subjects

There are clear scientific reasons to justify the use of human subjects in research projects. The information derived may be unique in that there may be different results when an experiment, (e.g. the testing of the efficacy of a new drug) is performed on laboratory animals or *in vitro*. Furthermore, the results of the human testing that will be applied to other humans may be knowledge which cannot be obtained in any other way.

Does this argument provide a sufficient moral justification for using human subjects in medical research? One way of examining the problem is to argue that the knowledge obtained will be used to improve the general good; many people will benefit and the benefits will outweigh the risks. The weakness of this utilitarian argument is that there is a possibility that the wellbeing of the minority (the research subjects) may be subsumed to the good of the majority.

In support of this minority, Immanuel Kant's teaching may be used which states that human beings should always be considered as ends in themselves (i.e. having an intrinsic value by virtue of being human) rather than merely being considered as a means to achieve an end (the research project).

Generally, human beings are capable of independent reflection and of making decisions based upon various considerations. They are capable not only of thought but also of the ability to experience sensations, feeling and emotions. Humans, therefore, act in an independent and autonomous manner. Contemporary moral values require that due attention is given to these considerations. Respect for persons and human dignity are integral grounding features of ethical research and remain perennial values.

Assuming that, given the necessary conditions, it is morally right for humans to serve as research subjects, is there an obligation for an individual to serve as a research subject as part of a wider duty to society? Members of contemporary society do benefit from the contributions of previous generations. It could be argued that there is a type of social contract operating where, by virtue of being a member of society, there is an obligation to act to benefit society in order to repay some of this debt. Participation in medical research projects would seem to satisfy this obligation. Such a requirement, however, is not individually or legally enforceable in a democratic and civil society. Each individual is permitted to make an autonomous and informed decision as to participation. Against this argument, the goods of medical research are not necessarily available to all members of society equally. Furthermore, in a government-funded health system, the costs of research form a substantial proportion of public outlays on health to which individuals contribute through the tax system. There are, therefore, other means by which an individual may reciprocate benefits derived. There should be no compulsion to contribute to research as a subject.

Therapeutic and non-therapeutic research

A distinction is made between research from which there may be a derived benefit to the subject, who is generally a patient in a clinical situation (therapeutic research) and where there is no direct benefit to the subject, but where the objective would be a benefit to the general good of society through, for example, the addition of new knowledge (non-therapeutic research).

For therapeutic research projects, the risks and benefits may be individualised to the subject who, with the aid of information provided, can make an independent decision as to whether he or she wishes to participate. The researcher should satisfy himself or herself that there is a genuine equipoise within the medical community; that is, a genuine uncertainty about the relative value of each of the treatment arms proposed in the research. Generally, therapeutic research is seen to be less ethically challenging than non-therapeutic research owing to the potential for individual benefit. For non-therapeutic research projects, the potential for individual harm becomes more important as no direct benefit is likely to accrue to the subject. This potential for harm, often to the health and wellbeing of volunteers, is weighed against the likely accrual of a general benefit. The process of weighing may require subjective judgments by a majority over a minority and care needs to be taken not to violate the autonomy of the latter group.

The lines blur, however, as not all subjects in a therapeutic research project may obtain even a potential benefit. One example of such a situation occurs in placebo-controlled randomised clinical trials of drugs where both subjects and researchers are blinded to which subjects receive the trial drug or the inactive placebo. In the construction of such trials it is unethical if the subjects in the placebo arm receive no therapy, assuming some treatment is possible. All subjects should receive best conventional therapy, with a trial drug or other intervention being additional.

Autonomy and consent

It is axiomatic that the subject of a research project should provide consent to the researcher as a condition for entry to the project. Yet this has not always been so and there are numerous examples of medical research in earlier times, indeed not so long ago, where the subjects were not made aware of their inclusion in a study.

Examples of such unethical studies were the Tuskagee syphillis study and the Willowbrook hepatitis study in the USA. In the former study, which was conducted between 1932 and 1972, 400 black males were used to study the untreated natural history of syphillis, although penicillin, which would have been an effective treatment, was available after the 1940s. The study continued, without the consent of the subjects, until publicity caused the project to be discontinued. The Willowbrook School was a facility in New York for mentally handicapped people, a sample of whom — all children — was inoculated with hepatitis virus in order to test various treatments. The school was overcrowded and parents were offered an earlier admission if they consented to their child being included in the study. Each of these studies, one on black males and the other on mentally handicapped children, provides examples of exploitation of vulnerable groups by researchers.

The ethical justification for strictly requiring consent to participation in a project is that of autonomy of persons. This is the right of individuals, as far as reasonable, to be self-determining. A person should be free to make his or her own decision as to whether to participate in a research project and there should be no protocol-driven conditions attached to that decision. In addition, during the course of the project, the subject should be free to withdraw at any time without penalty. The weight applied to autonomous decision-making is great because it recognises that involvement in research may not be without harm. The harm and potential benefit (or lack of benefit) should be available for measurement by each individual subject, rather than by the researcher or other individuals on behalf of the subject. Such a process minimises the likelihood of exploitation of research subjects. This is a particular problem in non-therapeutic research where the subject takes up a burden on behalf of others. An autonomous and informed decision emphasises and defines the voluntariness of the process.

Informed consent implies both an autonomous decision and agreement to participation. The process requires that sufficient information be provided, that the subject is able to understand the information and is competent to decide. Therefore, the information provided should be in lay terms, as simple and as comprehensive as possible. There should be no duplicity or deception. Information should include the reason the project is being undertaken, the goal of the research and the expected good which may accrue. Specific information as to exactly what will happen and when to the subject during the conduct of the project, the inconveniences, any pain or suffering and possible harm should each be disclosed.

Understanding involves assisting the subject to assimilate the information provided and places an obligation on the researcher to ensure that the process has taken place. Understanding is unlikely to be full (in the scientific sense) but it must be sufficient for comprehension of the central issues. Competence is linked to understanding in that the latter is a necessary condition for the former and is best considered as the ability to carry out a particular task, such as making a decision. Competence may be affected by a variety of factors including age, educational status, physical or mental disability or impaired consciousness. The inclusion of potentially vulnerable groups in research projects is a major ethical problem and is discussed below.

The final ethical requirement for informed consent is that the decision made is voluntary. This means that the person makes a free choice to be included or excluded from the project. Where research is part of the clinical trial of a drug or therapeutic device, the subject may feel in a vulnerable position, exposed to possible sanctions if he or she does not wish to participate in the project. The construction of the research project should aim to exclude any possible coercive situations, particularly where the researcher is also the clinician who has a responsibility for ongoing care of the patient/subject. The inherent inequality in the relationship between clinician/patient and researcher/subject requires acknowledgement. By virtue of both knowledge and position, the clinician/researcher is dominant; a notion which may cause tension by undue influence upon the autonomy of the patient/subject. That such potentially conflicting or coercive situations may occur does not render research projects unethical. However, it would be unethical not to recognise the potential for conflict and act to resolve any such tensions.

Justice

The notion of justice in research is concerned with fairness and equity in the manner by which the burdens and benefits of research are shared by members of society. Procedural justice requires that the study design provides that individuals should, where possible, be selected in a disinterested manner, giving each person eligible for the sample an equal chance of inclusion or exclusion and an equal chance of receiving the treatment or technology under investigation. The methodology should include the opportunity to discontinue involvement in the study without penalty and a mechanism for conflict resolution which is external to the study structure, that is 'at arms length' and independent of the research group.

Vulnerable groups require special attention to ensure that requirements of distributive justice are met, that they are not exploited and that burdens do not fall unfairly upon them. These groups include children, people with mental or physical disability, institutionalised individuals such as those in the armed forces or in gaols, or people in dependent relationships such as those in nursing homes, State wards or the elderly. The selection of research subjects from such groups might be an avenue for exploitation, as might selection from low socio-economic classes. This type of maldistribution of burdens and resulting injustice can be extrapolated globally where research in under-developed or third world countries may see the research subjects less likely to benefit from the results of research and less likely to be compensated for harms done. Research involving vulnerable groups should be considered only where the proposed project is therapeutic, of potential value to the individual participants, where no alternative less vulnerable subjects are available (who could give a more informed consent) and where the information cannot be obtained by other means. Distributive justice also requires that the benefits of the research be made generally available to the community, if a benefit be shown, after the trial concludes. Were the treatment to be withheld on the basis of cost, or were it to be restricted only to those who were prepared or able to pay for the service, the outcome of the research could be considered unjust and unethical.

The types of research that require special consideration include projects in emergency care such as trauma, acute vascular or neurological disease, where there may be insufficient time to obtain informed consent or where the subject may have impaired consciousness (e.g. head injury). The research should be therapeutic (i.e. of potential benefit to the subject and inclusion in the project should, as far as possible, pose no more risk than best alternative treatment). The subject's relatives should be informed expediently and provided with the option of continuing or withdrawing. In most States of Australia, Guardianship Boards may act as surrogates and particular representations should be made to those groups, if required by law, as a part of the methodology and ethical consent process. Innovative interventions including newer technologies and new surgical equipment should be considered as research projects until of proven value and their use is best considered within the structure of a research protocol.

Finally, notions of compulsory or punitive justice in research require that compensation be made available for harm done as a result of participation. This harm may not only be physical, it may be psychological or economic. While one of the groundings of ethical research is non-maleficence, there may be unforeseen occasions where unintended harm does occur. Unfortunately, there may also be instances of harm resulting from irresponsibility, poor study construct or fraud, which deserve both censure of the research and adequate compensation for the subject.

Health research ethics committees

Contemporary societal pressures for the regulation of medical research grew out of the atrocities of German and Japanese doctors and other workers on subjects during World War II, research which both denied rights to the subjects and inflicted suffering and death. The Court at Nuremberg, as part of its findings in these matters, expounded 10 points of justification necessary for medical experimentation. These included proper scientific design and methodology of research, the likelihood of meaningful results, the exclusion of unnecessary suffering or pain and the absolute requirement for free and voluntary consent by the subject to inclusion. In 1954, and later in 1964, the World Medical Association adopted a code of ethics for medical experimentations (The Helsinki Declarations), but it was not until 1989 that the Association established as an international standard the requirement of an independent committee of review for each research project. Such committees, now widely established, are known as Human Research or Institutional Ethics Committees (HREC or IEC).

The primary purpose of the HREC is to ensure that the interests of the subject are protected, including both protection from harm (non-maleficence) and ensuring equity in selection justice. A secondary purpose is to ensure that research is performed to appropriate ethical standards.

In Australia and New Zealand, all health-related research involving humans must be considered and approved by a duly constituted HREC. In Australia, an institution which conducts research is obliged to establish a committee and to register it through the Australian Health Ethics Committee (AHEC), a principal committee of the National Health and Medical Research Council (NHMRC). The requirements covering HREC are detailed in the NHMRC publication, *National Statement on Ethical Conduct in Research Involving Humans*.[1]

In Australia, the composition of an HREC is quite specific and it is to be composed of men and women of different ages to include: (i) a lay man not associated with the institution but from the community in which the institution is located; (ii) a lay woman not associated with the institution but from the community in which the institution is located; (iii) a minister of religion or person performing a similar community role; (iv) a lawyer; (v) a person experienced in the types of research regularly considered by the committee; (vi) a person with experience in the professional care, counselling or treatment of people; (vii) a chairperson.

In practice, this is a minimum number and most HREC have a larger membership. It is an important principle that members are appointed as nominees for their expertise rather than in a representative capacity. In this way, they represent the public rather than sectional interests. In New Zealand, lay members must comprise 50% of the membership of an HREC and the chairperson must be a lay member.

The functions of an HREC are to consider and to approve, reject, or require modification of research projects to ensure they conform to ethical standards. It must also maintain a record of such decisions and monitor research in progress. The monitoring function requires a written report, at least annually, from the principal investigator covering the status of the project, compliance with the protocol and data security and handling. Adverse events and protocol amendments must be notified to the HREC promptly to enable review.

For such a committee, an ongoing cause of uncertainty is its responsibility to approve or reject projects based upon judgments of the scientific design of the protocol. While it is clear that poorly designed research is unethical research, the obligation of the HREC to determine the balance of benefit over harm may rely on a determination of the validity of the scientific construct. The HREC members may not be adequately qualified for this purpose, notwithstanding medical membership, for determination of scientific validity and to make subsequent judgments about the rightness of the science. A resolution of this problem might be the delegation of purely scientific matters to a scientific research committee or the seeking of expert external advice. Having reassured itself of the scientific rigour of the project, the HREC may then proceed to the other ethical issues concerning the humanitarian value of the research to society and details of the protection of the subjects.

All this has not been without controversy. The HREC system has been criticised as being too rigid, too legalistic, too adversarial and too slow, acting as an obstruction to, rather than a guardian/facilitator of, research. As a result, the potential arises for researchers to become discouraged and not pursue worthwhile projects, particularly if difficult ethical questions do arise. They may respond with progressive indifference to ethical issues, without ever connecting to the process of ethical review. Maximal utility would see the adoption of a non-adversarial, non-police role for the HREC, with provision of assistance and advice for improving the project, together with education of the research community in ethical issues as they touch on research. Such a move has the potential to lead to a position of mutual trust and might allow more autonomy for the researcher.

Ethical responsibilities of the researcher

What, then, are the ethical responsibilities of the researcher when planning a project? How should the various issues be addressed in order to ensure that research is conducted in accordance with both moral and scientific principles set out in the various covenants and guidelines including the Helsinki Declaration of the World Medical Association and the NHMRC statements?

The methodology should be sound. The research question should be framed in a rigorous manner with the researcher being informed by a literature review and assured the project is relevant and not a repetition of other work. The project design should enable the research question to be answered unambiguously. The researcher needs to give consideration not only to the scientific value of the research but also to the wider applications of the knowledge obtained and consequential value to the community.

The central ethical principles for the treatment of research subjects are respect for persons and preservation of dignity. The good of research is the knowledge gained through meaningful results and their subsequent application with a minimum of harm. Another relevant issue is fairness in the selection of subjects, particularly if the project is non-therapeutic. Special consideration is required where vulnerable groups are involved. When selected, subjects should be given sufficient information, provided in a simple, concise manner, as free as possible from scientific language and on which a free, voluntary and informed consent can be based. There should be freedom for the subject to withdraw from the project without penalty and provision of compensation for harm done.

The conduct of the research requires the collection of accurate and valid data and compliance with the experimental protocol.

The principal investigator should be experienced with the various facets of research and act as a supervisor of the other researchers. Regular peer review at a department level with discussions of the 'research in progress' ensures transparency of the process as well as useful feedback, within a collegiate atmosphere. Where confidentiality is required, adequate controls must exist to ensure appropriate de-identification of the data. The protocol should include a pathway for data storage during and following the project, for its ultimate disposal. The researcher must comply with the requirements of the institution's HREC which both approves the proposal and is responsible for ongoing monitoring. Regular reports, at least annually, are provided to the HREC by the principal investigator who also notifies the HREC of adverse events and protocol amendments.

The results of the research, regardless of the findings, should be published in a medical journal or communicated to peers orally, the latter being a minimum requirement. The report should make clear that ethical issues have been considered and included in the experimental design. Not only is the publication of research in a reputable journal a monitor of the ethical values and scientific integrity of the researcher, it is an important means by which the activities of an HREC may be indirectly audited.

Conclusion

The proposition that ethical medical research which adds to useful knowledge is an ultimate good to society is undeniable. Such knowledge can often not be obtained in any other manner than by using human subjects. The means by which knowledge is obtained, therefore, requires careful reflection by the researcher and a measure of regulation by society. There is a constant tension between the researcher, the subject and society where the general good and particular harm lie uneasily. It is the obligation of the researcher to design his or her work so as to ease the tension and provide the balance. It is by following this path that autonomy and trust among the three will ultimately be enabled.

ACKNOWLEDGEMENT

The author acknowledges with thanks the critical reviews of this chapter by Emeritus Professor JM Little and Dr BM Tobin.

REFERENCE

1. National Health and Medical Research Council. National Statements on Ethical Conduct in Research Involving Humans. Canberra: Australian Government Publishing Service, 1999.

FURTHER READING

General references

DeCastro LD. Ethical issues in human experimentation. In: Kuhse H, Singer P (eds). *A Companion to Bioethics. Blackwell Companions to Philosophy.* Oxford: Blackwell Science, 1998; 379–389.

Freedman B. Equipoise and the ethics of clinical research. *N. Engl. J. Med.* 1987; **317**: 141–145.

Kieffer GL. Human experimentation. In: Edwards RB, Graber GC (eds). *Bioethics.* New York: Harcourt, Brace, Jovanovich, 1988; 196–215.

Lock S, Wells F. *Fraud and Misconduct in Medical Research.* London: B. M. J. Publishing Group, 1996.

McNeill PM. Experimentation on human beings. In: Kuhse H, Singer P. *A Companion to Bioethics. Blackwell Companions to Philosophy.* Oxford: Blackwell Science, 1998; 369–378.

National Statement on Ethical Conduct in Research Involving Humans. Canberra: National Health and Medical Research Council, 1999.

Pearn J. Publication, an ethical imperative. *BMJ* 1995; **310**: 1313–1315.

Spece RG, Shimm DS, Buchanan AE. *Conflicts of Interest in Clinical Practice and Research.* Oxford: Oxford University Press, 1996.

Health research ethics committees

Chalmers D, Pettit P. Towards a consensual culture in the ethical review of research. *Med. J. Aust.* 1998; **168**: 79–82.

Charlesworth M. Bioethics, committees, experts and the community. In: Charlesworth M. (ed). *Life, Death, Genes and Ethics. The Boyer Lectures.* Sydney: ABC Books, 1989; 96–116.

Jamrozik K. Ethics committees: Is the tail wagging the dog? *Med. J. Aust.* 1992; **157**: 636–637.

Little JM. The bioethic committee. In: Little JM. *Humane Medicine.* Cambridge: Cambridge University Press, 1995; 108–121.

McNeill PM. *The Ethics and Politics of Human Experimentation.* Cambridge: Cambridge University Press, 1993.

Animal welfare and the ethics of animal experimentation

J. LUDBROOK

Purposes of animal experimentation in surgery

Scientific research conducted by surgeons

Scientific research conducted by surgeons can be in fields ranging from applied anatomy or physiology, to transplantation immunology, to cancer research. The important features are that the research is original, it is conducted by a trained surgeon or a surgeon-in-training, and that it is scientific. There have been some notable scientists who were trained as surgeons, who carried out highly innovative research in animals, and who sometimes continued to practise surgery. For instance, Alexis Carrel, Nobel prizewinner in 1912, showed how vascular anastomoses could be performed and used these in attempts at organ transplantation. Charles Huggins, Nobel prizewinner in 1966 showed that cancers of the breast and prostate are under hormonal control. Lester Dragstedt showed in dogs the importance of vagal control over gastric acid secretion. John H. Gibbon Jr in the USA and Denis Melrose in the UK spent years developing pump-oxygenators that would permit open heart surgery.

Development of new surgical procedures

Charles Huggins performed the first adrenalectomies for breast cancer, Lester Dragstedt the first vagotomies for duodenal ulceration, and John H. Gibbon Jr the first open-heart operation. But it has often been others than those who made the fundamental biological discoveries who systematically developed new surgical procedures by way of animal experimentation. Some examples are John Kirklin, then of the Mayo Clinic, who spent a year perfecting techniques of open-heart surgery in dogs, using Gibbon's pump-oxygenator, before undertaking the successful repair of interventricular septal defects in humans. Lester Dragstedt spent years testing the effects of vagotomy in dogs before treating patients with duodenal ulcer by this technique.

The training of surgeons and intending surgeons in established surgical techniques

Not so long ago, one learned as a surgeon-in-training, or even as a trained surgeon, how to execute established surgical techniques by trial (and sometimes error) in patients. Nowadays, this is not acceptable. Instead, if the established surgeon wishes to learn a new operative technique, for instance in fields such as microsurgery or endoscopic surgery, the proper way is by practice in animals. Surgeons-in-training are expected to learn the basic elements of their craft by enrolling in surgical skills workshops, or are required to obtain certification in the Early Management of Severe Trauma (EMST) by attending courses sponsored by the Royal Australasian College of Surgeons (RACS).

In summary, laboratory animals have played an essential part in the invention of new surgical therapies and in the development of these to the point that they could be used safely in patients. And laboratory animals continue to be used, fruitfully rather than frivolously, in the training and re-training of surgeons.

The animal welfare movements

From the mid-1970s onwards, there have been strong movements of resistance against the use of animals in industry, research and teaching. These have been active worldwide, under banners such as the Animal Rights Movement and the Animal Liberation Movement. Among the evangelists of these movements were Ryder,[1] Singer[2] and Reusch.[3] It is not only pet-lovers and anti-vivisectionists who have participated in these movements, but also moral philosophers such as Singer[2], Regan[4] and Rollin.[5] One compelling argument is that laboratory animals are often housed under conditions that are so different from their natural physical and social environment that this must cause distress. The same argument is extended to intensive methods of food production, such as the use of battery hens and concentrated pig farming. Other points of focus have been on the use of animals for testing cosmetics, and for testing new drugs in the pharmaceutical industry. The moral philosophers have drawn attention to the similarities, rather than differences, between the social structure and behaviour patterns of mammals (especially sub-human primates) and humans (especially the handicapped or the very young). On this basis they argue that animals have similar moral rights to those of humans when it comes to their use in experimentation. The activities of the animal rights movements have ranged from public protest to physical invasion of animal research facilities and even 'physical liberation' of laboratory animals. These matters were drawn to the attention of Australasian surgeons more than 10 years ago.[6]

Even the staunchest animal experimenter has to admit that the activities of the animal welfare movement have been beneficial. Practices such as the collection of stray cats by students for sale to universities, the unrestricted use of pounds as sources of supply of dogs, and the importation of sub-human primates have largely disappeared and been replaced by closely monitored breeding programs. Trivial uses of laboratory animals, such as the testing of cosmetics, have been abolished or severely curtailed. There have been some restraints placed on the wholesale use of animals by the pharmaceutical industry. There is now close regulation of the use of animals in scientific research, to ensure that pain and distress are minimised and that scientists refine their experimental designs in order to economise on the use of animals. Yet, paradoxically, the enormous growth of molecular and cellular biology and gene technology has made animal experiments more, rather than less, important. It is unthinkable that the products of the new biology should be transferred directly from the laboratory to humans without extensive testing in animals.

The use of laboratory animals in the education of biomedical students has been greatly reduced. For instance, the use of animals in undergraduate teaching at the University of Sydney was reduced by 65–99%, depending on the species, between 1970 and 1995.[7] The practice of allocating one animal to each ill-prepared and technically ill-equipped student per practical class has disappeared, and been replaced by demonstrations in animals by qualified staff and the use of computer-simulation. But, somewhat paradoxically, the use of medical students themselves as subjects for class experiments has also disappeared from the curriculum. In my days as a medical student (*ca* 1950), we were required to ascend to >16 000 ft in a decompression chamber; to experience extreme pain by injecting each other with saline sub-periosteally and by inflicting burns on ourselves with hot brass cylinders; to inject ourselves with crude posterior pituitary extract to illustrate its antidiuretic effects; and to be exposed to 60° foot-down tilt until syncope occurred. Such experiments have been removed from medical curricula chiefly, one supposes, because of a fear of litigation rather than for moral or ethical reasons.

Measures to protect the welfare of animals

Over the last two decades of the 20th century a number of measures were taken to protect animals from the previous excesses. These have been somewhat different in detail in Australia and New Zealand, in part because of the differing bodies responsible for setting the rules and monitoring compliance with them. In both countries, an essential element is the institutional or regional Animal Ethics Committee (AEC), the function of which is to receive, evaluate and give or withhold approval to applications for the use of animals in research or teaching. In both countries, there is emphasis on evaluating the scientific or educational merit of proposals, and on ensuring that distress to animals is minimised, especially when they are studied unanaesthetised. In Australia, the approach has been rather more to issue codes of good practice, in New Zealand rather more to legislate.

Australia

One of the first measures was the development of a Code of Practice for the use of animals for scientific purposes.[8] It is now in its 6th edition, and is sponsored by the National Health and Medical Research Council (NHMRC), the Commonwealth Scientific and Industrial Research Organisation (CSIRO), the Agricultural Resource Council of Australia and New Zealand (ARCANZ), the Australian Research Council (ARC), and the Australian Vice-Chancellors' Committee (AVCC). This Code is obligatory reading for anyone involved in the use of animals for research or teaching. It covers such issues as the acquisition or breeding of animals, anaesthesia and pain relief and, notably, the composition and functions of an Animal Ethics Committee (AEC). It contains a comprehensive bibliography. The NHMRC has a standing Animal Welfare Committee (AWC), which is responsible for monitoring the welfare of animals used in all instututions that receive NHMRC funding. Information on its activities can be obtained via the Internet (www.health.gov.au/nhmrc/research/awc). There is also legislation in the States and Territories that is concerned with animal welfare.

Without exception, all experiments on animals must gain prior approval from an institutional AEC.[7] *The Australian Code of Practice for the Care and use of Animals for Scientific Purposes* requires that these be set up in universities and hospitals, and indeed in all institutions in which experiments on animals are conducted. There are four essential members of an AEC: a research scientist who uses animals, a veterinarian, a person who is active in animal welfare, and an independent person (usually from outside the institution).[7]

Special guidelines have been developed by the NHMRC in conjunction with the RACS to cater for the use of animals in training surgeons and developing new surgical equipment and techniques.[9] These Guidelines recognise the need to train surgeons and aspiring surgeons in new therapeutic procedures, to accredit trainee surgeons in techniques of EMST, and to evaluate new equipment for such specialised purposes as endoscopic surgery and microsurgery (though not the commercial advertising of such equipment). These

Guidelines are supplementary to *The Australian Code of Practice for the Care and use of Animals for Scientific Purposes*.[8] They explain the need for using animals in this way, but at the same time require rigid adherence to approval by AEC, and compliance with animal welfare legislation in the Australian States and Territories, and in New Zealand.

The RACS has an Ethics Committee, the responsibilities of which include animal ethics. It was originally formed to cope with courses in EMST. Approval of the latter has devolved on institutional AEC. The RACS Ethics Committee ensures that holders of RACS Fellowships, Scholarships and Research Grants-in-Aid, and who propose to use animals, have gained approval from a properly constituted institutional AEC.

Quite apart from the Code and Guidelines described above, most States and Territories of Australia have new legislation that governs such matters as facilities for breeding and holding experimental animals and just who should be permitted to experiment on animals. This legislation almost always enshrines *The Australian Code of Practice for the Care and use of Animals for Scientific Purposes*[8] within it.

New Zealand

There are two main sources of guidelines regarding the use of experimental animals in New Zealand.

Animal ethics committees in New Zealand operate under the terms of the *Animals Protection Act 1960*, and its subsequent amendments (1983, 1987). There is a standing National Animal Ethics Advisory Committee (NAEAC), responsible to the Ministry of Agriculture and Forestry. It has published *Guidelines for Institutional Animal Ethics Committees*,[10] *Model Code of Ethical Conduct for Animal Ethics Committees*,[11] and *Code of Recommendations and Minimum Standards for the Care and Use of Animals for Scientific Purposes*.[12] The last prescribes the terms of reference, operating procedures, and membership of institutional AEC. The prescription for membership is somewhat more detailed than it is in Australia. It must include a scientist capable of evaluating proposals; a staff member responsible for procuring, breeding and maintaining animals; an institutional veterinarian; another veterinarian nominated by the New Zealand Veterinary Association; a nominee of the Royal New Zealand Society for the Prevention of Cruelty to Animals; and a layperson.

The New Zealand Health Research Council (HRC) is the governmental body that provides grants for research in the biomedical and clinical sciences. Its functions are similar to, though not identical to, those of the Australian NHMRC. It has a standing Health Research Council Ethics Committee (HRCEC), established under the *Health Research Council Act 1990*. It has published *Health Research Council Guidelines on Ethics in Health Research*, which is available on the Internet (www.hrc.govt.nz).[13] The HRCEC provides ethical guidelines for health researchers, and lists accredited regional and institutional ethics committees.

Summary

The use of laboratory animals for scientific research, education and training remains essential. Regulatory and advisory guidelines have been developed by governmental and semi-governmental bodies in Australia and New Zealand to control the use of animals. These guidelines are not static, but have been repeatedly updated. In Australia, special guidelines have been issued to cover the use of animals in the training of surgeons and aspiring surgeons.

ACKNOWLEDGEMENTS

I am most grateful to the following for information, documentation, and advice: Professor Warwick Anderson, Chairman of the Research Committee of NHMRC; Associate Professor Michael Perry, immediate past-Chairman of the Animal Welfare Committee of NHMRC; the secretariat of NHMRC; Dr Bruce Scoggins, CEO of the Health Research Council of New Zealand; and Ms Kate Horrey, Secretary to the New Zealand National Animal Ethics Advisory Committee.

ADDENDUM

In New Zealand, a new Animal Welfare Act was passed in 1999. In accordance with the New Zealand approach of legislating rather than the Australian approach of advising, this new Act prescribes penalties for breaches of conditions of animal experimentations which range from fines of up to NZ$25 000 and/or 6 months imprisonment for individuals, and fines of up to NZ$125 000 for corporations or institutions. The text of the Act can be obtained from the Internet site: www.knowledge-basket.co.nz/kete/database.html.

REFERENCES

1. Ryder R. *Victims of Science*. London: Davis-Poynter, 1975.
2. Singer P. *Animal Liberation: A New Ethics for our Treatment of Animals*. New York: Random House, 1975.
3. Reusch H. *Slaughter of the Innocent*. New York: Bartain Books, 1978.
4. Regan T, Singer P. *Animal Rights and Human Obligations*. Englewood Cliffs, NJ: Prentice Hall, 1976.
5. Rollin BE. *Animal Rights and Human Morality*. Buffalo, NJ: Prometheus Books, 1982.
6. Anderson W. Animals in medical and surgical research. In: Crisis. *Aust. NZ. J. Surg.* 1987; **57**: 797–800.
7. Anderson WP, Perry MA. Australian animal ethics committees: We have come a long way. *Cambridge Qrt. Healthcare Ethics* 1999; **8**: 80–86.
8. *Australian Code of Practice for the Care and Use of Animals for Scientific Purposes, 6th edition*. Canberra: Australian Government Publishing Service, 1997.
9. *NHMRC Guidelines on the Use of Animals for Training Surgeons and Demonstrating New Surgical Equipment and Techniques*. Canberra: National Health and Medical Research Council, 1997.
10. *Guidelines for Institutional Animal Ethics Committees*. Wellington: National Animal Ethics Advisory Committee, Ministry of Agriculture, 1988.
11. *Model Code of Ethical Conduct for Animal Ethics Committees*. Wellington: National Animal Ethics Advisory Committee, Ministry of Agriculture 1994.
12. *Code of Recommendations and Minimum Standards for the Care and Use of Animals for Scientific Purposes*. Wellington: National Animal Ethics Advisory Committee, Ministry of Agriculture, 1995.
13. *HRC Guidelines on Ethics in Health Research*. Auckland: Health Research Council of New Zealand, 1997.